True Human Freedom

The Inspiration and Argument for GaiaYoga® Culture

by
Ano Tarletz Hanamana

GaiaYoga Gardens
Pan Piper Press
aloha@gaiayoga.org
www.gaiayoga.org

Fifth Printing

Copyright © 2016, 2017, 2019, 2021
by Ano Tarletz Hanamana

I consider this vision and writing to be part of Gaia, therefore un-ownable.
I've copyrighted this book to protect it from someone else claiming ownership of it.
These texts may be freely quoted if my authorship is acknowledged.
Please send me a copy of any public expression that contains any of this material.
Thank you.

"Carried in the Blood
Ancient Memory
The wild-eyed Thirst
Of Humanity"

True Human Freedom
Is Dedicated
To the Thirsty

To those Longing
To live their Fullest
Expression of Humanity
As an Individual
In Community
Sustainably

LONGING

Longing for what I don't have
Longing for those not here
Longing for what I fear might never be
Longing for the beauty I see in my dreams
   In my dreams

Longing every day
And it's getting in my way
Of enjoying what is
My life and my kids

Longing right now
I yearn but I don't know how
  To have it
   Or find it
    Or fake it
     Or replace it
      Or transcend it
       Or create it
        Or not want it
         Just not want it

Where is he
Where is she
Where is we
And where is me?
   Where is me?

I know they're out there
 But I don't know where
  Every day I stare
   But it's like thin air
    And it's way too rare
     To meet ones who'll dare
      To bare and care
       In more than pairs
        In more than pairs
         In more than pairs

Longing for what I don't have
Longing for those not here
Longing for what I fear might never be
Longing for the beauty I see in my dreams
   In my dreams

    I pray my dreams come to be
    I pray my dreams come to be

••• PREFACE •••
by
Melekai

When Ano first asked me to write a preface for *True Human Freedom*, I felt inspired to share at an intimate level how I came to align myself with the GaiaYoga Vision. What I have found challenging in the vision, as elucidated in this book, is to take theory and apply it to life - which is dynamic, unpredictable, and complex. In writing this preface, I am hoping to convey that every expression of GaiaYoga Culture is going to have its own "face." I want to share intimately with you what ours looks like in this pioneering stage so you can use that as a reference for your own experiments.

My story begins in 2008 when I first arrived at GaiaYoga Gardens. Up until this point, I lived in a polite culture, in a polite family where yelling did not exist. When I came to GYG, I experienced yelling fights filled with raw emotion, and I saw Ano mediating amongst the involved people with such a presence of allowing and honoring of their raw feelings while facilitating an actual resolution of immediate issues. I also saw him giving attention to people involved who needed to address deeper wounds and he supported them in delving deeper into their pain in attempts to really address the healing that could occur. Although I wasn't romantically interested in Ano at the time, I came to deeply respect his ability to support healing.

During the last week of my stay in the fall of 2008, we did a plant spirit medicine journey in which I connected to what I consider the Spirit of the Big Island, Pele, and had a profound experience of love and connection. Ano was present, and he and I and another friend discussed Ano's dreams for GYG. I felt a deep kinship and appreciation for him.

Fast forward six months... I am gardening, after having spent the last six months in California finding a job, securing hospital privileges, renting a home, furnishing it, and undergoing a entire shift into a life of 48-hour-call at the local hospital, weekly clinic shifts, and an integration into a MD-based midwifery practice that is embroiled in local small town politics. Almost constantly I had been daydreaming of Hawaii, experiencing daily signs of Hawaii in the most unusual places, having dreams of the people I met in Hawaii, and feeling uninspired in the life I was leading.

While I am gardening, I see a vision of Ano playing with two children, and intuitively know they are our children. I decide to call him that night, after having struggled to reach him for the last six months. He picks up. During our conversation, sensing my energy, he asks inquiringly, "Are you interested in being my lover?" I simply say, "yes", and the flirting begins. Reconnecting with Ano put me in touch with a sense of meaning and purpose in my life, and after getting to know him at a deeper and more intimate level over the phone, I decided to move to GYG to begin a new life.

Once I moved to Hawaii, Ano and I immediately become intimately involved. The drama I had experienced when I was first at GYG was settled, and I focused on developing my relationship with Ano. I started eating an all-raw diet, including raw meat. We were making love frequently, and working hard to maintain GYG and earn an income at the local farmers market. During this time, however, Ano's previous intimate partner and co-owner of GYG decided she was uninterested in owning GYG, and evicted us in order to sell the property. And she was refusing to even consider selling us the property! All of a sudden, my dreams were shattered, and I felt confused as to what my vision had been alluding to. Ano began a constant stream of emails to her, negotiating and processing what was going to transpire. During this time, I became very jealous for I saw that his motives, although mostly practical in purpose, were serving to maintain a deep entanglement with her. I had entered into a relationship with a "polyamorous" man without the slightest clue as to what that really meant. I questioned where my vision of living in Hawaii had really come from.

During the subsequent weeks of Ano and her emailing practically 40x daily, she rescinded the eviction and then reestablished it. I felt hopeless in having the kind of relationship I wanted with Ano, yet felt completely motivated to continue my involvement. Finally, I was able to convince Ano to consider buying another property. We were in negotiation with a nearby landowner when she decided that she was willing to consider selling GYG to us at a reasonable price. We called her bluff. We set a date, and entered into an 8-hour, facilitated negotiation in which she refused to listen to Ano and thereby I was elected to be the main voice for our side in the negotiation without having any real knowledge of the relevant financial issues and other matters that were being discussed. This was only the beginning of episodes like this, and I deeply questioned why I was even willing to do it. I struggled so deeply, and came to a breaking point so many times, I can't even count. And I remember one particular time when I saw what was happening so clearly, and I was mourning so deeply the loss of a "dream," but I stopped and connected to an understanding that THIS was exactly what I was supposed to do. I absolutely could not do anything else. This was actually painful for me emotionally because I was not experiencing the love I wanted to have in a relationship, or the ease and happiness I wanted to have in my life. I was totally confused as to why this was happening to me. But like I said, it was crystal clear that this was exactly what I was supposed to do, and I trusted Spirit was guiding me.

As the process of actually buying the land ensued, we experienced a lot of abundance and generosity, especially from close family. We had a long 60-day escrow, and we were able to close in much less time, narrowly missing our eviction date. We were even given a last minute "gift" of $27,000, wired directly to our Escrow account. Fate was certainly with us!

Over the next few years, Ano's and my relationship deepened, and I felt happy to be co-creating GYG with him. He and his ex-partner were still in frequent communication, and I struggled to support our open relationship. I was brought into many emotionally charged discussions, and felt entangled in a sticky web that was not mine. I engaged many times for hours on end with him and her, feeling constantly jealous and confused as to why this was happening. I was told I had to speak in NVC, and endured hours of screaming directed at me and Ano. Finally, I began to speak my truth, and these episodes became less and less frequent, and less and less volatile.

In the early months of Ano's and my relationship, I had a vision while making love. The vision was as follows: There was a fruit tree, and many people relaxing underneath it. Some of us were eating its fruits, and some were playing with children, and some were relaxing under her shade. Most of the people were naked. Everyone was happy. I saw that we were eating the raw fruits directly from the tree; the tree was the representation of Gaia, and that by eating her fruit raw while naked and directly from the tree that we were worshipping Gaia completely and experiencing the greatest joy possible in a mutual exchange of giving at a deeply spiritual level. I still hold this vision close to my heart, and when I remember it, I feel strongly connected to the vision of GaiaYoga.

Meanwhile, life continues and in the summer of 2010 Ano and I conceive a child without Ano ever ejaculating. And when our son is four months old, we make passionate love without me ever having had a moon cycle and conceive our daughter. Thereby begins four years for me of deep service to my children.

Raising children is a powerful teacher and bringer of power, and I can barely begin to elucidate here what motherhood has done for me, but needless to say, two children radically changed our reality. We began to create what we thought a "Continuum Concept" culture could be. The importance of people who were living with us took on a whole new meaning, and we integrated everyone who was willing into our family. We mourned the lack of an integrated culture here because we experienced that we, as parents, were not always capable or available to provide for all of our children's needs. During this time, we had a few blessed individuals who showed up for our children in a way that deeply served our rejuvenation and our children's hearts, (thank you Mae and others <3). We also experienced the pain of being judged for parenting practices that we thought would best serve our children. In the Continuum Concept, children are trusted to have a survival instinct, and we found this to be true, so when our children wanted to emulate us by using tools, we let them while holding safe boundaries. And while our children rarely even hurt themselves slightly, the fear that some people had to the point to where they couldn't live with us was startling. Having children seemed to bring the values of GYG to the most practical level.

As far a polyamory goes, Ano had only engaged at an emotional level up to this point, and I had struggled deeply with that. Being pregnant and nursing infants had totally exacerbated my need for security and trust and commitment. Then, in the fall of 2013, Ano met a woman who wanted to engage him more fully. My children were about one-and-a-half and two-and-a-half. This was the beginning of my real training in polyamory. Although I suffered through the process, in actuality I discovered joy at connecting at a deep emotional level with the three of us, and I enjoyed a level of intimacy that I had not experienced before. I learned to advocate for my needs to be met, and I found Ano to be a better husband and father for me and our children. I started to trust in his vision that raising children with multiple intimate partners was optimal for everyone involved.

Although that relationship eventually faded, it set a precedent for me to understand life in a whole new way. I had a concrete understanding of what Ano was talking about when he spoke of a tribal community where there aren't social contracts around sexuality and where children were raised by the whole of the tribe instead of just their parents. I caught a glimpse of the profound intimacy, meaning, and depth of human-ness we could experience living that way. I became a believer! It was at this point that I told Ano, "I am totally aligned with your vision of GaiaYoga!" - what is being expressed in *True Human Freedom.*

Months later, in the fall of 2014, I met a man who became my lover. For over a year he, Ano, and I were a "triad." We shared hopes/intentions of creating a group marriage in which he would find an additional partner to have children with, and Ano and I would possibly add another woman or couple or more to our intimacy. I find extreme excitement in imagining that I can support my lover in expanding our family by finding a partner he can have children with, supporting all of us to have access to a range of possibilities of intimate connections. Through the challenging growth and healing, I have discovered feelings of joy in polyfidelity, where I can nurture and be nurtured in deep intimacy by multiple people.

Now, as the year turns to 2016, we are four months into the process of discerning how a woman, who has become intimate partners with my lover, is going to integrate into our group relationship. I am watching our relationship dynamics change. It is a profound process of growth for me, and while doing emotional work around old childhood wounds, I am discovering a truer me in this process, and I am deeply grateful. I find myself welcoming the challenges because I believe that real emotional freedom and deep intimacy are going to be the results of my efforts.

As I write this, people arrive and leave GaiaYoga Gardens almost on a monthly basis, and we have the beginnings of a community container with four other adults who have demonstrated a commitment to our community with a strong intention to become members. We have established a strong social container with two meetings per week in which we discuss and plan any current and upcoming projects and another meeting purely for heart connection and delve into and process any emotional content. We have structures to house approximately twenty people. I am hoping to soon add to our infrastructure with a new community kitchen and more small cabins.

So, while our life has it's share of pain and frustrations, we have a container here of healthy food, healthy communication, real intimacy, sustainable food-growing practices, sustainable energy systems, and an experience of communality that grows us each day to be better humans. We practice living aspects of *True Human Freedom* principles in a way that we imagine will create a life that is beautiful, abundant, and rich beyond all worldly measures!

The GaiaYoga Vision, as expressed in *True Human Freedom* and Ano's earlier booklet about GaiaYoga, provides a template that covers all areas of life. Ano offers arguments that, although sometimes cannot be scientifically or historically proven, do provide logical explanations for our actions, and for actions that can possibly and/or probably give us more access to what we really want (what we are calling Domain 9 or GaiaYoga Culture). One reason it's important for me to explain the "synchronicities" and spiritual messages that I received at GaiaYoga Gardens, in the time leading up to my return, and for months after my return, is that I believe these transitions into a different paradigm are genuinely spiritual and guided by a deeper force than we may be aware of. Living more in the ways of Domain 9, I believe, is to be more connected in this way to "Spirit." Once one is guided to live differently than the typical way we have grown up in the USA, then this book can be a great reference guide to the next steps one can take.

So, in conclusion, I want to express gratitude to you for your efforts at creating a more beautiful world. If this book resonates with you, then I suggest that practicing any of these ideas may lead you to a more meaningful and rich life. It is only for you to decide. I cannot claim that I am perfectly practicing anything referenced in this book. In many areas of life, perfection is not often a reasonable or even possible goal. The path is never a straight line, and any movement is an opportunity for growth and learning. So, with that, I lend my heartfelt support to you, and may you be truly guided by your highest good in all that you reach for!

Blessings on your journey.

Aloha from Melekai

••• TABLE OF CONTENTS •••

Chapters and Sections

FRONT MATTER

Dedication	ii
Preface (by Melekai)	iv
Acknowledgments and Appreciations	x
Introduction	2

THE CORE ARGUMENT

Getting Started	5
The Eleven Domains of GaiaYoga	8
Domain 5	9
Domain 6	11
Domain 7	13
Domain 8	15
What Is a Natural Human Social Structure?	22
Getting Culturally Sober	28
Sexuality and Security in the Domains	32
How Is Security Generated in the Different Domains?	33
Oy Vey! What Can We Do?	38
The "Spiritual" Domains of GaiaYoga	43

~~~~~~~

I Can See above the Smog! What's Next?	45

DIVING DEEPER

Navigating and Designing the Spheres of Community	46
The Relationship Between the Domains and the Spheres of Community	50
Money and Economics in the Domains and Spheres of Community	51
Spirituality within the Domains (Practice, Realization, and Internal Experience)	57
A Journey through the Spiritual Qualities of the Domains	60
Sustenance within the Domains	63
The GaiaYoga Approach to Diet and Health	66
The GaiaYoga Perspective on Birth	70
Explaining the Single-Source Imprint	72
Polyamory from a GaiaYoga Perspective	76
Competition, Jealousy, and the Single Source Imprint	77

OBSTACLES, INSIGHTS, & CONSIDERATIONS

The Great Obstacle: The Pursuit of False Human Freedom	88
Surpassing our Natural Limits	89
The Not-So-Great Obstacle: Creating Domain 9 While Loved Ones Recreate Domain 8	90
Creating a Community of Intention and Affection	91
Sustaining Relationship through Polarity and Conflict	91
Two Relationship Insights	92
Accepting our Genes, Re-assessing our Memes	93
Cultures of Preservation Versus Cultures of Acquisition	95
Avoiding "Traps" with Gurus and Leaders	96
The Limitations of Eco-Villages	96

NOW WHAT?

The Foundational Social Agreements of GaiaYoga Culture	97
Holistic Health and Healing	100
Holistic Intimacy and Sexuality	102
How Do We Create GaiaYoga Culture?	105
Tying the Bow around the Gift	106

BACK MATTER

Recommended Reading List	151
A Closing Thought	153
About The Author	154
Also Published by Pan Piper Press	154

Nagdeo Song Lyrics

Longing	iii
The Final Frontier	1
Suburban Refugee	20
Cradle-To-Grave	21
Fluid Bonding	31
The Errors Of My Way	42
Stuck In The Middle (For Melekai)	69
Mono-Mom Imprint	71
More Than One-And-Only	75
To Be Or Not To Be The True Me	108
Elate	150

Diagrams and Charts

The Eleven Domains of GaiaYoga	7
Domains Comparison Chart	26
The GaiaYoga Matrix	115
The Five Spheres of Community	115
Feelings List	126
"Universal Motivators" or "Needs" List	128
Nonviolent Communication Reference Guide	129

Appendixes(°°°)

What Is Instinctive Eating?	109
Why We Choose to Eat Raw Meat	111
GaiaYoga (The Introductory Teaching)	114
What is GaiaYoga?	115
An Overview of the Five Spheres of Community	118
What is CBGI?	119
What Is Nonviolent Communication?	123
Strategy Versus Needs	125

Glossary(°°)

Bonded Relationship	130
Buddha, Dharma, Sangha	130
Burning Man	131
Charge (also see Projection)	131
Container	131
Contracts	132
Contribute	132
Co-Parenting	133
Cultural Consciousness	133
Dagara, The (Malidoma & Sobonfu Somé)	133
Dietary Teachings	134
Primal Diet	134
Weston Price Diet	135
Egoscue Method	135
Ensoulment	135
Family Constellations	136
Integral Science	136
Intentional Community	137
Interdependence (Dependence/Independence)	137
ManKind Project, The (MKP)	137
Michael Teaching, The	138
Modern Spiritual Teachings & Teachers	138
Natural Giving	139
Network for New Culture (NFNC)	139
Nuclear Family System (Isolated)	139
Permaculture and Other Sustainable Agriculture Teachings	140
Plant Spirit Medicines	141
Polarity/Polarized Energy	141
Projection (also see Charge)	141
Rainbow Gathering	142
Re-evaluative Co-counseling (RC)	142
Rituals	142
Sexuality-Intimacy Styles	143
Polygamy	143
Polyandry	143
Polyamory	143
Polyfidelity	144
Shadow Work (Light on Shadow)	144
Shivalila	145
Social Agreements	145
Spiritual Energy Cultivation Techniques	146
Survival Needs	146
Tantra/Tantric	146
Transparency	147
Triggered	147
Waking Down	148
Hypermasculine	148
Zegg Forum	149

°° After the first occurrence of a word or phrase, indicates that that word or phrase is discussed in The Glossary. I've included an extensive glossary, because many of the concepts, teachings, and practices that are part of GaiaYoga Culture are probably unfamiliar to a large percentage of readers, and without some basic understanding of them it might be hard to move forward with following my inspiration or argument.

°°° After the first occurrence of a word or phrase, indicates that word or phrase is discussed in The Appendix. Entries in The Appendix are longer and more detailed than those in The Glossary.

••• Acknowledgments and Appreciations •••

Like all creations, this book would not be possible without collaboration, support, teaching, and mentorship from others. While I am certainly the person responsible for creating this book and birthing GaiaYoga, I can only do it because of the presence and effort of others who care about me.

Firstly, I acknowledge and appreciate my intimate-life-partner, Melekai. We've been together since May, 2009. She has made it financially possible for me to still have the land we live on, GaiaYoga Gardens, has given me/us two children, Elohi (4/22/11) and Iolanthe (6/8/12), and has fully joined me in co-founding GaiaYoga Culture. Delightfully, my love and attraction for her keeps growing as the years go on. And while I've had two long-term relationships before her, I consider her the first real partner of my life, as we can actually co-create a harmonious and juicy living reality together, that includes more than just the two of us, and our children.

Next I acknowledge and appreciate Ma'ayag Polihronopulos, who took me under his wing in 1992, helped me in my transition into living in Hawaii. He supported me in healing and developing my consciousness and he transmitted the Shivalila dharma to me. I deeply resonated with the vision that he expressed, and I devoted myself to its manifestation. I helped him coalesce the second incarnation of the Shivalila community (though I wasn't ever a full participant in it myself.) Ma'ayag gave me a model of what it means to be devoted to a vision as a leader and as a follower simultaneously, and planted in me an understanding of what our potential is as social animals, and what it takes to bring that into life. Without Ma'ayag carrying the torch of the Shivalila teaching, GaiaYoga Culture would not be a living vision in me.

I acknowledge and appreciate Marshall Rosenberg, the man who developed the Nonviolent Communication (NVC) teaching. I was first exposed to NVC in 2000 and I had an immediate devotional response to it. I studied NVC intensely for the next five years, including numerous workshops with Marshall. I consider NVC to be the most important single teaching for creating peace in this world at the internal to interpersonal to international levels. Marshall's contribution to humanity, in my opinion, at the level of Gandhi, Martin Luther King, Nelson Mandela, and the like, because besides offering inspiration, he has also given us utterly practical tools and a language to heal our minds so that we can create a deeply connected world based in natural giving. I would have almost no confidence in creating GaiaYoga Culture without NVC.

I acknowledge and appreciate Guy-Claude Burger who re-discovered Instinctive Eating in the 1960s and 70s in Europe. I started eating instinctively in 1990, and I've been doing so ever since. It is the foundation of my new life, the brick that everything else has been added onto. Though we've never met, he's had a huge influence on my natural well-being and capacity to bring the GaiaYoga vision forward with such clarity and confidence.

I acknowledge and appreciate The Mankind Project (MKP), the international men's group I've been in since 2010, and its founders, Rich Tosi, Ron Hering, and Bill Kauth. More directly I acknowledge and appreciate the men who, along with me, are the founding core of my weekly MKP Kumukahi i-group: Clive Cheetham, Roy Lozano, Scott Middlekauf, Lorn Douglas, and Daniel Moe. Even though they weren't directly share my mission of creating GaiaYoga Culture, these men, "mid-husbanded" me into fatherhood, into living my life in integrity with my values, and facilitated untold hours of effective shadow work to help remove my blocks from living my mission. Deep deep gratitude I have to these five men, and beyond them, the rest of the men in my i-group, and beyond them all the men throughout the islands that are involved in MKP Hawaii.

I acknowledge and appreciate Saniel Bonder and the Waking Down Sangha°°. I worked with Saniel during the late 1990s, and his teaching liberated me from practicing hypermasculine°° dharmas, brought me into a Witness Awakening, and gave me the spiritual foundation that I had been seeking. Saniel's approach to spiritual realization was unique, in that he was not interested in ascension out of mundane life into Spirit, but rather the descent of Spirit into mundane life. It was very liberating to realize I didn't have to change or purify myself to be fully spiritually realized, and this understanding has influenced the way I practice and teach GaiaYoga.

I acknowledge and appreciate Mercedes Kirkel, my intimate partner from 1999 to 2007. We met in the Waking Down community. Our relationship was a catalyst for immense growth and healing and the birth of the GaiaYoga teaching. We got into NVC together, bought and developed the land that is GaiaYoga Gardens, and co-wrote the first teaching booklet about GaiaYoga.

I acknowledge and appreciate Bill Mollison, Dave Holmgren, John Jeavons, Masunoba Fukuoka, and Dr. Cho Kan Hyu. These men pioneered sustainable agriculture, developed worldwide teachings, wrote books, and inspired me to grow food and develop a homestead sustainably.

I acknowledge and appreciate all the folks who've stayed at GaiaYoga Gardens over the years leading up to publishing this book, and have given their energy and input towards our home. I particularly want to honor Amor Rays and her children, Mae Desmond, Ürbāh Sullivan, Galaxy McDonald, Dominic and Shivani Dahl-Bredine, Evelyn Tanner, Isabel and Stefano Quarta, Kana Covington, and Zai Scruton who have graced our community with their devotion.

I acknowledge and appreciate Riley Ann Doyle for drawing the eye on the cover, Damian Cannamela for laying out the Domain diagram, and Mica'el Cerveny for creating the background of the cover and re-working the Domain diagram to fit over the eye. (Overall cover layout is by me.)

I acknowledge and appreciate all those who have edited this book as a gift to me and to GaiaYoga. i'm most grateful to Natec Harijan, who, along with Ma'ayag, was part of the original Shivalila community and lives here in Puna, Hawaii. She "came out of the woodwork" to make sure I accurately represented the Shivalila dharma, and helped me evolve that transmission into something I believe will be more effective in the world. Each of my other editors gave me much gold in their efforts to refine and re-organize what I wanted to say. Kaniela Lurie edited the first draft. The second draft was edited by Melekai. The third draft was edited by Ingo Suppan, Alan Conrad, Natec, my mother Braja Tarletz, and partially by Happy Om and Gary Zamber. (I edited the fourth and later the final draft.) The fifth draft was edited by Zai Scruton, and partially by Braja and Natec. The sixth draft was edited by Melekai. The seventh draft was edited by Boinn Quarta. And then further editing and structural re-organization was done by Julia Sokolyansky.

In early 2017 I re-edited the entire book and did a bit of re-writing here and there. From the clarity I got sharing and teaching out of the book for a little over a year I realized there was more I wanted to say about True Human Freedom, so I also added three new sections that I consider necessary to fill out the book. They are 1) *Competition, Jealousy, Insecurity, and the Single Source Imprint,* 2) *Holistic Intimacy and Sexuality,* and 3) *Holistic Health and Healing.* These sections also went through rounds of editing. The first draft was edited by Aleanu Matthee and Mae Desmond, the second draft by Zai, and the 3rd draft by Melekai, and partially by Boinn and Natec.

In mid 2018, during the lava flow that covered 10 square miles of our area (and about ½ acre of GaiaYoga Gardens!), I began an intimate relationship with a woman named Omya. She is the first person I've met in my life who truly and fully shares all my values and life-practices. Her presence has definitely strengthened and refined what I/we are doing at GaiaYoga Gardens and the development of GaiaYoga Culture.

In mid 2019, Omya and I, with Melekai's support, wrote the new essay and Appendix section called *What is CBGI?* Omya and I also did some re-writing in the sections about intimacy and sexuality to integrate the term CBGI into them, and Tydyn Rain St. Clair edited the entire book a final time.

For the 2021 printing Omya's ongoing research into new teachings to shore up gaps in our cultural practices has led to the addition of a two new books to our reading list, an indigenous culture-based parenting book and a cutting edge book about multiple adult intimacy.

Also during the time between the 4th and 5th printings Melekai and I transferred the ownership of GaiaYoga Gardens to a religious non-profit, and, with support, have created a financial and legal system to allow others to have equal power, security, and sense of home here. As of June 2021, we have 7 members and about 5 trial members in our community

Finally, I acknowledge and appreciate you! Thank you for taking the time to read this book and deeply consider my message. I might never know you, or perhaps you will directly join me in my mission of creating GaiaYoga Culture. Either way, it is for all of you that I've found the inspiration to put this forth, hoping to make a huge contribution to your life and the world. If this book contributes to you, I would love to hear from you. Feel free to email me at aloha@gaiayoga.org.

THE FINAL FRONTIER

We've gone to the moon
Can zoom zoom zoom
Built towers and tombs
Could boom boom boom

Get things and ka-ching
Boastin' bling bling bling
Latest ride without a ding
Smart phones ring ring ring

Type and Skype the hype
Sculpted bodies tight and ripe
Lost in lights, and seeing sights
And every erotic delight

*But we won't get along
So I wrote this song
We're hanging on by a tether
'Cause we won't live together
Ain't trekking out there, it's right here
Face-to-face is the final frontier*

Ice caps we climb
Sky and scuba dive
Bet our last dime
For crimes, risk doin' time

Got Guantanamo's
Growin' ghettos
Shoot first the negros
Give the res's casinos

Drill deep to drive our cars
Get drunk and laid in bars
Might colonize mars
Or fly to the stars

*But we don't get along
So I sing this song
We're hanging on by a tether
'Cause we don't live together
Ain't international, it's right here
Heart-to-heart is the final frontier*

Rock stars and star wars
Barge loads of more and more
Bigger and better than before
And did I mention more and more

With IQs so so high
Yet EQs too too low
Led by toddlers in suits
Screamin' "mine" and "no"

Dare any feat
Risk every bone
But don't dare ask me
To share my bank, babe, or home

ABC, FBI, KFC, REI
CEO, UPS, WHO, IRS
DDT, GMO, ATT, TRO
LOL, NRA, NFL, IRA

Re-mastered Mean Mr. Mustard
Every kind of sauce and custard
Billion buck blockbusters
Galas, glitz, 'n' lots o' luster

We got enough technology
To save the world or maybe three
Now let's make the maturity
To use it to serve all humanity

Here's a radical vision
To end the division
Put us all in one place
Lock the doors no escape

Jews and Muslims, Repubs and Dems
Rich and poor, us and them
Sexy ex's and current squeeze
Best buds and worst enemies

No one leaves 'til the conflicts end
All hearts open, make amends
Relate to each as a dear friend
Happy together, no pretend

*Yes we can get along
So I share this song
Weave strong bonds out of these tethers
As we choose to live together
Beyond our fear, right now and here
Hand-in-hand is the final frontier*

*Functional family is…
Inner peace is…
Peace on Earth
Is the final frontier*

What you fear is your final frontier

True Human Freedom
The Inspiration and Argument for GaiaYoga Culture

Introduction

Aloha. My name is Ano Tarletz Hanamana. I have a very precious dream that I've been yearning to manifest for over twenty years. My life-partner, Melekai, and our two children, Elohi and Iolanthe have joined me in this dynamic mission. We've also been joined by other individuals and families - for varying lengths of time, with different depths of commitment. In simplest terms, this dream/mission is to create a new human culture, from the ground up that is based on a sustainable-and-holistic vision, which honors and cultivates our deepest and fullest humanity. What we're doing is something that's hard to articulate without potentially sounding naive, utopian, grandiose, or even offensive to folks making other choices, but I'm going to take the risk anyway and share what I have to say!

Ever since I was in college, I've been tuning into my "yeses" and "nos." I asked myself questions like, how do I want to live; how do I feel about the world I grew up in; what actions and systems are in alignment with my values? Sadly, as I left college, I had a "no" for pretty much everything around me, a very strong "NO!!!" In 1990, I moved to Eugene, Oregon, to be around other hippies and to participate in the three "yeses" I had – friends, music, and organic farming. At the time my diet was a mess, and soon after moving there I stumbled onto one of the biggest "yeses" of my life – Instinctive Eating°°° — eating a natural diet of only whole, raw food, guided by my instincts. This "yes" trumped everything else I was doing, so I devoted my life to it. This devotion eventually led me to Hawaii in 1992, to the life I'm living now, and to more and more "yeses."

Over the 20+ years since I moved to Hawaii, I've been privileged to have free time and attention to deeply meditate on culture, communication, family-systems, healing, health, the natural world, ethical and ecological businesses, cooperative community, and our deepest nature as humans. This meditation has led me to discover and integrate my "yeses" in all the different areas of life. Over the years, it's become very clear to me that most of the suffering in the world is "by design."

Allow me to explain: Humans create cultural designs - and they are predominantly what define our life experience. One design shapes our experience one way, another design a different way: A capitalistic culture versus a gift-economy°° culture; a culture that is disconnected from nature versus one rooted in nature; a culture whose language is based on the mind and our judgments versus one based on heart connection and revealing our feelings°°° and needs°°°; a culture where people eat an all-raw diet versus one where people eat a cooked food diet; or a culture where people live in isolated nuclear families°° versus living in either a nomadic tribe or a rural village.

It's become clear to me that the "problems" we experience in life are mostly because of our lifestyles we choose and the underlying consciousness that both generates and is generated by the lifestyle. This is what I am referring to when I say "by design." Our problems are not because of something inherently wrong in us as individuals or a species. To me this is both "good news" and "bad news." It's good news because this means there is a possibility for change. We can change our lives and the lives of our descendants by creating a new cultural consciousness°°, a new cultural design, and a new cultural experience. I believe if we are living within a cultural design that is in harmony with our full nature as humans, then we will have a profoundly more enjoyable and sustainable experience in life.

The bad news is that this is a HUGE project. It's not one that can be done alone, nor can it just be done in a weekend workshop, nor just by changing one or two things in your life. We're talking total deconstruction and reconstruction of self, family, community, and culture!!!

I've been pioneering this ever since I got to Hawaii, and I've gone through more trials and errors than I can remember. I've fallen down a lot, with a lot of different people, in a lot of different community configurations. I've gotten back up, learned from my experiments, and continued forward. I'm now ready to come out of the closet, so to speak, and show up with all my truth, spread these seeds around, and hope that they grow. I'm calling this seed GaiaYoga°°°, the poetic term for the practice of living sustainably and holistically, which came to me in 2001 when I was looking for a phrase to express and represent this vision and teaching.

I believe this is the teaching and practice most needed by the world at this time. I pray GaiaYoga consciousness and practice spreads like the light bulb or the cell phone, and that GaiaYoga becomes the common understanding of humanity and the mainstream cultural pattern. Imagine a world where humans act in conscious alignment and harmony with the Earth and all the other creatures on it, instead of in a cancerous relationship with our own greater body. I, for one, trust it would be pretty fun and beautiful. We'll see....

~~~~~~~~~~~

One way to understand GaiaYoga, like I presented in my first teaching booklet, is as a vision and practice of creating sustainable-and-holistic culture, that integrates Spirit, self, community, and Earth. In order for this kind of culture to succeed and flourish, a significant dilemma must be solved -- how can we create a way for people to live together that truly and simultaneously honors all of who we are as social, emotional, physical, psychic, sexual, spiritual, and animal beings? In other words, is there a way that is stable, yet also dynamic enough to support each social unit (whether a family, clan, or tribe) in being able to cooperatively co-parent°°, grow food, educate children, operate businesses, foster creativity, grow and change together, handle conflicts, and, of course, enjoy and celebrate life?

Before I articulate a more full expression of the GaiaYoga vision or dharma°°, I will paint a picture of the main archetypal human social structures that have existed on Earth and articulate what their basic strengths, weaknesses, errors and/or limitations are. I'm trusting that if you understand what I'm going to share about humanity's past, our genetic/biological predisposition, and the cultures and consciousnesses we developed along the way, that you will recognize the wisdom behind what I want to create. It's my argument... In other words, what I want has real grounding in our humanity (our past, present, and potential), and thus there is universality to it.

And while these ideas have plenty of merit, they are not the reason I want to create and participate in GaiaYoga Culture. I want what I want because it's in my heart and soul to live this way. I see it as the cutting edge of integrated human evolution, and super juicy and fun! ... It's my inspiration.

My hope is that through reading this treatise, the same inspiration and desire will be ignited in you. That you'll come to see that the lifestyle and culture that truly resonates with your soul and your deep humanity might be vastly different than the way you grew up, and vastly different than the way most humans are living on Earth at this time. Furthermore, I hope that you'll be motivated to change your lifestyle and cultural foundation of your life to give yourself and your loved ones the gift of a life in full congruency with all of your being.

A significant percentage of what I'm about to say is based on the books *The Book Of The Mother* and *The Tantric Transmission Of The Shivalila Kinship Society*, written by Gridley Lorimer Wright (aka "Abralut") in the 1970s. Shivalila°° is a teaching that very radically looks at the nature of the human experience, emphasizing the way children are born and raised and how that impacts culture, and how cultural consciousnesses shapes our experience of life. Abralut proposed a way to create a free and enlightened society based on this teaching. The Shivalila teaching (I prefer the word "dharma") was the basis for two communities. The first one during the 1970s and early 80s in California, India, and other places, and the second one (after Abralut's death) from the mid 90's to early 2000s in Hawaii (based a few miles from where GaiaYoga Gardens is located).

Other external influences are Robert Lawlor's book about Australian Aborigine, *Voices Of The First Day*, Lynn Saxon's *Sex At Dusk*, my exposure to the spiritual teachings of both Adi Da (Da Free John) and Saniel Bonder, the work I've done in The ManKind Project°° (MKP), what I've integrated and uncovered through practicing and teaching Marshall Rosenberg's *NonViolent Communication*°°° (NVC), Pianky's *Integral Science*°°, my own life experiments in Instinctive Eating, practicing Permaculture°° in Hawaii, living in and founding intentional community°°, and other Tantric°°, social, and consciousness research I've done over the years.

An author is supposed to have "author-ity" on a subject – something that gives them the right, rank, or respect to tell a story for others to accept as true. So where do I get the authority to write a book called, *True Human Freedom*? I've accomplished, healed, and learned a lot pioneering GaiaYoga in Hawaii, but this is not where I generate the chutzpah to make the claim that I'm articulating *True Human Freedom*. It's not authority in the way/manner/context most people think of it. What I'm sharing with you is a myth, a soul song, a way to frame reality that generates beauty, meaning, and clarity for me. I ask you <u>not</u> to trust me. Don't project authority onto me. Instead, let my words guide you to a place in your own heart that might validate what I'm saying. I will make many arguments in this book, and I'm not going to reassure you of their validity with a bunch of footnotes, references, college degrees, or scientific evidence. I refrain from doing this because what really matters is if you're moved -- if your hunger and longing is sparked.

Ultimately, it's not my argument that matters; it's the inspiration that you generate from taking in these ideas and vision. The argument is just a bone to give your mind so it can chew on it and let the deeper process proceed without being blocked. Your mind can easily doubt and refute me. I don't want to wrestle with your mind. I'm using my mind to communicate these ideas, yes, but it's a communication from my heart and soul. It's with your heart and soul that you will either find value and inspiration in what I'm saying, or find that it doesn't resonate deeply with you. It's about what you find in yourself upon reading what I've said, not about the precise historic accuracy of what I'm saying. For indeed, anytime people talk about what occurred thousands or millions of years ago, it's just speculation, abstraction, myth-making. No one knows for sure, but we can know what's alive in us now, and if exploring our cultural past activates something valuable in us now -- that's what matters to me.

I'm not right, nor am I wrong, I'm just singing my song and hoping you'd like to dance.

••• THE CORE ARGUMENT •••

Getting Started

One of the first questions to ask is this: What does a natural human social structure look like in real life? Or, in other words, how are people genetically, biologically, socially, and instinctively predisposed or designed to optimally live?

It's pretty hard to answer this question looking outward because almost all of the evidence is lost in the distant past, and there are so few tribes of people living truly naturally and "off the land" anymore. I believe that to find clues it's worthwhile to meditate on what other species are doing. There has been a lot of observation of our close genetic relatives, the primates. They exhibit a fairly broad array of social forms, from the matri-centered, poly-sexual, more-cooperative bonobos, to promiscuous chimps, to the alpha-male-polygamous°° gorillas, to the lone-male, camp-invading orangutans and baboons. Monkeys have many forms of society which are worth considering as potential clues to what ours might naturally be.

Expanding beyond primates, other species such as bees, ants, dolphins, wolves, and giraffes have a close-knit social organizations that are larger than a nuclear family (one male, one female, and their offspring). Their social groupings are bonded; they work together for survival, play intimately with each other, and raise their young within the group.

Given the patterns of social structure displayed by most mammals, I believe it's worth seriously considering that the isolated nuclear family (one that is not living as an integrated part of a larger close-knit social organism) is not the natural social foundation of humanity. Perhaps our nature is also to live in, and as, a bonded unit that extends beyond the nuclear family, whether as an extended family, a clan, a tribe, or some other kind of kinship group. If this is the case, it isn't something that was only true a long time ago; it's just as true today. Our genetics and primal needs have not changed just because we've developed more tools, can watch TV, participate in "social media," go to the supermarket, or live in suburbs. Our genetics haven't been altered by these outward changes of modernization; thus, our core social needs or the structures that meet those needs haven't really changed either. Our genetics, our very nature, contain patterns for group living, even when it is not apparently necessary for our survival.

There are many dynamics to consider in the foundation of a social structure.

- How/why/when does mating occur?
- How is pair-bonding handled in relation to how extended-family and community bonding is handled?
- Who raises children (and how and why)?
- How is food acquired and stored and who feeds who (and why)?
- How is power held (is it through violence, rank, sex, age, skill, charisma, the joy of cooperation, by men, by women, by wisdom, etc.)?
- How big is the group?
- How is incest-caused pregnancy avoided?

- How are decisions made within the group (whose needs are considered, who makes decisions, are there fixed hierarchies, are men's and women's voices both (equally) valued)?
- How does the group split (from either population growth or unresolved conflicts within the group)?
- How and why does it merge (through sex-bonding, heart-bonding, food cooperation, mutual-protection, shared survival, or other reasons)?
- How do groups (families/clans/tribes) relate to other groups?
- What is the relationship of the group and the individuals within the group to a "higher power" or Spirit (however that is understood in that culture)?

Lots of questions! Human history and all the cultures that have existed within it are experiments that attempt to effectively answer these questions in life. Over the eons, billions upon billions of humans have participated in these cultural experiments. Given the vast number of cultures that have existed, and the lack of records of what they experienced or wisdom they gained, a truly exhaustive/thorough anthropological study is impossible. However, there is evidence available to draw on.

Keeping this in mind, it's definitely worth considering several questions: What kind of social forms has humanity lived in over the eons (from millions of years ago to ~10,000 years ago?) What kind of shifts have occurred in our more recent past (10,000 years until today?) How and why did we change from living in larger, bonded, social units to most of humanity living as an isolated nuclear family in a suburban or urban environment? And the most important question -- what do we do now?

I trust that much of this knowledge and clarity is held in our bones, blood, sperm or eggs, dreams, and souls. This is where I have looked for truth. I've used my ideas and other people's ideas as guides, inspiration, and maps or frameworks to make sense of what I find inside (especially the books and teachings I mentioned previously). But I don't stop there; I always go back inside to validate any theories. If they don't harmonize with my bones, blood, sperm, dreams, and soul, then I set those ideas aside and look for ones that do.

The approach I want to take to answer these questions is to describe the five archetypal human social forms (or types of human consciousness), and six other domains of manifestation that exist independent of, and prior to, humans. This is a modified map of what Abralut called The Nine Dimensions of Shivalila. I have found the word Dimension to be a bit misleading, so I've opted for the word Domain instead, but this doesn't change what I'm referring to. I've reorganized Domain 1 and 2 a bit differently than Abralut originally did. I've also added Domain 0. In his teaching, Abralut considered all the other Domains to be in relationship to a center of here-now/no-thing/no-form/no-structure, but he didn't include it in his Nine Dimensional map and by this omission it was easy to overlook. I'm also splitting Shivalila's Domain 9 into two domains to emphasize and clarify some issues around spirituality and metaphysical experience. These eleven Domains are symbolized by the diagram that's both on the front cover and the following page. It expresses the core teaching of this book.

As we travel through the Domains together, imagine that they express a timeless truth that links us all together. When our journey together ends, when you finish reading this book, hopefully my vision of sustainable-and-holistic GaiaYoga Culture and how and why to create it in your life will be apparent. Blessings on your journey!

THE ELEVEN DOMAINS OF GAIAYOGA

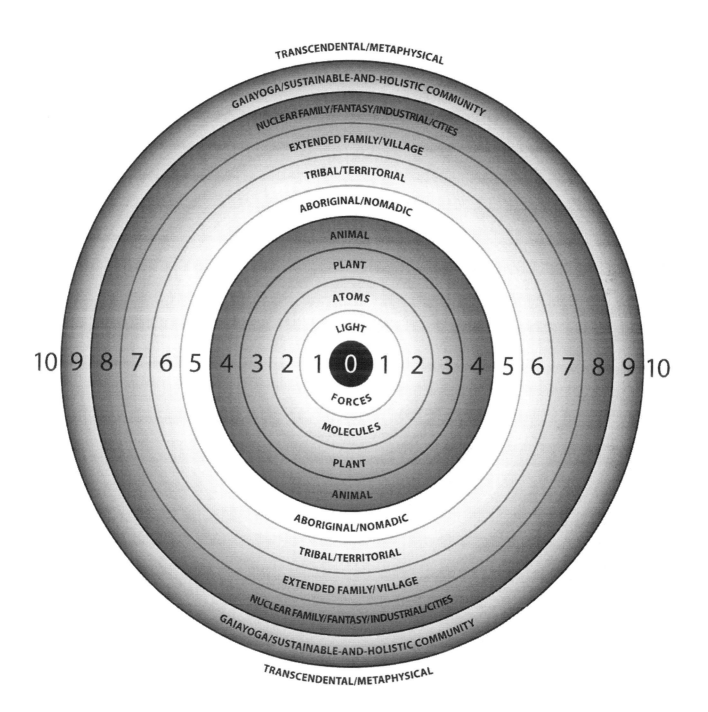

The Eleven Domains of GaiaYoga

First, I will briefly introduce the 11 Domains; then I will discuss at length Domains 5 - 9. I'll go into detail about Domain 0 and 10 later in the book, as they aren't directly relevant to the main points I'm making in the next few sections, and I don't want to create unnecessary distraction. I also want to make clear that the "lines" between the Domains are not solid, there are organic transitions between them, gray areas, permeable skins. I present these as a broad-stroked map to help us navigate and understand life; they are not to be wielded as a rigidly defined absolute truth.

"Outside" and "prior" to all of the other domains is:

Domain 0 - Emptiness/Non-Existence/The Witness/Consciousness

There are four foundational, pre-human, Domains of Life:

Domain 1 – light/energy/forces
Domain 2 – atoms/molecules (elements, minerals, gasses, liquids, solids, atmosphere, water)
Domain 3 – plants (from single cell to huge trees)
Domain 4 – animal (from single cell to whales)

The next five Domains are an articulation of the distinct archetypes of human culture and types of consciousness that individuals have within these cultural forms.

Domain 5 – aboriginal/nomadic
Domain 6 – tribal/territorial
Domain 7 – extended-family/village
Domain 8 – nuclear family/industrial/cities
Domain 9 – GaiaYoga Culture/Permaculture settlements

The last Domain is a "spiritual" Domain that exists beyond any particular human cultural form.

Domain 10 – transcendental/metaphysical

(Before I go further I want to clarify that this map is human focused, for us to navigate life, frame reality, and consciously create culture. Obviously there's a vaster difference between plants and atoms than between different types of human society. So while it might be more "scientifically sound" to not call each of these categories a "Domain" I find it useful to organize it this way. But I could just as easily lump all human culture into one Domain with many subdomains or whatever.)

Whether you use the lens of science or intuition, one doesn't see any fundamental alteration in how the four foundational Domains of manifested life (1 – 4) have functioned over the eons. Yes, new elements have formed and species have come and gone, but the way matter, energies, and living beings function in and of themselves, and in relationship to each other, are pretty much unchanged. These four Domains, in total, are what we refer to in layman's terms as "nature."

Why do we call this nature? Well, I would say that it's because there's a deep recognition that all light, gravity, magnetism, atoms, molecules, soil, plants, and animals exist, reproduce, interact, and express themselves within a single, relatively-harmonious structure. There are "rules," or "habits," that are consistent and shared. One can feel the difference between a wilderness, a natural cave, the stars, or a wild ocean versus a human construct. There is a natural order in the world, and everything and every being, with the exception of nearly every human, is fully integrated and surrendered to it. There are no straight lines in nature, no boxes, no forged metal objects, no computers, no cars, and no cooking. Humans are doing something quite different; they are attempting to live outside of nature.

I'm not going to spend much time talking about Domains 1 – 4 as I hold these Domains to be self-evident and people can meditate on these Domains and how they function and relate to each other. Indeed, there are thousands of books about energy/light/forces, atoms/molecules, plants, animals, biology, soil, fresh water systems, oceans, stars, astronomy, and physics, so if anyone wants to explore aspects of these Domains there's lots of wisdom and research out there. I'm going to focus on the human Domains (5 – 9) because this is where I see that the confusion exists, where most of our breakdowns occur, and where we have the power to make most of our choices.

Domain 5:

I trust that that there was some point in humanity's past when humans were still fully integrated and surrendered into the natural order. It could have been as recent as 50,000 years ago, or maybe 600,000 years ago, or maybe 2,000,000 years ago. There are numerous theories that seem sensible. To make the point I want to make, it doesn't really matter when, it just matters that this was true, and it lasted for a very long time. Let's call this type of human being an aborigine and call that consciousness/culture/lifestyle Domain 5.

What are the essential qualities of a Domain 5 (aboriginal) human being?

In no particular order: There was no written language, no money, and no sense of ownership as a social construct. Ownership, as it were, was generated through here-now aggression and physical possession of an item (much like an animal "owns" its kill). Language was profoundly simpler than modern language, without abstractions, concepts, tenses, etc. Most likely basic nouns and verbs were the extent of it (similar to the language of a baby or toddler). Paternity, the identity of the father of a child, was unknown or hard to determine at a mental and cultural level because people didn't understand sex led to eggs being fertilized by sperm, which led to babies. Somehow male animals "know" what offspring carry their genes and which don't, but it's at an instinctive level. So Domain 5 men probably had that same gut sense of which children they had sired.

I've exposed myself to many different theories of what Domain 5 "society" looked like. I see two possible social foundation scenarios: 1) People lived in multi-generational, matrilineal kinship groups of 20 to 100 people or so, and children were raised communally. There was an absence of sexual contracts (marriage/fixed-pair-bonding) that created anything like marriages that excluded a couple from other people in the kinship group -- in other words, a form of "group marriage" (everyone sharing food, sexuality, decision making, child-care, resources, etc.). Or 2) People lived in networks of small bands/families, as pair-bonded adults and alliances between people grew from inter-connection to "in-laws" on either side of the pair-bond. Probably these bands had a gravity that kept them close enough for protection and cooperation. Greater cooperation existed through in-laws (extended-family), but people were less cooperative and group-bonded than in scenario 1. (This whole topic is gone into at length in the books, *Sex At Dawn*, by Christopher Ryan, Ph.D. & Cacilda Jethá, M.D., and the response book, *Sex At Dusk*, by Lynn Saxon.)

Either way, these early humans were not enlightened or acting out of some high ideals or cultural savvy. They were functioning out of their genetics and instincts and whatever consciousness they had developed (which was probably not much in the dawn of humanity).

One thing that's become obvious to me is that our first human cultures were completely rooted in nature (without all the added intelligence, technology, and complex cultural stimulation). We were mostly "gene-driven" in how we lived; and the expression of our genes was limited by the container°° we lived in –- Domains 1 - 4. According to Richard Dawkins' selfish gene theory, the drive for genes and the person with those genes to replicate themselves and insure genetic continuity is very strong. Unfortunately, according to the theory, genes seem to be rather "short-sighted" and don't consider their impacts beyond their single-pointed purpose to continue and pass themselves on to the next generation, regardless of the quality of life this propagates. It's "selfish" because its purpose is very limited in scope – to effectively reproduce regardless of the costs. Think of a vine that grows so intensely that it kills the tree it's climbing on to get into the sun and with the tree's demise, falls back into the forest to die in the shade.

Until my mid-forties I clung to the idea that in the past there existed an idyllic, utopian human society "before the fall" out of "Eden"/nature. Between raising two babies and reading *Sex At Dusk*, I now realize that, much like childhood, our early ways of being were simplistic, unrefined, less conscious, with a very here-now attitude. The consciousness required to live in a utopian manner is being slowly sown and nurtured in humanity, and though Domain 5 exemplifies humans living in, and as, nature, it is without much of the consciousness that modern people take for granted.

Regardless of which of the two possible Domain 5 scenarios humans were living in, there were no individuals that lived outside of the kinship group. In the same way you don't see bees going it alone without a hive, there weren't lone humans without a people.

Going further, in Domain 5 there was also no agriculture; people hunted, gathered, scavenged, and roamed to find food. Until transitioning into Domain 6, people had no fire, so all food was eaten raw and without condiments. There was no refrigeration, canning or other type of modern food storage. People were naked all or most of the time and like wolves usually slept altogether for warmth and protection. There were no permanent settlements; camps or nests would be made and left as needed. People, as a rule, were fully expressive of their feelings and desires, without shame, inhibition, or repression. While it's impossible to verify this, in the same way other animals are fully expressive, there is no reason to believe early humans would inhibit their expression, even though they lacked a sophisticated language like we have today.

The primary time known to these humans was <u>now</u>. While most could plan a group hunt or remember a foraging site and return to it, even the sense of cyclical time (the movement of the seasons) was not probably present at an intellectual level; they knew simply the eternal now. There were no tools beyond sticks, stones, bones, and such. You probably get the picture.

There's a tendency to want to romanticize this way of being, and while there is certainly a lot of beauty in this consciousness it also represents limitations that, for some reason(s), humans had the drive and ability to transcend. The rest of Domain 4 has remained true to their instinctive and genetic limitations. Dolphins haven't built underground cities and domesticated fish. Cows didn't learn to open up gates so they can escape. Chimps don't drill for oil and forge metal. Ants haven't become able to live on their own, in apartments, so they can have freedom from the colony, etc…

Domain 6:

How did we grow out of this? Probably the biggest agent of change was fire. For better or worse fire changed man in a profoundly significant way. It allowed us to cook food (which was a radical change from our previous 100% raw diet), brought us out of the trees, allowed us to move to colder climates, offered us protection from predators, and gave us other powers too. It's important to realize that fire's power was received by primitive humans, who couldn't comprehend all the ramifications of what they were doing (much in the same way 19th/20th century man didn't understand the ramifications of using petroleum for making fuel and plastics). So, for better or worse, using fire became the thing to do… and we've never looked back.

There are a lot of theories out there about when man first tamed fire; most range from 2,000,000 to 100,000 years ago. And while Domain 6 isn't simply Domain 5 plus fire, the taming of fire was probably the first of many steps towards the full expression of Domain 6. (Of course this change wasn't uniform planet wide, some human groups shifted much more recently than others.)

But fire wasn't the only agent of change, so it's valuable to consider what else could have helped instigate this great change in humanity. Environmental changes could have pushed humans into a different niche. Perhaps it was psychedelics in the form of plant spirit medicines°°. Perhaps it was increased tool use (besides fire). Perhaps the human race became en-souled. If ensoulment°° did in fact happen, that means before this occurred humans didn't have a soul that re-incarnated from life-to-life, and learned lessons over the course of lifetimes. So ensoulment could have altered the vehicle of its incarnation (the human animal), increasing its drive for new experiences, intelligence, and capacity to step beyond natural limits. This drive also could have been caused by aliens, angels, or any number of other possibilities.

Whatever combination of factors was at play, humans developed into Domain 6 -- tribal. While it is commonly held that there is no difference between an aboriginal kinship group and a tribe, in fact there are many differences. In Domain 6 there is an increase of material power and freedom through greater tool use, control of fire, an expanded circle of cooperation, the establishment of fixed territories, the building of semi-permanent camps, some domestication of animals (like horses for travel), and more of a sense of cyclical time (past, present, future, seasons, ancestors and generations to come, within the cycle of nature). Language increases in sophistication and intelligence, and while the sense of family remains similar to aboriginal communality, there are probably social norms or agreements for how to "appropriately" relate to different categories of people (e.g. close family, people from other tribes, elders, children, warriors, mothers, etc.)

Instead of only participating in an intimate sphere°°° (a here-now, fully expressive, shared social circle), there is now the addition of a larger personal sphere°°° (relationships that are cooperative and friendly, but have limits for amount, depth, and continuity of sharing of time/energy/resources/power). Within Domain 6 there are different types of social contracts that fundamentally didn't exist in Domain 5. Examples of this might include: 1) cultural recognition of paternity and therefore clans within the tribe (clans being an intimate sphere within the personal sphere of a tribe); 2) use of ownership as a social construct (e.g. my teepee and your teepee, my spear and your spear, my sex-partner(s) and your sex-partner(s), our tribes territory, your tribes territory; 3) withholding expression of certain feelings or needs with people outside my clan (what we now think of as social decorum or manners); 4) people have simple, natural clothing; and 5) councils of elders or other types of personal sphere governing bodies.

Relative to food, Domain 6 ushers in more advanced forms of food storage; more manipulation of plants and animals for increased food supply and consistency of food availability. The biggest change is probably the advent of cooking, which takes place primarily over open fires in tribal cultures. Other forms of food manipulation also developed (e.g. fermentation, juicing, drying, combining, spicing, etc.) Thus humans went from using our instincts to eat food and choosing from food as given by nature (whole, raw, and wild) to consuming "indigenous" diets°°.

In Domain 5 consciousness, there is no trade or barter as we think of it, because there is no concept of ownership, but in Domain 6 there can be inter- and intra-tribal trading or barter.

Rituals°° begin to have use in the tribal societies of Domain 6. Ritual and shamanism are ways to intentionally shift from one Domain consciousness and awareness to another (usually downward from one's "home" Domain or up to Domain 9 or 10). Since Domain 5 people are naturally fluid in Domains 1-4 (and don't know the higher Domains) there isn't a need to have rituals to shift Domains. In Domain 6, there can be blocks to accessing any of the first five Domains. This is because of the various changes that developed going from Domain 5 to 6. The social constructs and use of fire and tools have the cost of taking people out of the full fluidity of presence and natural health of the here-now. Thus, there becomes practical need for rituals and shamanism to dissolve the contractions that block fluid consciousness. Examples of this are a Sun Dance ritual, sweat lodge, vision quest, or an ayahuasca or peyote ceremony.

Sexuality in Domain 6 varies from tribe to tribe. Some tribes have open sexuality within the group, culturally supporting various types of poly-sexuality. Some tribes have restriction of poly-sexuality to certain members, such as a chief, while others remain monogamous. Before marriage, for teens and young adults, there may have been no restrictions on sexuality, leading to more open and free sexual expression for the youth. The important thing is to realize that there is a shift in how a typical person relates to their sex partner(s) as we step away from Domain 5.

This change most likely occurred in one of two ways, depending on which possible scenario of Domain 5 we follow. If we take possible scenario 1 (a group marriage type culture) then there is decrease in overall bonding within human groups and an increase in social contracts dictating who can be sexual with whom as we move into Domain 6. These are ways of owning/possessing other people, not necessarily in an effort to overtly treat them as property, but as a way to insure the security in a mating relationship. At a primal level the motivation is to guarantee intimacy with them. On the other hand, if we started in possible scenario 2 (a more mating-pair-based culture), then it might be that there's an expansion in cooperation moving into Domain 6. Less organized and cooperative bands would come to see the advantage of bonding as larger social units (clans and tribes). There still would be an increase in the use of the social structure of ownership, because owning is something that happens over time, and is a psychic and social event that is different from here-now aggression of physically holding something from another who wants it. Ultimately, we can't really own or possess anything, we can only get people to agree we own things, and act as if that social agreement is true.

Intimacy, in fact, is about mutually having authentic and deep access to another person. Many people mix up ownership (particularly of a lover) and intimacy. Ownership is a strategy°°°. It is used primarily to meet one's need for dependable access (to a person, land, or a resource) and for security. As a strategy it has advantages and disadvantages; in other words, when the strategy is asserted, some needs are met and others are not met. Ownership is a way to control free energy, resources, things, land, or people. Besides the apparently positive result of dependable access, there is the stress of maintaining ownership. A schism is created between you and those who aren't owning that person/thing/property. One symptom of this schism is that we don't get to create the trust and deep security by cooperating and sharing with others around vulnerable and precious things (like lovers, babies, land, food, etc.). So owning impacts our social/emotional body, altering how we experience and handle jealousy, insecurity, vulnerability, and trust.

Relative to security, it's a simple formula. The more whole and bonded a people are, the more they get security via their group intimacy, and the less they are inclined to own or possess a single person. If a group is less whole and bonded, they can get less security and intimacy via the group as a whole, and the more they'll seek security in a single intimate partner. (In Shivalila dharma, this is called the "single-source imprint," which I'll discuss in depth later, starting on page 71.)

A baby who is nursed by multiple mothers and has many intimate-caregivers (men/women, older children, and elders) has a "multiple-source" childhood experience. Because of this, they will tend to enter the world of adult intimacy and sexuality with a very different sense of how to engage in life and relationship than a baby who had only one mother as an intimate caregiver. The mother-child relationship (especially around nursing) is the predominant template that is echoed in the lover-lover relationship of adults. In other words, how we are loved as babies is the primary influence of how we will treat our lovers and how we will want to be treated. (I'm only considering structure here, not the quality of the care and relationship, which could be anywhere from enlightened to highly dysfunctional, regardless if there is one source or many sources.)

The deep security Domain 5 and 6 babies get from being part of a bonded people, especially if they have multiple nursing mothers (and multiple men relating as a father), deeply nourishes the human being. This foundation of nourishment in infancy and childhood makes them immune to so much of the dysfunction we see in the modern world of relationships – where adults seek from their adult lovers and intimates what they didn't get as infants. There's nothing "wrong" with folks who are doing this. They are simply suffering from a cultural design error that has profound impact. One of my deep intentions in analyzing Domain 5 and 6 at this level is to address the dysfunction we see today and provide a cultural template for health and healing in our intimate relationships. Alter the foundational cultural consciousness and we can prevent dysfunction and trauma from ever starting. Plant a different seed; a different plant grows. More on this later.

Most of the indigenous cultures that people today respect, wish to emulate, or idealize are Domain 6 cultures. Books like *The Continuum Concept*, by Jean Leidloff, *Voices of the First Day*, by Robert Lawlor, *Nomads of the Dawn*, by Wade Davis, Ian MacKenzie, and Shane Kennedy, or *Mutant Message Down Under*, by Marlo Morgan, or the teachings of the Hopi, the Mayans, and the Dagara°° are all about and by tribal cultures, and express Domain 6 consciousness.

Domain 7:

Over time, tribes gave way to Domain 7 (extended family/village culture). Though village cultures share many elements with tribal cultures, they differ in many important ways. Domain 7 cultures began to emerge between 10,000 to 30,000 years ago, as some tribes developed agriculture and permanent settlements. Certainly by 5,000 years ago there were many examples of Domain 7. In the village, people tend to live in extended family units; grandparents, parents, uncles, aunts, children, and other relatives all living in the same home, compound, piece of land, or very near each other. Villages are usually "close to nature" and mostly rural, but they can be somewhat urban. Villages contain private and extended-family land-holdings whereas a tribe's territory is almost always held by the whole tribe. There is a larger sphere of cooperation in Domain 7. This increases material power, but it decreases the wildness and intimacy within our connections.

Villages have a fixed location; they are not at all nomadic. This physical stability is made possible by, and supports the growing of, food crops (farming) and the keeping of livestock (animal husbandry). This combination of farming and animal husbandry mostly replaces hunting, gathering, and roaming. A huge shift occurs in our relationship to food. Grains and roots become a huge part of the diet (rice, wheat, millet, amaranth, corn, potato, cassava, taro, quinoa, etc.). Stoves, ovens, clay pots, metal pots, etc. become essential elements of life. Grains and roots mostly can't be eaten raw but can be stored for long periods. They become the primary staple of most villages, allowing people to be non-nomadic and to move settlements further from the equator.

Linear time kicks in (the tracking of time on a clock or sundial), though it's used in a "softer" way than we see in Domain 8. Paternity is now the primary way family is recognized and organized (surnames in most of the "world" religions and first-world cultures come through the father). There's a huge advancement in tools and weaponry, as well as in mining and forestry. There's metal forging, carpentry, roads, wheels, various forms of water control, and a much greater permanent infrastructure that people live in. Domain 7, as it first developed on the Earth, precedes plastic and petroleum, electricity, and phones. Humanity's original villages predated these. Some Domain 7 cultures were so large that they developed towns and cities (London, Athens, Rome, Ur, Tokyo, etc.) though living in urban centers was not the norm.

Within villages, there is barter and trade. From village to village there is also barter and trade, but there is a dramatic increase in currency (a.k.a. money) used to exchange goods and services. Prior to Domain 7, there really isn't money the way we understand it now. Yes, gold, silver, and other precious minerals held value and were traded, but this is a different than using currency primarily.

In Domain 7 there is written symbolic language. Where a tribe's children are mostly integrated with the daily life of the adults, in villages you begin to see schools where children are segregated into their own culture. Education often takes place separately from adult life and this starts to make it harder for children to follow in the footsteps of uncles, aunts, older children, parents, and grandparents. Most villages blend these two forms of child education and enculturation.

In Domain 6, there might be treaties and agreements between different tribal groups, but each tribe is fundamentally autonomous, not answering to a greater governing body. At times there is an expanded sense of unity or allegiance within groups of tribes. For example, the Cherokee Nation was much larger than what one would normally think of as a tribe. However, even in this kind of situation there wasn't the kind of top down control structures that we see in Domain 7 cultures. For example, Britain up until the late-1700s was a Domain 7 culture. Kings, queens, dukes, barons, sheriffs, and others, who did not live in a particular village, ruled that village and other villages as part of a larger dominion (county, district, kingdom, etc.) In many cultures, there was outside law and rule enforced on villages. This is a huge shift from the kind of governance, or rather lack thereof, found in Domain 5 people.

There is a definite movement in how force, violence, and weapons are used as we step up through the Domains. In Domain 5, "violence" is used to kill for food, and in here-now aggressive acts.

These instances are complete once the act is over, and don't escalate into long-term grudges, feuds, and wars. In Domain 6 there are territorial conflicts between tribes, but it's not at the level that war is. In Domain 7 there is war. This includes religious war, economic war, resource exploitative war, and territory expanding wars. In Domain 8, which we'll talk about soon, there are the same kind of wars as Domain 7, but the weapons are much more powerful and the scope of the wars are much greater. In Domain 7 there can also be slavery, which doesn't exist to the same extent in Domain 6, where people are limited to the personal sphere and don't have the same capacity to dominate other races or groups of people. Slavery in many Domain 7 cultures was the key to their ability to prosper and expand their empires.

In summary, to many folks, Domain 7 represents the "good 'ol days". Extended families lived together, with much less technology, food was still exclusively organic and almost always local, the word of most villagers had real meaning and could be trusted, and villages were safe places to live and raise families and get a generous amount of support from other folk within your village.

The village helped birth the local sphere°°°. The word "neighbor" best expresses the relationship in the local sphere. There are people in the village you may not interact with, but there's a social awareness of all the people in the village and their relationships. Prior to village life, a person's day-to-day life existed solely in the intimate and personal spheres. In the village, there's the intimate/personal sphere of a multi-generational extended family. Outside of that is a personal sphere of the friends and close associates of that family, and surrounding that is the local sphere of the whole village. While a tribe is one economic unit, for the most part, a group-organism working as one to survive together, the village has much more division between families, requiring each household to have its own economic system to maintain the distinction between extended families. Hence, the economic energy in a village goes primarily toward supporting each extended family's autonomy, and secondarily toward supporting the larger group-level communality of the village. In other words, the personal sphere trumps the local sphere in a village. Thus, the all-for-one-one-for-all disposition that spread out to the tribe in Domain 6 is limited to the extended family in Domain 7. Again, more people cooperating together, but less intimately bonded.

Domain 8

A pattern is emerging of increasing technology and decreasing bonding between people. As we all know, we didn't stop in Domain 7. For better, worse, or both, the adventure continued... Big shifts occurred in the Western world beginning in the mid 1700s and continuing into the1800s. The most significant one being industrialization! More than any other external factor, this initiated the birth of Domain 8 (nuclear family/industrial/technological/fantasy) consciousness and culture.

Domain 8 is the dominant cultural pattern and consciousness on the planet at this time. As with the other Domains, there are many elements, patterns, and agreements that define and epitomize Domain 8. Socially, Domain 8 is based on the isolated nuclear family as the foundational structure of society. Urban and suburban households are filled with endless pairs of people living alone or with their children. In Domain 8, it's not that children don't have grandparents, aunts, uncles, and cousins; it's that they don't live together as a whole family. They might live near each other, but in general, every couple (and their young children) has their own household, own economics, and the extended-family gets together for special occasions or for specific reasons, rather than living with continuity as an extended-family. The very architecture of homes, apartments, and condos concretize this family system.

Even more than technology, the isolated nuclear family system (which is based on monogamy or serial monogamy) is the water people swim in. This family system, as the basis of society, is rarely challenged, or considered as something changeable, or as a source of suffering.

The ability for families (and governments and businesses) to maintain connection via technology, such as mail, telegraph, telephones, the internet, cars, and planes, has helped foster the isolated nuclear family model and the collective sphere°°°. Prior to these inventions, families were much more likely to live together. Whether intentional or not, living together supported us in maintaining connection, and enjoying the strength and security that comes with that connection. People have aggressively explored this new-found "freedom" -- the ability to move about the planet while maintaining a semblance of connection. Ironically, these new powers actually decrease a family's capacity for deep cooperation and conflict resolution. The "muscle" has atrophied from lack of use and apparent necessity. Now, blood/DNA is often the only bond, not sharing the rhythm of day-to-day life together. I argue that these changes have disastrous impacts, further isolating us from each other, and undermining our capacity to connect.

Why and how did the isolated nuclear family replace the extended family of Domain 7?

There are several factors that helped precipitate the changes from living in extended families to isolated nuclear families that occurred from Domain 7 to 8. First and foremost, industrialization made it possible for people to survive without needing to directly cooperate with others, namely their extended family at close quarters. Machines and collective sphere cooperation also eliminated the need for overt slavery. It was psychically made possible by shared abstractions, social agreements, and mind control around religion, corporation, state, nation, race, ethnicity, and class. It was materially made possible by oil, coal, electricity, and all the inventions and machines that people bought and sold. Thus it became a realistic option to live outside an extended family system and be able to survive or even thrive. Indeed, the whole way we see individuality today and the dominance of the collective sphere is based on the "freedom" granted by machines and the indirect cooperation of people that don't live in the same region, yet provide goods to strangers from strangers. A Domain 5 or 6 "individual" couldn't even begin to conceive of living alone. In short, the tribe and the village has been traded for, and made obsolete by, machines, tools, long distance transportation, and global markets. Another byproduct of this "freedom" is that individuals and isolated nuclear families became easier to control and overt slavery was replaced.

Without a tribe or village, and the intricacies of different relationships therein, a Domain 8 person needs an outlet for these fundamental social needs. Clubs, bars, festivals, soap operas, romance novels, movies, and now the virtual world of Facebook, Skype, email, texts, etc., attempt to fulfill us socially and emotionally. (While I don't consider it another Domain, the information age could be called "Domain 8.1".) Without real, in-person relationships, a human being must find some way to satisfy his or her deep need for connection and meaning. So this "freedom" to live alone, made possible by machine servants (cars, tractors, supermarkets, cities, the phone, all sorts of industries, light bulbs, televisions, computers, refrigerators, lawn mowers, etc.), has also crippled our cooperation and relationship skills and diminished our ability to experience and participate in relationships.

This has become a cycle that perpetuates itself, while each successive generation of Domain 8 children become less and less able to engage in deep and cooperative relationships or live without various anesthesia such as fantasy, substances, and authoritarianism. The need for these pain reducers is increasing as well, as the trauma in our childhood and fragmentation of our humanity also increases generation-by-generation, due to the changes happening in Domain 8 society.

Another factor is fantasy. Fantasy is the acceptable anesthesia of Domain 8. The message is, "Just choose your favorite escape (aka drug), and you can easily numb out to all the profound needs that are not met in your life." Take away peoples' fantasy fix and we'd have some massive eruption of emotion and probably social revolution or uprising, or anarchy. Fantasy is a distraction from both the external environmental and social reality, and our internal emotional and psychic reality. It's easy to become addicted to fantasy; it's so bright and shiny and clean and safe, not messy and challenging like life. The problem is that it's "junk food," and has little real nourishment; but in the same way junk food fills one's belly up, fantasy fills peoples' time and attention and keeps us distracted from our real needs. While imagination is certainly a wonderful part of being human, the profound imbalance of our use of fantasy has become instrumental in allowing humans to live far outside nature and a natural social structure.

While Domain 6 and 7 cultures did have myth and story, theirs were integrated with daily life, farming, hunting, seasons, and community. Story and myth were not used as a substitute for the real world, but rather a way to make sense of life, so it could be lived better. Storytelling was a living art and part of the glue of a people, shared within the personal or intimate sphere by other people within that sphere. Fantasy is different from storytelling or myth, though it certainly acts as a pseudo-glue. Nowadays, many children and adults spend much of their time absorbed in fantasy. Examples for children include thematic Legos, comic books, computer/video games, cartoons, cartoon cereal, movies, action figures, recorded music, etc. For adults it's pornography, fantasy-based sex, web surfing, virtual reality games, novels, television programs, movies, magazines, following professional and school sports teams, and valuing meta-concepts that come through national politics, religion, and the internet over real-life, intimate experience.

If fantasy isn't enough, we also have mind and body altering substances, addictive substances, and pharmaceuticals. Most of us can easily see how substances, (including nicotine, caffeine, alcohol, marijuana, refined sugar and other junk foods, prescription drugs, anti-depressants, and hard drugs) are used by most people, most of the time, to numb themselves, distract themselves, and avoid feeling pain. Many of these substances were available to people in Domain 7 cultures and some Domain 6 cultures, but their use has greatly expanded in Domain 8 cultures. Also in Domain 6 and 7 cultures, substances were more often used in a conscious container or ritual space, as opposed to recreationally as they're often used in Domain 8.

I'm not suggesting that there is no value in mind-expanding or psychedelic "drugs" and that they can't serve people's health, healing, and consciousness. I am suggesting, based on my experience, that other than psychedelic plant-spirit medicines and raw plant or animal products (like coca, kava, or organ meats), most substance use disempowers people more than it empowers them.

But there's even more…

Authoritarianism. Domain 8, at least as it is currently manifested in most places, is a power-over authoritarian system, which separates people into the haves and the have-nots. There are slaves (mostly through mind control and economic pressure), serfs, and workers on one end and people of wealth and power on the other (the "1%"). And, for sure, the people on the bottom have it pretty tough. Now clearly, this consciousness and mode of power use and political system has its origins prior to Domain 8. But since it is in full-blown expression, amplified by all of our technological prowess, I'm choosing to address it as a feature of Domain 8.

As I hinted at earlier, in the introduction, the first six letters of the word authoritarianism is "author" -- the one who writes the story. The boss, the owner, the teacher, the doctor, the politician, the priest, the father, the news (in paper and on screen), the wealthy, these are the ones who write the story. Where is their story written? Intentionally or unintentionally, the story is written upon the weaker minds, the poorer in wealth, and those with less personal power.

In authoritarian organizations (e.g. families, schools, clubs, religions, corporations, and governments) the needs of the few (or the one) is what matters; and their power is wielded over the many. Also, instead of people being motivated by intrinsic reasons, such as natural giving°° and desire to contribute and grow, people are motivated by extrinsic reasons, such as hope for rewards and/or fear of punishment. This dynamic encourages people to fragment from their hearts or whole beingness, and instead operate primarily out of their minds and a sense of what is right-or-wrong or good-or-evil/bad. This leaves people susceptible to mind manipulation and mind control. The extreme version of this is literally killing others because they are told by the authorities (the authors) that there are others who are "bad" or "evil", and we are good, and good must stop evil, and indeed kill the evil, or risk being evil oneself for not stopping the evil. (This is my re-expression of NVC's teaching around authoritarianism.)

Sadly, people submit to this. Indeed, authoritarianism cripples people's hearts and souls, and makes them easier to control, whether it's children seeking good grades instead of having the joy of learning, soldiers killing with a shutdown heart just following orders, zealots following the bible because their pastor said "Jesus said they'll go to hell if they don't," or people enslaving themselves to a false personality out of fear of being rejected or shamed (by others doing the same thing).

Being under the spell of authoritarianism or casting the spell on others is a huge distraction from feeling, understanding, and acting upon our true nature (which deeply fulfills our humanness). So it also serves as a form of anesthesia that permeates the whole culture.

A few more points...

A human is biologically and socially a Domain 4/5 being at birth. To be "civilized" into Domain 8, a baby human must be denatured and molded and experience the loss of their primal nature. This starts with how birth is handled and how parents and families relate to babies. Most people born into Domain 8 experience a huge amount of trauma from hospital birth. This comes in many ways: by very bright unnatural lights, being removed from parents, being poked and prodded, induced labor, drugs for the mother, unneeded C-sections, sterile environments, strangers in this most intimate space, disrespect for the pacing of the baby coming into the world, circumcision, etc.

Moreover, most parents aren't identified with the real needs of a baby human, so they unwittingly do things to their child that they don't realize the impacts of. Some of this includes feeding them non-organic and highly-processed foods, isolating baby in cribs and even its own room, feeding baby formula instead of breast milk, training baby to suppress its sound and feelings, lack of extended-family tribe, authoritarian schools and governments, lack of real connection with the Divine and Nature, and so on. If you think about it, raising a child is probably the hardest most sophisticated "job" a person could ever have, and most people enter into it with almost no training or deep understanding of infants, babies or how to raise the kind of child they would want. This is a huge topic that we could look at much more thoroughly, but this enough for the moment.

In the 21st century, we have actually gone beyond nuclear families, to what I call sub-nuclear families (another "Domain 8.1" phenomenon). This includes single-mother (or father) families, all kinds of artificial insemination, and children who are not breastfed and are pretty much raised by computers, the internet, television, daycare, schools, and don't have any real intimate social skills or contact. The ramifications of what I just said and the impact on these people's lives is profound. It is crippling our capacity to be in relationships and to be truly self-connected.

Similarly, industrialization has gone way beyond where it began in the 1700s. Now there's genetic engineering, sci-fi level technology in many areas, and an inconceivably vast network of interaction going on through the internet and cell phones, most food is grown completely by chemicals and planted and harvested using huge machines, many people spend their whole lives without directly communing with wild nature, and the air, water, and soil are polluted and toxic in many places. There are EMFs, radiation, smog, pesticides, oil spills, etc. The level of disassociation from the Earth, community, families, and indeed ourselves has reached an unprecedented height.

This means most people in Domain 8 are in a lot of pain, pain that is buried beneath all of the anesthesia, denial, and disassociation. Fear and lack of skill in facing and feeling this pain keeps people stuck in their lives, recreating the same situation day after day. Domain 8 is profoundly effective at keeping people captured and captivated in it. In fact, when people attempt to escape or reach outside of Domain 8 they often experience pain. Why? Because their energy systems are clogged with unfelt pain, and when we open up those channels of energy and relatedness they empty out like a clogged drain, and the first movement of energy is often the yuck that's been stuck in there for a long, long time. Unless a person understands this process, this pain can easily be misinterpreted as a reason to not open up.

Hopefully when people open up and face these old pains they also experience a sense of expansion and freedom from releasing the contracted consciousness. The "bad trips" that people have on psychedelics are very much this kind of thing, where the release of inhibitions also creates a flood of pain, paranoia, feelings of separation, rage, grief, etc. The issues that come up in intentional communities and intimate relationships are the same kind of thing. These issues are often tough to work through, and it requires a lot of skill and clarity to realize it's about the past and our conditioning and not the present moment.

It's easy to see the "problems" in Domain 8 culture and consciousness, and I don't wish to dwell on them, but it's important to delineate them sufficiently so we can be discriminating and understand what we're working with when we attempt to heal from it and evolve out of it. What most folks are facing is that literally their survival is dependent on being a member of a culture that is designed to enslave them, control them, distract them, keep them disconnected from each other and nature, and have no free energy to make any significant change. To put it lightly, most of us are in a very difficult, very compromised situation in life, and getting out of it takes a lot of risk, courage, support, and quite literally, a place to go to that's a sanctuary from the madness, where the kind of culture I'm suggesting can be developed. This is the kind of sanctuary we've created at GaiaYoga Gardens and this is the kind of culture we are actively co-creating here.

Suburban Refugee

Suburban Devotee
Is what you've grown to be
Muted and molded from infancy
In a fragmented family
Without wise community
Tricked by a paved reality

It all falls on you and me
Eons of insanity
Who's gonna heal this mess
And pay the karmic debt
Yeah, now's our time to choose
We all win-win or lose-lose

Your anesthesia is starting to wane
What you gonna do when you feel that pain
Keep the ship steady towards coma and death
Or dare to change course towards life and breath

Suburban Devotee
With dreams of being free
Yet you invest in university
Or tread caged in your city
Drunk on oil ignorantly
And media mythology

The sacred birds and bees
Got warped by pornography
Your elder is a t.v.
Supermarket mentality
Virtual intimacy
Science rules divinity

It takes faith to walk away
When your friends intend to stay
But when you choose to live free
You become a refugee

Your anesthesia is starting to wane
What you gonna do when you feel that pain
Keep the ship steady towards coma and death
Or dare to change course towards life and breath

Suburban Refugee
Of course it ain't easy
When all you learned is to consume
And maybe clean your room
To make a whole culture now
When you got no know how

Suburban Refugee
Heroically
Leave your security
To secure your future free
For the walls cannot contain
A being who's truly sane

Your anesthesia is starting to wane
What you gonna do when you feel that pain
Keep the ship steady towards coma and death
Or dare to change course towards life and breath

Suburban Devotee
To New Indigeny
Create this with my friends and me
We have skills for living free
We don't have to live like a refugee
We don't have to live like a refugee…

Cradle-To-Grave

Cradle-to-grave
Born to ride this wave
Cradle-to-grave
I bet it's what your heart and soul craves

Tracked by your tribes' elders from the other planes
All the way into your womb to be born again
Welcoming songs fill your forming ears
Blessing your return with joy and tears

The rituals of birth are a sacred time
When ancient bonds are re-entwined
This longest journey ends in loving arms and eyes
Skin-to-skin, trees, birds, rain, sunshine

Days turn to weeks and months to years
Following in footsteps so wise and clear
Of a people wed to Nature and Spirit strong
Hunt, gather, build, ensure all belong

    Cradle-to-grave
    Be brave - leave your cave
    Cradle-to-grave
    The greatest gift we were given and gave

Children, elders, women, and men
Used to be ancestors, and will be again
Now here on the Earth as a whole tribe
Celebration, ritual, the rhythm and vibe

Rites of passages, wisdom guiding choices
Deep cooperation, an accord of voices
Finding your purpose with elders support
Living your mission with real rapport

I wasn't born like that, so it's hard to know-and-trust
Raised without a whole tribe, so create one I must
To find my true way, left my past in the dust
Carrying my sign: "Cradle-to-grave or bust"

Cradle-to-grave
In a tribe no slaves
Cradle-to-grave
All-for-one-and-one-for-all is "saved"

Dagara, Eskimo, Yequana, Navaho
Shinto, Beduoin, Hopi, Tibeten

Lakota, Saami, Aztec, Yanomami
Fijian, Jamaican, Anuak, Penan
Buryats, Incans, Hadza, Mayan

Dolphin pod, hive of bees, lion pride, ant colony
Kangaroos, giraffes, bonobo troupe, wolf pack

Aborigine, Samurai, Cherokee, Maasai
Zulu, Maori, Naga, Kanaka Maoli

    All together - none the same
    Human nature - whole and sane
    Sovereign souls, choosing life
    Wed to their clan like man-to-wife

What about you? What about me?
What about our kids and our elderly?

When is the time? What's the delay?
Are you healthy and whole how you live today?

Who makes the change? Is there a map?
If I stay put, is there a slap?

Calling all souls, some to me
Create a sane society
A natural human social structure
Designed for rapture not to rupture
A humble and conscious society
One you're proud to hand to humanity

    Cradle-to-grave
    Always was the rave
    Cradle-to-grave
    The greatest gift goddess and god gave

What Is a Natural Human Social Structure?

Deep down, I believe most of us still know in our bones, in our hearts, in our instincts what our natural/innate social expression is. It just takes some digging and feeling to connect with it. I believe this is because that information must be inherent in us, just like the ability to breath, circulate blood, digest food, and grow our bodies from uterus to adulthood. The information and patterning for how we connect socially is also within us, even though it's expression is very obscured in Domain 8. So, it helps to have a language or a map to make sense of and frame our experience. This is a big part of what motivates me to write *True Human Freedom*, and to articulate the GaiaYoga teaching and vision altogether, to enable people to create their lives with clarity and deep self-connection.

If we look at other species we can find a lot of clues. Aside from humans, there's a complete consistency within all the other species in how their social structures manifest. For example, dolphins live in pods, wolves live in packs, bees live in hives, ants live in colonies, lions live in prides, etc. There's no deviation within a particular species. There might be different sizes of bonded social units, like a larger or smaller hive or pack or pride, but the essential pattern is the same within each species.

Almost all of the most sophisticated species, such as apes, elephants, dolphins, whales, wolves, and pigs, live in larger bonded social units. There are variations from species-to-species in style, structure, and most definitely in how dominance and sexuality are handled. I postulate that human beings are very sophisticated, and that we are biologically predisposed by genetic design to thrive in bonded social units that are larger than a mating pair and their offspring.

As far as I know, there is no pure Domain 5 culture left on Earth to observe, as all of them have interacted with Domain 7 and 8 cultures and have either been changed or exterminated. Where they've held their ground and survived they've turned into Domain 6 or 7 cultures. An example of this would be a nomadic people, like the Penan of Borneo, who have been removed from their jungle habitat and forced to live in permanent settlements against their will. Without the home and resource system their wild habitat provides, they cannot help but "lose their way" and have to learn a new way to survive. This coerces them out of Domain 5/6 and into Domain 6/7.

If we use our imagination and intuition we can visualize and grok how Domain 5 culture and consciousness would look, feel, and act. I find it useful to imagine or intuit the gap between a Domain 6 culture and the various primate cultures of Domain 4 -- gorilla, bonobo, chimpanzee, and orangutan. That's where I believe our natural human social structure can be discovered. Looking to indigenous Domain 6 cultures is extremely valuable, as they are much closer to a pure expression of our genetic/biological/animal nature than a Domain 7 or 8 culture. But we can overlook some of our essential human nature if we only look to Domain 6 cultures as our models and guides.

There have been thousands of examples of indigenous human cultures on the Earth. An indigenous culture (Domain 5 or 6) is one that "makes its living" through the local surroundings (Domains 1 - 4) and knows how to do so in a socially and materially sustainable manner. All of these cultures actually practiced GaiaYoga -- integrating Spirit, self, community, and Earth in a sustainable and holistic manner. Domain 5 people, in general, didn't have a "spiritual practice" and weren't even consciousness about "Spirit." Their connection to the divine is at a preconscious level, in the same way that a infant experiences itself as part of the whole, though it is not consciously or cognitively aware of this. This didn't make them "less spiritual." In fact, the infant comparison is a very good way to understand how Domain 5 is experienced. Later in our evolution, Domain 9 consciously re-integrates this quality of being, like an enlightened adult.

Domain 5 people can be considered "animists." They perceive life-force energy animating from everything, but don't make up the story that it's holy or divine (or that there are things that are not holy or divine). As such, they were likely ignorant of Spirit (and Domains 6 through 9). This was not intentional; it simply was not a conscious development yet. They were just expressing their nature like all other animals do, and how they lived together worked effectively over time. Their culture's lifestyle pattern and consciousness could be repeated generation-to-generation, without destroying their habitat, their natural health, their emotional and familial bonds, or their cooperation as a whole people. (In relationship to Domains 0 and 10, Domain 5 people, in general, probably connected what the Australian aborigines call "The Dream Time". The beginning-endless moment that is infused with life, energy, and consciousness.)

Humanity, en masse, is not practicing GaiaYoga. We are destroying our habitat by deforestation, mining, drilling, polluting the oceans and lakes and rivers, polluting the air, eroding soil, creating deserts, and creating radioactive dead zones. Our basic survival needs°° are met by transporting chemically-grown food across the planet. We're building homes and human settlements in the form of profoundly unsustainable cities and suburbs. Moreover, we have almost completely eroded and shattered our natural interconnectivity, relatedness, and cooperation that we had in Domain 5 kinship groups. Now, all that most humans have are the tiny nuclear families of Domain 8 that rely on machines, media, corporations, and agribusiness for their survival.

This begs the question: Are we suffering if we live outside of a natural human social structure?

For me, the answer is a resounding YES.

So, what can we do about it? Is there a way out of this situation?

I'm confident there's a way out! However, the road is paved with lots of work in many areas of life. This includes doing heroic amounts of personal growth work, (work ignored by generations of people); feeling deep emotions accumulated from generations of repressed and denied psychic, emotional, and spiritual pain from abuse, trauma, and neglect; and essentially re-designing and re-creating culture from the ground up. We can't just maintain our current lives in our current culture, put on some band-aids and spice it up a little bit and expect any lasting sufficient change.

The way out also requires "being." Being all of whom we are, reclaiming and integrating any and all aspects of ourselves that we've lost in this life or in past generations, and growing into a new and fuller expression of our humanity. And it requires bonding -- truly bonding with other people to form conscious and healthy, natural, human social organisms.

I've used two different phrases to name the kind of culture and consciousness I'm talking about. The original phrase I used from Shivalila was "Dimension/Domain 9." The phrase I've developed during the writing of this book is "GaiaYoga Culture." Though Domain 9 has the advantage of being a more objective, less "brand-name sounding" phrase, I prefer the poetry and particularity of

GaiaYoga Culture. I will use both terms throughout the book, and they are to be understood as essentially synonymous.

Regardless of the name, what I'm talking about is creating a culture and a consciousness that is both sustainable and holistic, and supports individuals in living the fullest authentic expression of their being, in relationship with other people who are also living their fullest authentic expression. Domain 9 is consciousness/culture that is similar to Domain 5, in that Domain 5 people are fluid through all the foundational Domains of 1 - 4, and don't require rituals to reconnect or reintegrate with these Domains. Similarly, Domain 9 people are fluid through all the other Domains. They have a consciousness that is liberated from the limitations of any of the previous Domains, and can use discrimination about what and how to include and exclude from Domain 5 - 8 cultures. To say it using Buddhist language, neither fixated by desire nor blocked by aversion. Instead, having the ability to intelligently, cooperatively, and compassionately choose with both discrimination and acceptance. A middle way, if you will.

What might GaiaYoga Culture look like?

Externally, in broad terms, it would most likely look like people living in Permaculture-type settlements (from Domains 6/7), using clean technology (from Domain 8), in clans and tribes (from Domains 5/6), deeply rooted in their primal animal nature (from Domains 4/5), connected in an integral way to the Earth (from Domains 2, 3, and 4), consciously awake and alive as the forces of the universe (from Domain 1), awakened spiritually with both individual and group spiritual practices (from Domain 10), and realized as Emptiness/The Witness (from Domain 0).

Internally, it would be the ability to recognize the different Domains, activate their energies and consciousness within our selves, and participate in each and all of them as is "appropriate" in life. So, instead of being either mesmerized by Domain 8 and all its "bling," or being disgusted by it and unwilling to participate, one (or a group of people) could enter into Domain 8 culture and/or consciousness, without getting over-identified in it and losing connection to the other Domains or to wholeness. Similarly, people could be equally "at home" in aboriginal kinship groups, tribes, extended families, wilderness, human settlements, spiritual realms, or emptiness. This is the liberation and fluidity I spoke of above. The consciousness is the internal experience, the culture the external manifestation or expression of the consciousness.

NOTE: The Shivalila teaching has profoundly inspired me, which is why the map of the 9 Dimensions/(Domains) is at the core of this book. Nonetheless, I have some fundamental issues with making the Shivalila teaching (or any other teaching) the umbrella teaching for the culture I am creating. Mostly the issues have to do with Shivalila being an incomplete transmission of a holistic and sustainable culture – it lacks clarity around food consumption and production, spirituality, communication, and doesn't clearly articulate Domains 0 and 10 (which I will discuss in-depth soon). It also easily comes across as a hypermasculine teaching that people can't really live up to, and within which people can't be their real selves. It almost hits the bulls-eye, but not quite. This is why I'm creating a new teaching, writing this book, and calling the culture and consciousness that I'm envisioning GaiaYoga.

ANOTHER NOTE: Realizing that all these differences are a lot to integrate into one's consciousness from just reading it in paragraph form, I developed the chart on the following two pages to help people wrap their minds around the distinctions between the different human cultural Domains (5-9). Hopefully this chart will make it easier to have a clear picture in your mind when I refer to Domains 5 – 9. So, feel free to refer to this chart while you are reading this book to refresh your understanding. Beyond that, I invite you to use this map as you navigate through or co-create human cultures in your life. I find it very practical and clarifying.

Quick Reference Comparison Chart of Archetypal Human Cultural Domains

	Domain 5	Domain 6	Domain 7	Domain 8	Domain 9
Food Acquisition And Production	Hunting and gathering	Hunting and gathering, some animal husbandry, some plant management	Some hunting, animal husbandry, crop production, grains, specialty shops, local and direct sales	Mechanized, chemical-based, large scale farming, super-markets, restaurants, food is a business	Sustainable agriculture systems (Permaculture), local organic food distribution
Types of Food Consumed	Only local, raw, wild, whole, unprocessed	Local, wild, raw and cooked, minimally processed	Primarily local, wild and cultivated, raw and cooked, grains, often processed	Mostly imported, cooked, highly processed, domesticated	Local, raw, wild or heirloom varieties, mostly or all raw, whole, unprocessed
Settlement Type	Nomadic, arboreal and terrestrial, temporary camps/nests	Semi-nomadic, medium-term camps built with all natural materials	Villages, stationary, homes and farms, local goods and services, some towns and cities	Urban, suburban, some rural, mass-transit and car-centered settlement design	Permaculture homesteads, eco-villages, intentional community, holistic settlement design
Property Ownership	N/A	Territory held by whole tribe	Extended family land holdings (e.g. farms, plantations, castles, manors), some individual or private property	Private property, real estate, land seen as just another commodity to be profited off of, almost all land is owned	Land trusts, intentional-community-owned properties, free lands, respect of wilderness
Base Family Unit	Kinship group based on birth and shared survival	Clan within a larger tribal unit	Extended family usually within a single village	Nuclear family with extended family elsewhere	Meme-and-love sharing community
Maximum Conflict Size	Individuals and bands here-now aggression	Tribal battles, feuds, treaties	Nation-nation wars	World wars	Nonviolent conflict resolution
Tool Use	Wood and stone	Fire, more complex natural tools built by tribe or traded for with neighbors	Metal, mechanical inventions, pre-petroleum powered engines, mostly locally built	Mass-produced power tools, plastics, appliances, high-tech devices, computers, heavy machinery	Clean and appropriate technology
Transportation	Foot	Animal assisted movement, canoes, rafts, sleds	Carts, wagons, larger boats, sailboats	Petroleum engines for cars, boats, planes, and trains	Non-polluting, sustainable transportation

	Domain 5	Domain 6	Domain 7	Domain 8	Domain 9
Awareness/Story Around Time	Primarily here-now, with capacity to plan	Cyclical time	Soft linear time	Hard linear time	Integrated/Holistic relationship to time
Currency-Economics	Human kinship groups cooperate together as a survival unit like other animal groups (packs, hives, colonies, pods, prides, herds)	Direct trade, barter, and gifting within and in between tribes	Trade, barter, local and national currency backed by precious metals, made into coins or notes held by national governments	(Inter)national currency held by (inter)national banks, backed by military, deception, and blind faith, stock markets	Gifting economy, need-based economy, needs of all people and planet valued over individual short-term benefit
Social Power Center & Unit of Functional Cooperation	Intimate Sphere – 10s of people – kinship group, band, or clan	Personal Sphere – 100s of people – tribal unit	Local Sphere – 1000s of people – village and multiple villages (some towns/cities)	Collective Sphere – millions of people – nations, corporations, us and them	Integrating all Spheres in balance - billions of people - one world family
Structure of Social and Labor Organization	"Might makes right" in the moment, no fixed social hierarchy	Tribal hierarchy, chiefs (male or female), people work for good of their tribe	Feudalism, empires, overt enslavement, kings, queens, etc.	Capitalism, theocracy, communism, covert mind control	Sociacracy or Holocracy (consensus decision making), "wisdom makes right"
Energy Source	Living energy from Domains 1 – 4, intimate human cooperation, at the end fire use begins	Fire, intimate and personal sphere human cooperation, some domesticated animals	Fire amplified by inventions, local sphere human cooperation, slaves, domesticated animals	Coal, petroleum, nuclear, solar, wind, collective sphere human cooperation	Clean and renewable energy, holistic cooperation, voluntary simplicity
Family Line Defined By	Paternity unknown at cognitive level, maternity defines family line	Mix of paternity and maternity defining family line	Paternity primary definition of family line	Paternity primary definition of family line	Both parents, and perhaps whole community, define family line
Parenting System	Children raised by whole kinship group without fixed social roles/contracts	Children raised by whole clan within tribe, with some fixed social roles/contracts	Children raised by extended-family with fixed social roles/contracts	Children raised by mother and father (or single parent) with limited outside support	Children raised by whole kinship group without fixed social roles/contracts
Understanding of Spirit/God	Connection to living energy in all things, Animism, no myth about God/Spirit	Spirit seen in natural forces including plants and animals. Myths about Spirit, shamanism, rituals	God seen as a great other, written spiritual doctrines, religions, priests, evil/good	Doubt of Spirit in many, God seen as a great other and not part of daily life, religions, priests, extremism	Beyond religions, spiritual realization, non-dualistic, holistic shamanism, Self/World/Spirit are one

Getting Culturally Sober

So, what do we do with all this information and new perspective?

Well, the biggest thing is to stop doing what we're doing already – individually and collectively! For most of us, that means to stop living a Domain 8 lifestyle. As long as a person is locked into one of the other Domains it isn't possible to enter into Domain 9 and create GaiaYoga Culture. Making this shift means generating huge changes from the core of one's being, consciousness, and lifestyle. To truly do this is a huge leap of faith into the unknown. The fears, doubts, and resistance that can come up around this can't be overestimated.

Why can it be so scary at first to move one's center of gravity into Domain 9? Because to live sustainably, holistically – to fully integrate our animal nature, our aboriginal self, our tribal self, our villager, our modern personhood, and our soul - requires living our life almost completely differently than most of us are used to. Certainly it is not the way we were raised to function if we grew up in Domain 8. It will probably require a change of how we create our home, how we parent, where food comes from, how we eat it, how we communicate, how we think, how we meet our needs for security, how we relate to power, how we use technology, how much and why we travel, how we consume, how we handle family, how we handle sexuality, how we understand disease and health, how we run businesses, how we make decisions and who we make decisions with, plus much more.

I opened up this book with this long description of the Domains 1 through 8 in order to contextualize what I'm saying now. The way we handle a particular area of life could emerge out of any of the Domains. In designing our GaiaYoga Culture we want to take a sober look at whether or not any given practice will support being stuck in one of the Domains or if it will support being fluid and healthy throughout the Domains.

Let's look at diet as an example. Most people who have looked outside of "the box" generally agree that a Domain 8 diet is not healthy. A stereotypical Domain 8 person eats a diet of mass-produced food, stocked with synthetic additives, and grown using chemical herbicides, fungicides, and pesticides, sold by big corporate supermarkets and chain restaurants that require food production at such a huge scale that it's all but impossible to do it in a humane and sustainable manner. This also includes TV dinners, GMOs, fast food, pre-packaged food, factory farmed meat, preservatives, artificial flavors and colors, and ingredient lists with words only a well-educated biologist can pronounce and derive meaning from. Eating this type of diet supports staying in Domain 8 consciousness. It's really the main "drug" people consume and it works well to keep people's attention and consciousness in a particular frequency.

Some people do seek a healthier version of a Domain 8 diet and are satisfied, but many folks have started looking to Domain 6/7 cultures for guidance. Examples of these kinds of diets are The Weston-Price Diet°°, The Primal Diet°° of Aajonus Vonderplanitz, Dr. Peter D'adamo's Blood-Type and GenoType diets, Ayurvedic diets, most modern vegetarian and vegan diets°°, and any indigenous diet based on a particular indigenous culture (like a Hawaiian diet, a traditional Japanese diet, any native American diet, a traditional Mexican diet, etc.) Some of these diets are simply regional diets that were practiced for generations successfully, others are modern re-expressions of how to eat based on broadly looking into various Domain 6 and 7 cultures.

As far as I know there's only one dietary approach that emerges from Domain 4 and 5, and that is Instinctive Eating, which is essentially a pre-cultural diet. In fact, it mostly emerges out of Domain 4, the biology of our animal body. (For full details on this you can read the book I wrote on this topic back in 1996 – *Instinctive Eating: The Lost Knowledge Of Optimum Nutrition*. For just a short explanation of Instinctive Eating see page 94 in the Appendix of this book.)

My point here isn't to go into teaching about diet, but to show an example of how a modern person can pick and choose how to change an aspect of their life by looking through the different Domains (in this case 4 - 8). Each diet supports a different consciousness and culture and has different impacts on individual and cultural health and the environment (the synthesis of Domains 1 - 4).

The more we can draw our life practices from Domains 4 and 5, then the more likely they are going to be fully in alignment with our biological and genetic predisposition/design. And obviously, if we are living in alignment with our nature (Domains 1 - 5) the more whole, healthy, happy, balanced, and integrated we will be in-and-with Life. I personally have a profound longing and drive to experience my deepest humanity. So I have chosen my individual practices to be ones that support me in being aligned with Domains 4, 5, and 9.

I'd like to make a parenthetical statement here. GaiaYoga Culture (Domain 9), in its fullest expression, is Domain 5 plus applied consciousness. A Domain 5 human (individual and culture) is not a conscious design by the people involved in it. It is simply the living out of instincts, nature, and genetic design. It's Domain 4, plus whatever it is you believe makes us different from animals (larger brains, tools, taming of fire, ensoulment, psychedelics, language, the ability to imagine, etc.) In the same way that a mature and healthy adult is very much like a child in happiness and purity, but far greater in consciousness and power, Domain 9 is an enlightened form of Domain 5. For the most part Domains 6 - 8 are a steady distancing, denial, and devaluing of Domain 5 (like an older child or teenager distancing itself from babyhood). It's a slow-and-steady distancing from our primal core as our foundation of life. At first some of this distancing was very selective (for example learning to use tools and fire to make survival easier and more comfortable). But over the eons all the baby steps have added up to make a very big difference and a very substantial forgetting. Domain 9 reintegrates that primal core (because without its living-awake presence there is great suffering) and invites us to consciously design our family and culture to be in alignment with our full humanity.

The renowned integral philosopher, Ken Wilber, has a concept called "expand and include." This is another way to consider GaiaYoga Culture. Instead of believing that the goal of humanity is to evolve beyond our animal self and natural limitations, I think our greatest "evolution" is to include them as we expand into greater material, emotional, spiritual, and psychic capacity. If we don't honor our Domain 5 self and our Domain 4 body as our foundation as we "evolve," it will end up being the force that topples us -- as it needs to be honored, heard, included, and valued. This is huge! And this understanding is lacking in most teachings and cultures. Indeed, "that which we embrace we erase" and "that which we resist persists." So if we resist including our primal self in our life it persists in asking (louder and louder) to be included through dreams, anger, depression, anxiousness, longing, acting out, fantasizing, etc. If we embrace it, then the drive to be heard and included fades and there is peace. The charge°° has been erased.

Consider sexuality for a moment. Sexuality is one of the strongest forces in humanity. Supposedly, according to most Domain 8 cultural and religious values, monogamy is the one and only way to be and any other form of sexual conduct is a sin or at least "weird." And yet, many people will risk almost anything to have sex outside of monogamy -- presidents, movie stars, priests, the guy next door, etc. I know one very wealthy international businessman (who will remain anonymous) who travels the world on business, secretly connects sexually with many different women, and has two distinct families that he has fathered that don't know about each other -- just because his drive to have sex with different women is so strong. If his first wife and children or other people in his above-board life ever found out, his otherwise very successful Domain 8 world would come crashing down on him. He knows this, and yet takes the risk because the drive is so strong. As a result, his life is embroidered in secrecy, and surely stress, at maintaining the separation and fearing he'll get found out at some point. I trust he is just an extreme example of what many others experience. And I also trust that the drive he has is actually a beautiful need, grown out of his humanity. It is being expressed in a tragic way because of his secrecy, shame, and stress, but that doesn't mean there's something inhuman or evil about him. In fact, I believe he is doing his best to express his natural (Domain 4 and 5) energy in the world, given the obstacles presented by the culture he's rooted in.

Because this man is living in a Domain 8 culture that no longer honors our nature (in this case our sexual nature) but rather tries to force-fit our sexual expression into the box of monogamy or serial monogamy as the only acceptable way to be a good citizen, he cannot find a home for his whole being. This is real suffering, and it's something that I imagine most people experience. They can't fit themselves in the box they've been taught they should be in by their culture and family, and at the same time they don't know another box or a "non-box" they can live in.

I, personally, have become very clear that my natural form of sexual expression is not monogamy, but it's also not whatever/whenever/however sexuality. What I long for is what I would call a group marriage, or something akin to a Domain 5 kinship group (the first of the two potential options for our early human social expression). Many needs are naturally and easily fulfilled through this kind of relationship structure -- diversity, security, economic ease, intimacy, safety, continuity, fun, ease of raising children, ease with survival, balance of freedom and order, the joy of deep cooperation, etc.

Obviously, it's a big risk to dismantle one's intimate relationship structure and explore something different. Additionally, this means dismantling one's family structure, economic structure, emotional body, and psychic sense of order. I find inspiration by seeing the overall results of the other forms of family, intimacy, and sexuality, and realizing that they just don't produce the results I want. At minimum, I'm left with many unmet needs, and at the extreme end many needs are not only unmet, they are denied, shamed, buried, and fragmented out of daily life.

Since I'm already talking about it, and it's such a big button, let's flesh it out some more. Why has humanity moved to isolated nuclear families and monogamy on the whole?

Fluid Bonding

Do you wanna slip?
Do you wanna slide?
Shine like the sun when you're young
So fun to twist in the tide

Now you wanna good grip
And a smooth ride
Not as bold when you're old
Too tired, mired, and fried

Been bound and betrayed
By a static quest?
Fluid bonding is a brew
That can surely quench

Been frozen and distant
In a fantasy fest?
Fluid bonding gives warmth
To breath and breast

We seek security
Like a fly to a fire
Elusive in this realm
Of death and desire

It can be found
Without a slick escape
Root to the ground
And feel life vibrate

When our fluids are shared
The bonding takes –
Us to the core
Of how we relate

Embracing who changes
Osmosis through time
Resisting, persisting
Insisting, sublime

Squeeze the womb water
Diffused into each cell
Decanting holograms
Of heaven and hell

Emerge as crying tsunamis
Or torrents erotic
Of "I want my mommy!"
Or archetypes exotic

When we share fluidly
The bonding forms –
A circuit to conduct
Calms and storms

Draws in a gravity
It hurts to ignore
Some drag, some race
To touch that tender core

I'm sure you wanna good trip
I'm sure you wanna glide
Fun keeps you young
Like new groom and bride

Security soars
Caressing winds and tides
Glow like gold when you're old
Eyes wild and wise

When our fluids are bonded
The electrons flow –
Our waters and planets
Orbiting to and fro

A Phoenix burns within
Smoke and steam implies
Out of our ashes
New orbs arise

Sweet intimate sweat
A kiss can ignite
The feel of the real
Is really in the flight

Fluid bonding is responding
Every day and night
Fluid bonding is responding
Surrender or fight
Fluid bonding is responding
To the current of life
Fluid bonding is responding…

Sexuality and Security in the Domains

I've deeply considered why it is that the dominant form of intimate relationship in Domain 8 is the isolated nuclear family. Obviously, I don't know all the reasons, but I believe I have some insights that support real clarity.

Think about how children play with each other. Kids often play very physically and passionately, together as one morphing organism. One can describe it as a (G-rated) orgy. I'm not saying this to prematurely sexualize children, but rather the opposite -- to show how adult sex play is actually very childlike in nature. Children are not sexually activated until puberty and there isn't overt sexuality or procreative drive in healthy children. But if we saw the level of physical, emotional, mental, and group engagement amongst adults as we see in children's play amongst themselves it would seem sexual. Children, in general, attempt to get as close to each other as they can and enjoy doing so in pairs and larger groups pretty equally. Think how common a slumber party is for children, and it's just as common as one child sleeping over with another. Children seek and enjoy intimacy.

Sexual energy is a primal expression of life energy -- it's bonding energy, it's playful and creative energy. If you take out all the taboo and charged energy around sexuality, it's easy to see that this same life energy that expresses itself in adults' sexual energy expresses itself through children in their play and in the ways they relate to each other and adults they feel bonded to. It's a different version of intimacy. Children at play can be very sensual with each other, without adult sex-play or the possibility of procreation, or all of the taboos and issues. There is also no connection of survival security to children's play with each other, since their parents are meeting their security needs (rather than the children with whom they are playing). It's "free play," not some sort of economic exchange. (This is part of the inspiration for the name Shivalila, which in Sanskrit means the play of non-attachment.)

The Bible quote, "To enter the kingdom of heaven you must be like the little children," it can be understood as an expression of Domain 9 consciousness/culture. Domain 9 culture is about creating a social-fabric where the deepest "goal" is to support the people within it to be able to live/play freely and have their survival, security, and other adult needs met. It's about integrating this childlike energy with the holistic responsibility of adults -- maintaining health and wealth as a multi-generational interconnected people. So in a bonded kinship group (the term I prefer over tribe, clan, or family) I can play more or less intimately or intensely or frequently with any other members in the group and it doesn't impact my overall security, the parenting of children, the care of land, the running of businesses etc. Adults are free to move in and out of intimacy, sexuality, different spiritual and personal growth practices, and other adult play, without a contractual linking of my sexual partnerships to my overall experience of home, security, survival, clan, and co-parenting.

Sexuality is the biological basis for family, period. Whom we have sex with is whom we bond with as family, and with whom we create children. It's also intimately linked with our sense of security. This is obvious, since many people stay in a relationship that's not working for them in order to meet their needs for security. In Domain 8, where the day-to-day family has been reduced to essentially one other adult and offspring, security and sexual intimacy are literally merged together, or should I say <u>appear</u> to be merged together because of the architectural limits of the chosen social structure.

How is security generated in the different Domains?

In **Domain 5**, security comes from the Earth, and from being part of a bonded, multi-generational kinship group that works together to survive. Additionally, it comes through being valued by the others in the group, manifested in their desire to care for you, take risks on your behalf, and care for and take risks with the kinship group as a whole. Now of course, ultimately, there is no immunity from accidents, predation, and death, but there is certainly the day-to-day experience of our needs for security being met as much as possible in the Earthly realm of life/death and change.

In Domain 5 (whether in scenario 1 or 2) there would not be much security gained by two adults completely separating out as an independent family. In fact, it would be a weakening of their security (and power). Thus, in Domain 5, there isn't the same advantage of merging one's security primarily with whom you have sex. Even in scenario 2 where people are more pair-bonded and less pack-bonded, larger groups would still be fundamentally cooperative around survival. Greater security is generated at a wider level of group bonding, and within that group bonding sexuality might or might not be shared, but deep cooperation and security is not limited to those with whom one is sexual.

In fact, in this kind of culture, there would actually be more security through being sexual with more people, as this physical intimacy would generate more bondedness within the group. This isn't to say there wouldn't be jealousy, insecurity, competition, or other issues surrounding shared sexuality in Domain 5 cultures. It is to say that handling these energies, while staying bonded as a whole group would increase the ease and capacity for survival, childcare, and continuing to enjoy the richness of a communal experience. If this was done historically, it wasn't as some highly conscious, spiritual practice, but rather it was a purely instinctive, biological, natural activity.

Within possible scenario 1 of a Domain 5 kinship group, people experience both the benefits of monogamy (commitment, emotional bonding, shared parenting and survival) and of polyamory°°, or being single and mingling. Monogamy, in Domains 7 and 8, creates the stability and security people want, but it's at the cost of sexual freedom and creating a greater field of interconnectivity and intimacy. Being "young, single, and liking to mingle" gives one sexual freedom, exploration, and growth, but doesn't support raising children, a stable life, or a social network to care for you when you are old and require physical support to survive.

It is apparent that people in their 20s through early 60s can "get away" with being single or in a couple-ship much better than children or elders can. Of course, if people in their 20s through early 60s are in a bonded relationship with elders or children, then they'll have a big "cramp in their style" if they're taking care of them on their own, without the support of a greater social network (extended-family, clan, tribe, or kinship group). What it comes down to is sacrificing wholeness at a social/family level for the appearance/illusion of independence. On the other side of the coin we have the problems of co-dependence that form when you don't have a conscious and large enough family system to care for everyone in the family, without too much "burden" landing on any one person's shoulders. Neither independence nor dependence is ultimately very functional. Conscious inter-dependence is what we want to manifest and support.

So that was a brief look at the relationship between security and sexuality in Domain 5 with some important diversions. Obviously, depending on which scenario (1 or 2) we are actually in, the path of our development looks different and the "argument" is different. Regardless of whether our early social units were more centered in pair-bonding or in pack-bonding, the way our social structure was generated was very primal, rooted in nature, and devoid of the kind of rigid social contracts that we have in today's world.

As nomadic hunter-gatherers, Domain 5 people didn't store food beyond bringing it back to camp, didn't have fire, and used minimal tools. Obviously having fire, tools, and storing food appeared to be an upgrade as far as power and security. Domain 5 people also didn't have fixed social hierarchies (chiefs, shamans, medicine men, or other rigid social roles.) Not to say there wasn't a "pecking order," perhaps there was, but I trust it was re-created through here-now living energy (aggression, speed, vocal display, and the like), not through social contracts that were held in peoples' primitive psyches.

In **Domain 6** fixed social hierarchies begin to appear and develop. Levels of human cooperation are slowly traded in for tools. For example, with a weapon a lone hunter could kill an animal that would require a team of weaponless Domain 5 humans to make the kill. Perhaps this lone hunter brought the meat back to his favorite woman and she liked this. While not a "bad" thing, this special treatment could lead to schisms in the group. This could develop into a relationship that has a degree of separation from the rest of the kinship group. If there wasn't enough to share with everyone, then this lone hunter might only feed this one woman. Once there's special treatment of one person over another, repeatedly over time, a "special contract°°" gets formed. While this is a great thing on the surface for the two in the special contract, it has subtle and not so subtle impacts on the sense of unity within the kinship group. (This is starting from possible scenario 1. In possible scenario 2 this had already been going on within Domain 5.)

Over generations this leads towards separate clans and separate marriages within tribes, where in Domain 5 it was closer to purely one-for-all-and-all-for-one. This also leads towards paternity (the social recognition of, and attributing great significance to, who is the biological father of a child). In an openly sexual Domain 5 culture, the identity of the father could be relatively unimportant, but in Domain 6 it definitely matters. This obviously creates a fertile ground for patriarchy and male power to dominate human cultures, whereas in many Domain 5 cultures matriarchal leadership is more prevalent.

As you can see, sexuality and sexual contracts are becoming linked with security. Of course this evolved slowly and in different ways across the world. There are thousands of Domain 6 cultures, and I'm no expert on all of them, nor have I done ethnographies of all of them. So I'm talking in terms of general trends in both culture and consciousness.

To a modern person, the difference between Domain 5 and 6 cultures may seem insignificant. Both cultures are living as a large group, deeply integrated with Domains 1 through 4, and without permanent settlements and agriculture (that emerge in Domain 7). But there are real and significant differences, and they are worth noting and understanding, especially when we are designing and creating a Domain 9 culture. If we don't understand the impacts of these different choices, we could end up creating a design that doesn't give us the result we actually want.

So in Domain 6, tool and fire use increased individual group power, and this started to change the feelings around ownership (especially of food, lovers, and children). Essentially, smaller intimate spheres started to emerge that were contained within the personal sphere of the tribe, whereas in Domain 5 there was essentially only an intimate sphere of which everyone was included. Land was still held by the tribe as whole, and close quarters cooperation was still the primary power source of humanity. Children in some Domain 6 cultures are raised by everyone in the tribe, with close to equal care, and cross-nursing is a common practice in many of these cultures, giving babies a much different sense of who its kin are than a Domain 7 or 8 baby. In general, there is more similarity in how children are raised from Domain 5 to 6, and more difference in how adults behave around food, sex, tools, fire, and adult roles from Domain 5 to 6.

Security and sexuality become more closely linked together in **Domain 7**, village culture. A Domain 6 person could fairly easily (at a material level, but not necessarily emotional level) shift-and-float around the tribe, change intimate partners, and still have the same personal sphere home in their semi-nomadic tribe. But once people settled on a particular piece of land in Domain 7, and land was held by separate extended families rather than by the whole tribe or kinship group, then changing sex partners meant changing your home. In most Domain 7 cultures the men are the lineage holders as far as surnames and land title. So women can "buy" land by marrying a man and his extended family, but then lose land if they divorce or have sex with another man or somehow break the relationship with the man. This single dynamic has huge repercussions in culture and in individual lives.

Many Domain 7 cultures have allotments for expanded sexuality – either through special holidays where sexual contracts are lifted (like Beltane or Carnival), or through mistresses, or temple priestesses and priests, or of course secrecy, prostitution, and adultery. On the other hand, in Domain 7 there are religions and laws that attempt to enforce social contracts that link security and sexuality through fear of God (going to hell, original sin, breaking the Ten Commandments, etc.), fear of punishment (stoning, burning at the stake, public humiliation, shame), or fear of consequences, (loss of wife or husband, loss of home, loss of family, difficulty in raising children in a fragmented family, etc.) It's apparent that even though security and sexuality get merged on the social contract level, this certainly doesn't mean they are merged within the human being! This makes it so the outside doesn't match the inside.

In Domain 7, children can still raised by everyone in the village, with the biological parents as the primary caregivers. But it's not nearly as free an exchange or flow as we see in Domain 5 and 6. Children tend to "run free" in the village, but unlike Domain 6 there is a local sphere of people that are less connected to other people. Villages are bigger than tribes or kinship groups, so not everyone can have a personal sphere relationship let alone an intimate sphere one. The main advantage of the village is that there's a greater diversity of people to explore connecting and cooperating with, but the cost is that there is less bondedness and cohesion with the larger group. This cost is also fueled by the social and economic contracts in the village that end up separating people more. By contrast, in Domain 5 or 6 there is either an extensive or complete sharing of the economics of survival. Because of this diminished sharing, in general, villagers are less willing to co-parent. They still often do to some degree or another with other families, but because of all the contracts, it is done with less ease and flow than in tribes and kinship groups.

So, I trust you can see the growing design error. Culture is being further and further entrenched in social contracts that don't align with our genetic truth. This leads, generally speaking, either into submission or rebellion, neither of which supports wholeness in one's being. This design also makes it more and more necessary to have outside authorities to enforce these laws (of man and "God") that aren't natural for people to live with. Shame and confusion arise when people are just following in the footsteps of those who've come before, and what they're following isn't really congruent with who we are as humans. We end up having to choose either between aligning with our culture or aligning with our core being. And since younger people assume that older people have good reasons for what they do, without much understanding of the source or cause of their life's dysfunction, they usually choose to align with the culture they were raised in. Often this has people thinking there's something inherently wrong with them. It has also led to the creation of many religions, governments, and other organizations and philosophies, with people championing them and participating in them, even though these various systems are not congruent with our nature and breed more and more dysfunction and disease of mind, body, emotion, and spirit.

Besides all of these contracts, there is also a new phenomenon that emerges in villages -- "strangers." Strangers are people who you see in public, but that you don't actually know. This was a very unusual occurrence in a tribal culture where everyone knows everyone and cooperates together and visitors are far less common. When they do come they are not just randomly walking around without escort or connection to the tribe (unless they're an unwelcomed "enemy.")

My philosophy teacher in college said the whole reason philosophy developed in Greece was simply to deal with the issue of how to relate with the stranger. This new kind of situation created a new dynamic that required people to be much more intellectually clear and savvy, hence, philosophy. They needed to determine how to handle the occurrence of having a significant number of people in their presence with whom they didn't have a life-long bonded relationship with and also didn't share a way of being that they all lived in since birth. Thus arose the necessity for all sorts of new and additional moral and ethical codes to handle this crisscrossing of different people and cultural habits and values.

Lao Tzu expresses this understanding quite eloquently in the Tao Te Ching verse 38:

"Therefore when the Way is lost, afterward comes integrity. When integrity is lost, afterward comes humaneness. When humaneness is lost, afterward comes righteousness. When righteousness is lost, afterward comes etiquette."

The need for laws (man's and "God's") is not really present in a Domain 6 culture in the same manner (they are either living in The Way or have integrity). In general, people are connected enough to each other and the natural world to deal with issues directly. Morality, ethics and social harmony are cultivated in people by how they are raised. So instead of needing an outside authority enforcing ethics, morality, and harmony, "good citizenship" comes naturally from the inside-outward in each person. If a person is raised holistically with their needs mostly met, they are less likely as an adult to act in a way that is disharmonious with the values and social health of their people. When there is a serious conflict or non-resolving polarity, often a council of elders is used to guide the situation back into integrity for all, as opposed to courts and punitive justice. (Again, these are general simplified trends, not specific cultural ethnographies.)

Now, on to the beast: **Domain 8...**

It's pretty apparent that security and sexuality are treated as one in the modern marriage contract. Who I have sex with, is who I own my home with, is who I raise children with, is who I share money with, is who I make important decisions with, is who supports me when I'm sick or old, is who I share my deepest honesty with. It's all on that one person (for the most part). The social and emotional physics behind this are very challenging. This dramatically limits acceptable behavior in the realms of sexuality, intimacy, honesty, emotional bonding, and deep cooperation, through intense outside structural pressure.

For example, if I don't want to sleep with my wife one night, and instead sleep with another woman, it's not like when I was a kid and had a sleep over with my friend and it was simple and non-threatening to the family security. Now, it's called "cheating," "adultery," "grounds for divorce," "a sign I don't love her," "sick," "sinful," etc. So, if I have those feelings I need to do something with them besides act on them or if I do act on them, do it in secrecy so I don't "ruin my life." (The whole AshleyMadison.com hack of 2015 has brought this dynamic to stark clarity. It revealed that hundreds of thousands of Americans, in all but three zip codes, were looking for affairs online.) It is quite clear that this is a no-win situation for most human beings, unless you happen to have the karma of a particular lifetime to be 100% fulfilled having sex and sharing intimacy with only your spouse. A small percentage of souls truly have this, but it's not the norm. So, I don't believe monogamy is a functional basis for every family and the entire culture.

The problem is exacerbated by several factors:

1) Domain 8 babies receive more trauma, neglect, wounding, and just plain not having their needs understood and met, than any other Domains' babies. So, they're already deeply hurting, insecure, needy, doubting their lovability and worth, etc. Therefore, they are easily triggered°° into profoundly deep material when issues that threaten their security arise. To top it off, as adults, they don't understand what's going on, can't make sense of the pain, don't have the skills to address it in a healing and connective manner, and just want to blame the trigger as the "problem."

2) Domain 8 folks tend to be more out of touch with themselves and nature, and more in their heads, than people from other Domains. As a result they tend to act with greater insensitivity to others when in pursuit of their sexual/emotional/security needs.

3) (This might be the biggest one.) There is no social/cultural container to hold the energy that arises when someone acts outside of a monogamy contract in Domain 8 (as it's lived day-to-day by most folks). So, here's what happens: all this pain comes up for the partner who's not having expanded sexuality/intimacy, and it easily appears that the source of the pain, not merely the trigger, is either their partner and/or "the other man/woman," <u>unless</u> they have a lot of training in doing their own personal growth, healing, and shadow work°°. As a result, they fantasize about condemning, hurting, or killing that person, or actually do kill that person. At minimum, they blame that person for their pain. Certainly, Domain 8 culture on the whole looks down on seeking intimacy outside of a monogamy contract, so that particular (lack of) consciousness is strongly supported. Without the live presence of a conscious Domain 5, 6, or 9 social container to support this process, a Domain 8 person is in many ways wise to want to maintain the monogamy contract, rather than open the can of worms without the skills, support, or vision to get through to the other side.

The kind of rage, fear and insecurity a Domain 8 adult would feel from a broken monogamy contract is an echo of what a sibling might feel having a new brother or sister being born to their parents. A situation where love and attention is already lacking, gets yet another person added into the mix. Why is love and attention lacking? Again, it's simple math; it takes more than two adults to raise a human baby to adulthood (no matter how much they love their children). As they say nowadays, "It takes a village" (or a Domain 7 culture.) I'd say, it actually takes not a village, rather, it takes a tribe or a kinship group (a Domain 5 or 6 culture). But today, none of those are really the solution. What it really takes is a GaiaYoga Culture or Domain 9 culture to raise a human being to its potential.

Moreover, when a person is sexual with another person, it energetically brings that other person into the family, into the intimate sphere. However, when it's done without the consent or knowledge of the other people in the family (like your spouse), then it is, de facto, a rupturing of or invasion into the family. Needs for inclusion, to matter, trust, consideration, choice, and understanding, as well as others, are not met. To the wounded inner child of the non-participating partner, it's like they're being forced into a relationship, with an apparently threatening person, without choice. That's a double whammy. First, the threat that there will be loss of intimacy and security, and second, the loss of choice and sanctuary within one's intimate sphere.

It's really quite an overwhelming situation. We're left with individuals who profoundly need more intimacy, connection and diversity in their lives, but their very attempts to get it inadvertently brings up huge pain in others (generations of repressed and/or ignored pain). There's this drive for something beautiful that only seems to create ugliness (and maybe a brief night of beauty). To top it off the very laws – "God's" and man's - are huge obstacles to honoring this core part of who we are, that's been alive in us since the dawn of Domain 5.

Oy Vey! What Can We Do?

Well, there's really only one solution I can see to functionally and systematically address our dynamic needs around intimacy, sexuality, parenting, and security. It's good news that there is a solution, but unfortunately it's nothing short of creating an entirely new cultural foundation to live one's life from!!! The solution is creating a GaiaYoga Culture and cultivating the health and consciousness within one's self to be able to participate in it, and indeed, birth it with others. I imagine to a lot of readers out there this is beyond overwhelming and seems very far from possible. Nonetheless, this is our predicament and the direction to go in regardless of where we are now.

Since the talk of sexuality is still fresh in our minds let's continue to look at it. If we stay in Domain 8, and practice polyamory to get our intimacy/sexuality needs met we will end up either spending a lot of time at Network For New Culture°° (NFNC) camps (or other types of free sexuality workshops/events) or hanging out in a similar container that supports this kind of relating (a short-term Domain 6, 7, or 9 cultural experience). And then return back to Domain 8, having tanked up on intimacy. Or, we can have a split life with several lovers living separately from each other. This split life eventually stops being worth it because of the fragmentation, travel, and lack of an integrated intimate sphere.

Or we can suck it up, stay faithful and whole in our intimate sphere, and maintain monogamy. Now, for many people, monogamy is not a dilemma in and of itself. Obviously, if it were an unbearable situation, people wouldn't be doing it with such gusto. But monogamy usually isn't life-long, so it actually becomes <u>serial</u> monogamy. Serial monogamy has some big repercussions on life that most people don't acknowledge. It deeply disrupts continuity in one's life and, in a different way than non-integrated polyamory does, it creates separate intimate spheres. The separation doesn't occur in a fixed time frame, instead it's a separation that is enacted over time:

my life with my first intimate partner, then later a life with another intimate partner, then later this other one. I get certain parts of me activated in one relationship, but not others, and then later it's another collage of parts of me activated with different pluses and minuses. This can be livable, and there are certainly some perks to it, but this separation over time is a strain on the heart. Additionally, when children are involved it makes a much bigger impact, with the complexities of stepparents, divorces, ex-stepparents, and the overall loss of continuity in the home. Like so many things, everyone's doing it, so it just seems normal, but as a relationship design it has major flaws.

There are other intimate relationship configurations, but those are the basic ones.

Sexuality leads to bonding and generates intimacy. When we have multiple sexual partners outside of a bonded group, as we do in Domain 8, then in one way or another, "gravity" moves people to either fully separate (and become like a lone atom) or fully come together (like in a molecule). A long-term orbit of being intimate, but not integrating intimate spheres, is unsustainable over time. If this orbit is maintained over time, it's at the cost of integration, transparency°°, and wholeness. It's certainly not a functional cultural or family model. So, unless you are already living in a culture/family that supports this full integration, or unless you're actively creating it, eventually the lack of this container will undermine engaging in such intimacy with multiple people in separate homes.

What generates this "gravity"? Sex is not just the coming together of bodies: it's the blending/merging of consciousness (emotions, minds, and soul) and karma (or the current of one's life). When we have sex with someone, this bonding starts to occur. Now, if we only have sex once or a few times and we're not so attuned to all of this, we can keep it superficial and this gravity doesn't kick in. But if we have more frequency of connection or if we feel more deeply, then this movement to be together (in time-space, as well as emotionally, psychically, and spiritually) gets stronger. If you're having sex with one person, this leads to pair-bonding and then a committed partnership or marriage. If more than two people are sharing that kind of intimacy and sexual openness then this can lead to a larger bonded configuration and a group marriage. I want to clarify that, though it might sound like it, I'm not saying sexuality is the only way to bond or blend consciousness.

At a community or cultural level I'm not talking about everyone necessarily being overtly sexual with everyone they live with. I'm pointing to human bonding, and to creating a type of family/community/culture that is a powerful enough container to allow, and indeed cultivate, our whole being -- without contracts, repression, or broken relationships. I'm calling us to re-create our selves, to be capable of going beyond the limiting contractual template for bonding, cooperation, and family laid out in Domains 8, 7, (and even 6); and to go beyond the gene and aggression based social forms of Domain 5. My vision is to expand outward to create delightful and dynamic intimate and personal spheres that are designed to be functional and nourishing, because they consider holistically who we are. Moreover, because of this holistic and natural design, we have a real chance to meet all of each person's needs. So the goal is to create and enjoy living in a fully functional culture.

It's about creating a container where forms of relationship and intimacy levels are guided by natural, living energy, love, and consciousness, as opposed to aggression, fears, contracts, social conditioning, and unconscious adherence to how our family-and-culture-of-origin practice relationship and create family.

Think back to that picture of a group of children playing naturally and effortlessly, physically and passionately. I'm saying we can have that same kind of freedom, connection, playfulness, and capacity for flowing together through conflict and into resolution that we see with children and be mature adults with responsibilities, missions, and adult needs. I call this a "group marriage" for a Domain 9 consciousness.

A simple way to look at it is this: we are born with a natural living song that emanates from our being, our heart and soul. As we are enculturated, that song gets attuned to the larger energy of our family and culture (which is out of tune with our natural song). People end up conforming and contracting to fit into the roles, actions, and levels of realness that are acceptable in their family and culture. They harmonize with the outer world at the cost of being out of harmony with their own true song.

GaiaYoga is about creating a culture based on staying in harmony with our own original song, and then bringing our true selves into the field of relationship and creating a culture based on that. BUT it's hard to know what our true song is when we've spent years, decades, generations living in cultures that essentially demand that a person not stay connected with their true song. So, in order to be stable in that connection, we need to experiment, try things on, make mistakes, explore creating community and culture, etc.

If you live your life following the status quo of Domain 8, you don't know what's beyond it. For example, if you choose to only participate in monogamous relationships, you cannot know what a non-monogamous experience would be like for you, and if that type of relationship serves you. On the other hand, if you step out of it unconsciously, without skills, and a supportive container, you're likely to get in over your head and perhaps regret it. Similarly, if you never step out of the diet you were conditioned to eat, you'll never know how it's impacting your health and well-being and what is truly in your best interest. But it's not just diet and sex that need to be looked at, this need to challenge and explore is "necessary" on pretty much every front – how we communicate, how we handle conflict and polarized energy°°, how we handle food production, how we handle parenting, how we handle economics and money, how human settlements are designed, powered, and maintained, how socially-deviant behavior is handled, etc. If we don't re-evaluate each area, it's likely we'll be living in a way that was developed by people who did not have a holistic vision and the intention to live in Domain 9.

As a person who's pioneering Domain 9/GaiaYoga Culture, my "sport" and spiritual practice is challenging most every social norm of Domain 8. I've run lots of dietary, communal, relational, sexual, and agricultural experiments. Some work out well and some are a painful education, but all of them are valuable in feeling my way towards the life I want and the container I want for my life and my children's lives.

So in simple terms, what do I want for myself (and am encouraging others to consider)? My soul longs to be living in a bonded, multi-generational, sustainable-and-holistic community. I long to live in a community that supports people healing from their Domain 8 wounds, and teaches the skills to live in and enjoy Domain 9; one that co-parents all the children within the community equally, regardless of who the biological mother and father are; and one that shares land, businesses, and finances. I want to create a "group marriage," a social network that is rooted in Domain 4 and echoes Domain 5, but with all the added social, spiritual, psychic, emotional, and technological blessings that humanity has developed over the eons. I want to be discriminating, and release cultural patterns and agreements that don't serve wholeness, Spirit, nature, and full authenticity and health, replacing them with ones that do. While I know this is my own personal desire, I truly believe that deep down, under people's confusion, pain, addictions, distractions, and cultural conditioning, it is many people's desire and longing as well. I trust it resonates with our primal nature and soul as the way humans are meant to live.

As Einstein said, "Problems cannot be solved at the same level of awareness that created them." In other words, we can't just tweak Domain 8 and expect to really have what we want. So, let's talk about that further. I know many folks who have found a relative peace and balance by living in the cracks or on the fringe of Domain 8, not really buying into it, but not really getting out of it. When people do this, they end up "spicing up" their life with workshops, spiritual practice, alternative health practice, men's and women's groups, pagan rituals, world travel, etc. With reluctance, resignation, or ignorance, they keep Domain 8 as their home turf and create as much meaning, health, and connection as they can within that structure. But, as long as the family system and social contracts remain the way they are, people will not be able to access the fullness of their humanity and will not be able to stabilize in Domain 9.

Domain 9 is not an experience an individual can maintain through the force of their will or mind. It's also not the same as individual "enlightenment." It's the day-to-day living energy that is generated when psychic, social, emotional, and sexual contracts between people are dissolved, and instead of living as lone cells rubbing up against each other, we start to live the way we truly are, cells in the same body, one living being.

When most people think of "enlightenment" they see it as permanently realizing that "I am a cell in The One Spirit Body." With that realization they are then acting from/as Spirit, not merely from self (what many traditions call [usually in a shaming manner] "ego"). But Domain 9 is about being one cell in the Earth and Community body as well. Integrating, Spirit, self, community, and Earth -- aka GaiaYoga. It's not just spiritual, it's holistic, including all parts of life.

The Errors Of My Way

I've been hiding from myself – This Feeling in my Gut, an anxious groundless shock
I've been hiding from myself – My recoil at embodiment, core collapsed bewilderment
I've been hiding from my Self – The Unconditioned, only-Free, Divine-One Who I also Be

I've been hiding in relationship – Ingratiating in the name of Love, force-fitting the wrong right glove
I've been hiding in Relationship – From my utter Loneliness, scrambling to be We in Surrenderedness
I've been hiding in relationship – In a sacred growthful womb, that to me too often was a toxic tomb

I've been seeking in Relationship – What there can't be found, the Witness Self's unmoving Ground
I've been seeking in Relationship – A panacea from the Pain of constant need, death, and change
I've been seeking in relationship – Utopia-Titty-Security, and my own essential Identity

  That didn't work, there's no Out – I've exhausted all my doubt
  The only path left to take – is to finally fully Wake
  But if I saw another way – I would take it right away
  An though I sense The Real Prize – Tacitly I'm terrified

I've been seeking in phenomenon – Liberation beyond it all by manipulating what's conditional
I've been seeking in phenomenon – A Satisfaction that doesn't wane, whether sacred or profane
I've been seeking in phenomenon – Confused to my identity, but never asking, "Who am I?"

I've been trying to transcend – Neediness and Ownership, humanness and worldliness
I've been trying to transcend – Arrogance and Ignorance, push-and-pull, offense/defense
I've been trying to transcend – That I hurt and do die and have a conditioned identity

I've been squirming from my Hell – The constant Crisis at my Core, the frantic Craving that is my Lord
I've been squirming from my Hell – Hoping It would go away – dispel, distract It any way
I've been squirming from my Hell – But It's not an "it," It _is_ who I be – no escape, for all I feel _is_ Me

  That didn't work, there's no Cure – My condition can't be Pure
  I never found as I sought – I never freed as I thought
  I dumbly did dissociate – And with help self-violate
  But now graced by Saniel's Grace – I radically re-evaluate

  I can't dissect, I can't ignore – I can't resist, unlike before
  I'm landing in and as myself – I am God…I'm trapped in Hell
  This ain't who I want to be – Crucified in identity
  The tread has end, now I drown – A death/rebirth, I'm Waking Down

I'm rotting out of hide-and-seek – In Dharmas Hypermasculine, that didn't reveal Who I Am
I'm rotting out of hide-and-seek – From able-to-dissociate, to I-must-Be-me-and-relate
I'm rotting out of hide-and-seek – Wielding all the best beliefs, that never yielded Real Relief

I'm green-lighting myself – As imperfect mortal flesh – unpure, upset, and ignorant
I'm green-lighting myself – As perfection Absolute – Being, Seeing as The Root
I'm green-lighting myself – As mysterious seamless All – that does and does not rise and fall

I'm clarifying my Self – The living, life, the who I _is_, now includes Who Witnesses
I'm clarifying MySelf – Awake, alive, a mobious strip of Human, Soul, and Infinite
I'm clarifying myself – Every day, more and more, as The Beloved Most Adored

I am myself – I am My Self – I Am The Self – i AM – i AM my Self – i AM myself – i AM The Self
i am – i am my self – i am The Self – i am myself – i Am – i Am The Self – i Am Myself – i Am my self

I AM

What's next?

The "Spiritual" Domains Of GaiaYoga

Now I'd like to introduce the last two Domains – Domains 0 and 10. These two Domains are what most people would call "spiritual" Domains. Abralut recognized 9 Dimensions/Domains when he developed the Shivalila dharma. What I call Domain 0 he did recognize, but instead of calling it a Domain he thought of it as what all the other Domains were in relationship to. I found this confusing and it made this aspect of reality easy to overlook. In the Shivalila dharma, Domain 10 was subsumed in Domain 9, and though I can see the logic in doing this I think it's important to delineate the distinctions between them, as Domain 9, to me, is a liberated group consciousness, and Domain 10 is spiritual one that can be accessed as an individual self.

Domain 0 (Emptiness/Consciousness/The Witness) is "prior" to Domain 1 (Light/Energy/Forces). It is the Domain that is free from change, birth, life, and death. It is what many Eastern religions and New Age religions are referring to when they talk about The Witness, or emptiness, or the Divine Masculine, or The Self. It is the aspect of being that Sees or Senses all of Life and Manifestation. In the GaiaYoga Matrix°°° Domain 0 is one "half" of the Spirit facet, with The Divine Feminine being the other "half." Domains 1 through 10 are Domains of the manifest in the realm of change. Domain 0 is not found there, it simply witnesses the other Domains.

Domain 0, unlike Domain 9, can be independently and stably realized or "awakened" into. Ramana Maharshi, several Adviatic teachers, Adi Da, Saniel Bonder and The Waking Down School, and other spiritual teachers I'm not familiar with have realized Domain 0 and teach the realization of it. (I had a "witness awakening" during 1998 when I was actively involved in Waking Down. So, I am not just intellectualizing here. Domain 0 is a very real part of our beingness, which can be realized or brought to consciousness. It's nothing "special," because it's a part of everyone's nature, but it is obscured to most humans at this time.)

Domain 10 (Transcendental/Meta-Physical/"Spirit" Realms) is a concept I've developed to compensate for an obscuration I experienced in using Abralut's original 9 Dimensional map. Domain 10 is a catch-all category that includes all the experiences people have with angels, channeled beings, the astral plane, the causal plane, subtle energy bodies, heaven, Jesus, God, Krishna, Allah, etc. It's the metaphysical and it is not directly connected with any human cultural consciousness (Domain 5 through 9).

Domain 9 is an integrated cultural experience, which is a platform for living our lives from. Domain 10 is a great place to visit, but not really a place from which your average human being can live. Many New Age seekers, and many spiritual practices support connecting with, or "ascending" into, Domain 10. I'm speaking very generally, as there are numerous different planes of existence and types of beings that I'm lumping into Domain 10. The maps/myths/dharma that I most resonate with around Domain 10 are laid out in The Michael Teaching°°. (There are many authors who channel Michael and there is a large body of work to study. The book *Earth to Tao*, by Jose Stevens, addresses Domain 10 more than any other Michael book.)

For my purposes, I simply want to acknowledge that there is a vast "spiritual," non-physical world out there, that can be accessed whether your home is Domain 5, 6, 7, 8, or 9, and that it is different than connecting into Domains 1, 2, 3, or 4, and different than Domain 0. I also recognize that it is very useful, beautiful, growth-promoting, and rejuvenating to experience and explore Domain 10.

However I have a "surgeon general's warning" about Domain 10…

In my opinion, many spiritual seekers and teachers are attempting to bypass Domain 9 and "camp out" in either Domain 0 and/or Domain 10. I believe people do this in hopes of taking the path of least resistance and minimizing the work they "have to" do and the pain they "have to" feel. While I appreciate wanting to minimize pain and work, I believe they will not be able to sustain the experience they want if they bypass Domain 9. Evolutionarily, Domain 9 is the pinnacle experience of physical embodiment. It's the integration and cultural culmination of all that humanity has been grappling with for who knows how long. It's the foundation our souls would require if there is going to be some sort of graduation into Domain 10 as our primary home. I'm not saying that this is definitely what is in store for humanity, but if it is to be part of our evolution, Domain 9 would be our launch pad, not Domain 8 plus "individual enlightenment." In this way, I disagree with a lot of Eastern and New Age religions, which promote individual enlightenment as the great liberation. On the other hand, what I'm saying is actually in deep alignment with the Buddhist principle of Buddha, Dharma, Sangha°°. Buddha is the enlightened individual, Dharma is the way or the teaching, and Sangha is spiritual community. All three are necessary for effective spiritual practice and growth. The main difference is that I'm talking about a different dharma (the GaiaYoga dharma) and a different type of community (a Domain 9 one).

We can't skip a grade. We need to do the work at the cultural level to bond as a free and conscious people. This karma must be completed before it would be possible for our souls to stabilize in "higher planes." The main reason for this is that "higher plane consciousness" is not an individual consciousness, but it's precisely about souls merging as cells in a larger soul body. Premature ascendance is a very shiny prize, but I deeply doubt its sustainability. I also doubt that humanity on the whole, or as individuals, will be able to move into Domain 10 unless we first move into and master Domain 9. I believe this is necessary preparation if we want to keep developing as souls, and not have big gaps of uncompleted lessons and "karma," or lack of skills.

So I fully support people in "visiting" and experiencing Domain 10 (and Domain 0) as needed (which might be for an hour a day, or a minute a month), and soaking up the wisdom, energy, insight, and empowerment that is "there." But bring it back home. You are incarnated now as a human Earthling, and you incarnated for a reason. The cosmos didn't go through this whole grand process of creating physical life for souls just so we could ascend, transcend, or otherwise get out of being a human being -- with all its limitation, vulnerability, and profound physicality. Illusion or not, this is where we are, and I believe the sooner we accept and embrace this, the sooner we will maximize our happiness, power, and wholeness.

~~~~~~~~~~~~~

I Can See above the Smog! What's Next?

Let's celebrate! So far, you have been introduced to all 11 Domains, some of the major structural problems with our current Domain 8 lifestyle, and my core argument for GaiaYoga Culture. Building from this foundation, let's explore other topics that I believe are necessary in order to thoroughly consider achieving *True Human Freedom*…

First, I will <u>dive deeper</u> into the Domains and the Spheres of Community°°° and then focus on key aspects of our lives (Money, Spirituality, Diet, Sustenance, Birth Practices, Parenting, and Intimate Relationships). This will complete the picture, showing how Domain 9 is the most effective and ideal way to engage with each of these key areas of life.

- Navigating and designing the Spheres of Community
- The relationship between the Domains and the Spheres of Community
- Money and economics in the Domains and Spheres of Community
- Spirituality in the Domains (practice, realization, and internal experience)
- Sustenance within the Domains
- The GaiaYoga approach to diet and health
- The GaiaYoga perspective on birth
- Explaining the single-source imprint
- Polyamory from a GaiaYoga perspective

Next, I'll address <u>obstacles</u> that folks will inevitably face as they pursue Domain 9, as well as several important <u>insights</u> and <u>considerations</u> I've integrated from my pursuit thus far.

- The great obstacle: The pursuit of false human freedom
- The not-so-great obstacle: Creating Domain 9 while loved ones re-create Domain 8
- Creating a community of intention and affection
- Sustaining relationships through polarity and conflict
- Accepting our genes, re-assessing our memes
- Cultures of preservation versus cultures of acquisition
- Avoiding "traps" with gurus and leaders
- The limitations of eco-villages

Finally, I'll consider <u>what to do now</u> with all this information and inspiration. I'll overview the social agreements that can generate and sustain GaiaYoga Culture, and look into the big question: Practically speaking, how do I/we go about doing this?

- The foundational social agreements of GaiaYoga Culture
- How do we create GaiaYoga Culture?
- Tying the bow around the gift

Alright, let's get to it!

••• DIVING DEEPER •••

Navigating and Designing the Spheres of Community

(If you are not yet familiar with the Five Spheres of Community, I suggest either reading the synopsis I've put in the Appendix on page 103, or read *An Introduction to GaiaYoga* before reading this section. A diagram symbolizing the Five Spheres of Community is on page 100 of this book.)

It's not too hard to understand the differences between the five different spheres in an abstract manner, but how do we move through and between these spheres in real life? The diagram of the spheres has dotted lines between each of them. This is to indicate that there is a "skin;" a permeable edge between them. The ultimate movement through the spheres is birth and death. In (re)birth we move out of exclusive presence within the universal and emerge as a self in an intimate sphere, nestled within a personal, local, and collective sphere. In death we exit our selves (our incarnated human selves) and exit all the other spheres and return to the universal sphere.

Indeed, all of our most significant life events have to do with moving through the intimate sphere. This includes having a baby, getting a new lover, getting married, breaking up, getting divorced, and the death of a spouse, child, or parent. A (usually) less emotionally charged shift out of the intimate sphere is a grown child leaving their parents home. I want to be clear that when I say "intimate sphere," I mean someone's home sphere, the stable integrated foundational relationship(s) of their life. I don't mean, "oh well I was intimate with so and so last week," or parents and their adult children who don't live together anymore. Adult children will always have a profound intimate bond with their parents, and vice versa (in most examples), but that doesn't mean they're living within the same intimate sphere. Parents and their adult children generally have a personal sphere relationship, which easily slides into an intimacy both energetically and in dialogue. This is a normal relationship process, and I want to have clear definitions of these dynamics that people can agree on so we can discuss these topics and be understood.

In order to move gracefully through the spheres we need effective rituals. Here's an example: Imagine being on an airplane. You sit down next to another passenger -- a stranger, another member of the collective. You introduce yourself (a ritual to enter the local sphere), and they introduce themselves. You ask, "Where are you from?" (a ritual to get more into the local sphere). Perhaps you find out they're from the same town as you. You share that connection and talk about different places in that town. Then you ask, "Do you have kids?" (a ritual to move into the personal sphere). They say "yes" and you both share a bit about your kids. After awhile your new friend confesses that he's really struggling with his oldest child and would like some advice. You ask if they'd like to express what's really going on (a ritual to move into the intimate sphere). They say "yes" and share the details of they're struggle. Now if you just sat down and said, "Hi, wanna tell me about your struggles with your oldest child?" that wouldn't go over so well, because you'd be skipping all of these rituals for passing through the different spheres of connection/community. Likewise, at the end of the flight there's a series of rituals for stepping back out of the intimate, personal, and local spheres, back into the collective. Or perhaps you might exchange contact info and stay in touch, creating a personal relationship. But if you just got up at the end of the flight and said, "Bye" and walked away, it would be a disturbance to the other person's heart because of the abrupt shift from an intimate/personal connection into the collective.

Another example is a man approaching a woman at a bar hoping to have sex with her. There are rituals to effectively progress towards this, which are sincere and enlivening for all involved. In fact, "picking up on someone" is exactly the art of moving through these Spheres of Community gracefully. It's pretty similar to our airplane story. Below I'll portray a typical man initiating such a scenario with a woman. This example is streamlined for efficiency's sake:

First the man might share some glances with the woman from across the bar and see if there's any facial responses. (This is a ritual of coming out of the collective towards the local.) If there's some indication of openness, then the man might come up and ask if he can buy her a drink (this is moving from the collective side of the local sphere towards the personal side of it). If she says yes, he'll ask her name and say some pick up line like "What's such a beautiful woman like you doing at a bar like this?" (This slides us into the personal sphere.) The woman will likely respond with some sort of flirtatious retort and ask some questions in return (moving deeper into the personal sphere). Maybe a great song comes on the radio and you ask her to dance. (This is a ritual to come towards the intimate side of the personal sphere). While they're dancing, the man notices how the woman is responding positively to his dancing and touch so he whispers in her ear, "I just love the way you dance, and how you smell, and the touch of your hand on my skin. I'd love to give you a kiss..." (This is an invitation to enter into the intimate sphere) And then she leans forward and...

Ahem... Besides these type of rituals we also need effective containers in our lives to maximize ease and flow in and out of intimate and personal relationships. One of the biggest issues with the isolated nuclear family living in a city or suburb is that each intimate sphere is surrounded only by a local sphere (a neighborhood); so when an intimate sphere dissolves there's no integrated personal sphere container to hold it. Additionally, most local spheres are highly un-intentional and hardly connected; so, they don't offer much support when an intimate sphere is in need.

This is one of my biggest inspirations around co-creating and living in a Domain 9 community: having an integrated personal sphere that is really a solid container for many intimate spheres, that can handle the birth, life, and death of intimacy without rupturing the container of the integrated personal sphere. Within such a container, the members of a dissolving intimate sphere don't need to exit their greater personal sphere they're both integrated into as a strategy to meet needs for peace, support for growth and healing, support for mourning, support for new intimacy, etc. In other words, if they live in a Domain 9 community, folks can move in and out of intimacy and still maintain the same integrated personal sphere that includes their home, gardens, orchards, co-parents, friends, community businesses, etc. This is what tribes do for clans and the lovers within them, they are the greater container in which people stay bonded together and cooperative in, even if intimacy doesn't work out long term.

In Domain 8 there's no "net" to catch people when they break up. Someone has to move out, or they both have to sell the home. Add children to the mix and it's a nightmare. This is part of the design flaw in Domain 8 that doesn't exist in Domains 5, 6, or 9. This is where the re-designing comes in, and this is what we're exploring at GaiaYoga Gardens. Instead of having the intimate sphere function as the basis of survival, (where our security and stability around economics, home and land, parenting system, businesses, emotional support, and intimacy and sexuality are held) we make it the personal sphere. I consider this a major upgrade in cultural design.

On a practical level it means property is held by a community, not by a couple. It means that the property is large enough for dozens of people, not just two. It means that infrastructure is designed around being together and sharing resources like kitchens, bathrooms, living rooms, gardens, orchards, pastures, play areas for children, vehicles, etc. It means that when a couple breaks up they can be "caught" by the same personal sphere they both live in. Independently they have both chosen this community and have gone through the rituals of transitioning out of an intimate connection and into a personal one. They do this within their community, without losing home, land, or family, without having to pick up their whole reality and move it elsewhere. It can simply mean that you sleep in a different hut than you used to, and maybe one or both of you take a trip to re-center your self. Obviously this takes a whole different cultural consciousness than most of us come from, and requires real skills and teamwork to make it actually work. It is very much possible, and it's much better for everyone involved, especially for the children who don't end up with a fragmented family, living away from one or even both of their parents.

Ultimately, an integrated personal sphere is a much more stable than an intimate sphere. It contains enough people to make survival easy and also provide a day-to-day home social network that is diverse and abundant. This is why it works more effectively to design our personal sphere to be the foundation of our survival and home, rather than our intimate sphere. When we do this, another benefit is that we can much more easily engage intimacy simply for the joy of it, without overburdening our intimate sphere by default. Imagine feeling secure in your future regardless of whether your intimate relationship survives long term. Imagine if you could freely decide with whom to be sexual without fear of losing your home and fundamental sense of security. Having this foundation is huge support for being authentic and honest with oneself and others. Really!!!

The closest equivalent I can think of to this in Domain 8 is the experience many people have living in a college dorm. In dorms people can "hook up" and "break up" and stay in the same dorm even after they are no longer intimate. The dorm acts as the integrated personal/local sphere or tribe. Also, in a dorm and at that time in most peoples' lives, they are just engaging intimacy (and personal sphere friendships) for the joy or experience of it, not linked to survival.

One big problem I see in the world is people's inability to exit intimate relationships with the same kind of care and passion that they enter into them. People come together intimately because they are attracted to and love each other. They want to be so close to each other that they live in the same house and sleep in the same bed. Yet often, when couples break up, the other side of the nation or even the planet is not far enough away. Indeed people leave the intimate and head straight into the collective sphere (hence the line in the hit song "Now you're just somebody that I used to know.") In a healthy, conscious situation people exit the intimate sphere into the personal sphere – to use common language they become "just friends."

Obviously, we have a lot more power to decide what our intimate and personal spheres look like than the other spheres. Our local sphere is also something we choose, though usually we have less influence over it. One of the reasons GaiaYoga Gardens is located in Puna, Hawaii is because the local sphere here is very friendly to the life we are living. If we tried to create GaiaYoga Culture in New York City or West Texas or in Southern California, then our neighbors would be looking down on us for being weird (at best) or shut us down for some sort of ordinance violation (at worst).

At the collective level we have the least amount of influence. These days it's harder to leave the country you were born in and make a home elsewhere, and even if you do, there's little people can do to change the course of governments unless they make that their life's mission.

We need to participate in all the Spheres of Community, as we are simultaneously family members, friends, neighbors, and citizens, and it benefits us to be able to move through the spheres gracefully. I see GaiaYoga Culture emerging as a personal sphere that contains multiple intimate spheres. Perhaps as the years and decades go on, we'll see a local or even collective sphere expression of GaiaYoga Culture. I'd be delighted to see that, but at this point, just creating a stable and functioning intentional community as a personal sphere is a grand enough endeavor!

Until we can intellectually separate the Spheres of Community, in the abstract, from how they've been lived in our culture of conditioning, it is basically impossible to re-design them. This is one reason this map is so important. If we understand the basic qualities of life and relationship that each sphere contains, separate from any particular cultural strategy, then we can be creative in crafting our social agreements within each of them, and meet the most needs for the most people.

A simple example of separating a particular cultural strategy from the intimate sphere is the national political discussion right now (in 2015) in the U.S. about whether gay/lesbian couples can be recognized as a bona-fide intimate sphere -- a marriage. (Fifty or so years ago, the discussion was, "Can a black and a white person be recognized legally as the same intimate sphere?") If we look at what kind of activity and sharing occur in the intimate sphere and separate that from the strategy of heterosexual monogamy between people of the same race, then it's obvious that gay couples and/or couples of different races are also participating in a committed intimate sphere relationship and it is in integrity to recognize it as such. Similarly, more than two people can participate in an intimate sphere, and this *can be* honored as a bona-fide form of intimacy. But we must let go of our fixation on the most common form of intimate sphere (heterosexual monogamy) to be able to see the empty structure of this sphere, without the influence of a particular strategy.

The same process can be done in the personal, local, and collective spheres, by pulling apart the strategies from the empty structure, really meditating on what will work for all of us and then co-creating something that works together.

Once we've let go of how the spheres of community manifested in our cultures of origin, (at least mentally) then we can consider what kind of social agreements we want in each of the spheres. I've already talked a lot about the intimate sphere's design, and there are also agreements in the personal, local, and collective spheres that we can re-evaluate and redesign. For example: Most people in America lack an integrated personal sphere that they live in with continuity. This lack in their personal sphere is a product of social agreements. In most local spheres there's no agreement to act in a sustainable manner or to truly work together towards sustainability. In the collective sphere pretty much all countries have agreed to a very unsustainable economic system that is beholden to central banks. Also most countries agree that violence is an acceptable way to attempt to meet needs for their country. Until we look soberly at the impacts of our agreements and choices, and really see if they're meeting our needs, it's hard to change them. Doing this re-evaluation process requires free attention and cooperation from others, so it's no surprise that most people don't take the time to do it, and just keep plugging away at the situation they're in.

As with many of these topics, there's certainly more I could say about navigating and designing the Spheres of Community, but I think I've said what is pertinent for the moment. Mainly I want to bring the process to consciousness, so people can start to be more deliberate about what they do in relationship to the Spheres of Community. I trust as people become aware of this, they will find their own way and their own wisdom around it.

The Relationship Between the Domains and the Spheres of Community

When I first developed the GaiaYoga teaching, I didn't include the Five Spheres of Community. I added it later when I realized people were really lacking clarity about the Community Facet. People, myself included, would throw around the word "community" meaning all sorts of different things. The use of the word, at the minimum, was confusing, and at the maximum deceptive to self and others. At the time I was well aware of the Nine Dimensional map of Shivalila, but I didn't see it as a necessary concept to express relative to GaiaYoga or the Community Facet. But, now I see that recognizing the Domains is crucial in being able to create a free, conscious, and holistic culture. So, how do these maps integrate with each other? It's actually quite elegant.

Plants, Domain 3, live in the intimate/personal sphere of their immediate surroundings, which are Domains 1 and 2. They grow and adapt to their habitat and the weather that passes by locally. Animals, Domain 4, have intimate relationships within their family groups (wolf packs, bee hives, beaver dens, etc.) and personal or local interactions with the other animals and plants in their local sphere (this could include the members of a large herd of one species). Domain 5 people are also limited to the intimate sphere (or the intimate edge of the personal sphere) in their kinship group interactions. Cooperation is limited to a fairly small band of people who can coordinate their efforts without sophisticated language or conceptualization.

Tribal, Domain 6, culture consists of clans within a larger tribe. Clans essentially function as an intimate sphere, and the tribe is a larger container that fundamentally functions as a personal sphere. In a tribe there are so many people that the energy of an intimate sphere cannot be realistically maintained. This means that humans expand their ability to cooperate outside of the intimate sphere and create psychic/emotional/social structures to allow for it. Because of this, tribal customs serve to support these two spheres' distinct levels of transparency in expression, sharing of power, and degree of cooperation. This creates more complexity in relationships and the need for more clarity via social agreements and customs.

In Domain 7 culture, the local sphere emerges and is made possible by an expanded ability to share a common story and cooperate flexibly with people we know to a lesser degree. In a village, the extended-family functions as an intimate sphere or as a blended intimate/personal sphere. Then there are guilds, affinity groups, and circles of friends that function as personal spheres. But again, there are too many people in a village for everyone to realistically be part of the same personal sphere. Moreover, because of sexual contracts, land ownership, economics, and the influx of more "strangers" the local sphere comes into being and so does a shared story within each person of having a larger identity as a village member. This is not possible in Domains 5 or 6.

The seeds of the collective sphere began in Domain 7 with people traveling from settlement to settlement. Additionally, some pre-industrial societies had manifested a collective sphere (of a state or nation). Examples of this are the Roman Empire, the British Empire, and the Cherokee Nation. The Cherokee Nation was a much larger association than a single tribal settlement. It included numerous tribes and these tribes had formal social agreements with each other. And as the saying went "The sun never sets on the British empire." So, prior to the birth of Domain 8, people around the world identified as British, and were sharing a common collective story, identity and culture, including political and military power. For both these cultures, there was a collective consciousness of citizenship that spread beyond the local sphere of the village or personal sphere of a tribe. So, while the collective sphere of community does predate Domain 8, it didn't really get into full expression until it emerged.

The collective sphere requires a vastly different level of flexible cooperation and shared story to maintain the larger power structure. Without the ability to internally create the concept or fiction of a nation or world religion (e.g. considering oneself Roman, Muslim, Catholic, or British) there is no possibility of a collective sphere. Indeed, only humans experience the collective sphere; and now the internalized stories are what pervade the day-to-day life of most people. The collective sphere's primacy and its power and influence over day-to-day life has dramatically increased through technology, electronic communication (starting with the telegraph), newspapers, national (and international) organizations, world religions, national currency, and now phones, radio, television, and the internet. This unique ability our species has to participate collectively has given us unprecedented power on this planet. Currently this power is being wielded rather unsustainably, but a sustainable and holistically designed collective is certainly possible.

Money and Economics in the Domains and Spheres of Community

How we handle money and economics is critical to the success of our intimate and personal lives, intentional communities, and our relationships with the world. A discussion of how to create culture would be incomplete without looking into it seriously.

So much has been written about money; how to get more of it, what's wrong with it, how it works, etc. The questions I want to look at are: how do we pay for things, why do we pay, and how does it vary amongst the different Domains and Spheres?

Economics comes from a Greek word "οἰκονομία" or spelled in English, "okionomia." It means "household management" or "one who manages household affairs." It has expanded to encompass how we manage whole nations – which are essentially a large collection of households. Since we've been seeing how differently households have been designed over the eons, it's obvious that our economics and currency have also changed.

Most of us reading this probably grew up in a capitalistic Domain 8 culture. Here's my favorite quote about capitalism: "Capitalism is the extraordinary belief that the nastiest of men acting for the nastiest of motives will somehow work for the greatest benefit of everyone." (The origins of this quote are not certain, but it's probably from E. A. G. Robinson in his 1941 book *Monopoly*.) I don't like judging people in the way the quote portrays, but it makes an important point. Capitalism, like everything people do, is an experiment. This particular experiment is certainly showing that it doesn't work for the benefit of all of humanity, and certainly not the Earth. At this time, the 85 wealthiest people in the world have as much wealth as the 3.5 billion poorest people. In other words, 85 billionaires have more wealth than half the human population combined. Meanwhile forests, oceans, oil fields, mines, ground water, and topsoil are being destroyed, depleted, and dispersed as corporate products at an unfathomable rate.

So how did we get here?

In Domain 5 there was no money or barter; there were only humans, their camps, and what they foraged, hunted, found, or simply made out of rock and wood. Now, these weren't new age folks choosing voluntary simplicity; these were primitive humans who didn't have the capacity to do anything else. Survival was a team sport, and people just did what needed to be done, and weren't beholden to any landlords or bosses or kings, or any sort of outside economic force – except the inherent demands of being alive. Energy resolved in the moment; there were no debts or credits. Sure, there might be appreciation and good will, or fear and hurts, but that's a very different energy. The household was managed much in the same way you see other pack animals manage their households – children are cared for, food is acquired, camps are kept livable, conflict occurs and is resolved, the household protects itself from other species and the elements, etc.

In Domain 6, we shift out of the primal here-now reality of Domain 5, into a complex system of territory, and families, within clans, within tribes and social contracts to maintain them. So the economics must be different as well. In Domain 6 the main form of economy is direct trade and barter, (e.g. "I give you one teepee you give me 4 bows and 10 arrows.") Of course, there is a difference between inter-tribal trading and intra-tribal trading, where relationships have much more integration and continuity than trade with someone outside one's tribe.

A particular Domain 6 tribe contains both an intimate and personal sphere. Another tribe would constitute a local sphere relationship. In the intimate sphere, the way we "pay for things" is by being intimate, being dependable and bonded, sharing everything and receiving that same level of sharing and continuity of relationship. It's not that things are free with our intimates, it's that the way we pay is invisible and not something around which we have to do accounting. We share and decide based on needs (in a healthy situation) and the all-for-one-one-for-all relationship transcends the need for trade, barter, and certainly money. We give, share, and receive fully and freely. That's what we still see within most isolated nuclear families. The adult sex-partners are one economic unit, which includes their children that are still living in the house. In Domain 6, this level of sharing usually occurs, not only with a mating pair, but also with their whole clan.

Trading within the tribe is, for the most part, a personal sphere activity. In the larger tribe there's not as much bonding and continuity as exists in the intimate sphere of the family or clan, but still a lot of the "cost" of the product or service is "paid for" by relatedness and shared commitment to the same larger human group. What many refer to as the "friends price." Some tribes function on a gift economy within the tribe, but may employ friendly trade and barter with others.

Trading from one tribe to another is a local sphere activity. Back when tribes were the dominant human social form, there wasn't a collective sphere, so the most expensive trade was in the local sphere. Nowadays, in some small towns, villages, and tourist areas there is a local price, which is less than the price for outsiders. The currency charge is lower because a percentage of the cost is covered by the relatedness that comes from people sharing the same locality. Neighbors have each other's back. This is the difference between a Domain 6/7 local sphere and a Domain 8 one.

In Domain 6 there really isn't money in the way we understand it. There might be valuable things like gold, silver, shells, and such that might be used as a more standardized unit of value, but not to the degree we see in Domains 7 and 8.

In Domain 7 there is currency (money), as well as active bartering. Historically, currency was backed by something real - usually gold, silver, or another precious metal or stone. As many of us know, this is no longer the case. Currency fosters a more consistent valuing of goods and services. Also, with currency, people can more easily store and build wealth in a way that facilitates the liquidation of assets. With barter, I need to find someone who wants what I have and has what I want, to get what I want. With currency, that search is not necessary. The efficiency of currency does have a cost – as currency becomes a thing in itself that can separate people from each other, and disconnect people from connection to real needs. People start to believe they "need money," when in fact money is just a strategy to meet our needs for food, shelter, fun, creativity, security, home, etc. So instead of people coming together to meet each other's needs directly they come together to get money, and often miss out on the living energy beneath the transaction.

More importantly, as money and economics become more and more sophisticated in Domain 7, and then in Domain 8, most people stop realizing that our economic system is a social agreement. For most humans, it's a tacit agreement that was made generations earlier that now has a momentum of its own. Money is not inherently real the way a nectarine or a massage is. It's only real because of the faith people put into it. This isn't an inherent problem, but because most monetary systems have been created to serve the bankers, the rich, the elite, rather than to serve the masses, it is a problem.

Here are a couple examples. Imagine if instead of countries collecting an income tax, there was a holdings tax. This means people would be taxed if they held on to their money, but not taxed if they spent it. This would discourage people from hoarding wealth and encourage the movement of energy throughout an economic system, radically reducing the gap between "poor" and "wealthy." And imagine if the Earth was paid for what it now gives freely. If a forest was paid for its trees, the ocean for its fish, a mine for its metals, an oil field for its oil, we'd see a very different end cost for these products. These are all limited resources that the Earth took decades, hundreds, or untold thousands or millions of years to produce. But the cost of the Earth's labor, or the time/work it would take to recreate the resource, is not included in the cost of the product. This really skews the actual value of things and allows them to be used up at a furious rate. This is possible because people have agreed, in a very short-sighted manner, to not value what the Earth makes nor how long it would take to re-create these resources. Unfortunately, taking "mom" for granted is a pretty common practice.

For the most part, the same basic dynamic around how we pay for things in the intimate, personal, and local sphere applies in Domain 7, except that because the local sphere is the container of the village, people often give "better deals" to people in their village rather than those outside of it.

In Domain 8 the collective sphere kicks into full swing, and currency is king. Trade-and-barter is almost completely absent from most Domain 8 cultures, and where it does happen its not at all part of the mainstream. Currency essentially erases the reality of human relationship as the heart of economics, creating the appearance of purely mathematical economic events. Most prices are pre-determined by the seller/merchant, and are not adjusted because of the relatedness within a shared locality. In most situations everyone is treated the same, as part of the collective sphere in economic matters. Certainly, friendship and family connections still matter, even in Domain 8 economics, and especially in shared business ventures.

One of the biggest things that occurs around money in Domain 8, and often in Domain 7, is that people lose sight of the fact that human beings want to do things because of their intrinsic desire to contribute°°. This happens because people end up doing much of their work to "make money," to "make ends meet," to "pay the bills," and to "keep a roof over their head." Most folks end up being, essentially, well-paid slaves and serfs in order to pay the rent and educate their children. Being in this situation, it matters little how the money comes in, but just that it does, and that there's enough to handle survival. In this situation it's so easy to think we work to make money and for selfish reasons, and to be oblivious that our drive to give to others and contribute is actually what is "supposed to be" behind our movement to work.

When individuals or nuclear families are all separated into their own isolated economic units, with their own rent or mortgage, their own car, refrigerator, utility bills, insurance, etc., they have to work very hard to maintain that separated survival reality. This separate reality requires working much harder than if people cooperated around these areas of life. This works very effectively to keep people stuck in a cycle of both having no real free time or energy to fulfill their deep creative dreams within the system, nor the capacity to revolt and re-create a new functional one.

I like to say there are two classes of people in the world: 1) those that work, in one form or another, to "make" money, and 2) those that print money. (Note the misuse of the word "make." People who print money are actually the ones who "make" it, and those who work in some way acquire, earn, or exchange for it – the money is already made.) Money is essentially printed out of thin air by The Federal Reserve Bank in the United States, and by similar entities in other first world countries. Neither these institutionalized banks nor their counterparts, "counterfeiters," want anyone moving in on their turf. The only difference between the banks and counterfeiters is that the banks have societal agreement (and the military) behind them so they can get away with it. And this social agreement, or mass hypnosis, is working very well. People know they can induce others to act if they have currencies, so people pass them around to get what they want, but we're not the one's generating the currency, so no matter how much we have, we're still playing with someone else's game pieces – and paying the price for it!

So how do we pay for goods and services in Domain 8? We use money, which is used as the unit of measurement for what is socially agreed upon to be valuable. Who decides what the value is? That is a direct or indirect negotiation between the buyer and the seller. Why do we pay? In general, we're not paying because we love someone and want to support him or her. We pay because we can't get the things we want unless we give other people the money they are asking for to get the things we want. So people focus on themselves, on meeting their own needs with their transactions, rather than being in touch with natural giving. This doesn't have to be the case, but one has to really rise above the system to change it.

So what do we have in store in Domain 9 with economics and currency? It could go several ways: one is a gift economy, another is a needs-based economy, and another is harmonious merger of several economic patterns depending on what sphere of community you share with the person you are exchanging goods/services with.

Nature is essentially a gift economy. All animals and plants are just freely giving whatever goods or services they "offer" or "produce." The sun gives light freely, the Earth gives soil and air and warmth and weather and minerals freely. There is lots of symbiosis in the natural world, but these are simply here-now exchanges. There's also lots of hunting and foraging and grazing going on, which is an act of aggression by the eater upon the eaten. While it can be argued that the eaten are not freely giving their plant or animal bodies to the eaters, the eaters aren't paying for their food. Trees give dead leaves to the ground, slowly building soil, and oxygen to the atmosphere so animals can breathe. Animals give carbon dioxide to the air, so plants can breathe, and they give their urine and feces to the ground, slowly building soil. At death, all creatures give their bodies back to the ground to build more soil.

This system works quite well, as most of us have noticed, and there's no reason to doubt that it can work for humans. The only challenge is to get the ball (re)rolling. It would take a critical mass of people to start doing this together to get it to spread beyond just a personal or local sphere and into the collective. At an intentional community level it is certainly a possibility to function in this way within the community. At the local and collective level it's going to take huge change that I imagine will grow out of intimate and personal spheres of people living this way successfully and then bringing it forward as a functional model to larger circles of people.

A needs-based economy is similar to a gift economy, except the focus is on the needs of those who receive a good or service, rather than the desire to give by the ones providing the good or service. In a needs-based economy, people receive a home, food, goods and services based on their needs, and people are in touch enough with their needs, the needs of others, and the needs of nature, to fundamentally only ask for things that serve all of life. The needs-based economy is what we see between a parent and a child. The child expresses its needs and the parent (in an ideal situation) provides that need freely and happily. If someone has a talent in art, then they are given what supports that; if it's healing, then that is supported; if it's ingenuity then those needs are supported. Obviously, the basics of clean food, air, water, and comfortable home are needs to provide. As the primary precept of NVC states: when people have their survival needs met, then their greatest drive is to contribute, to give in a meaningful and real way to the world. This spins back into a gift economy, because our greatest need is to contribute or give. We're hardwired to get our greatest joy from giving. Thus a needs-based economy and a gift economy are essentially the same system!

The expressing and meeting of needs is what bonds people together and makes life wonderful. Indeed, there is no greater wealth than a family/clan/tribe sustainably bonded together in love, authenticity, and mutual support.

For better or worse, it's unlikely the whole world is just going to wake up one day and recreate the current economic system into a gifting/needs-based one, so knowing how to participate with economic integrity in these different Spheres of Community is very important.

In the intimate sphere, we want to relate to others deeply, like we do with immediate family. And in our intimate sphere, we have lots of power to align our economic system with our values and dreams by creating a shared intention and practice with the others within it. If we're creating the seed energy of Domain 9 in our intimate sphere, then we can start to trust more in natural giving and make that the foundation of our intimate relationships.

In the personal sphere we also have a lot of say-so. But, since most people don't live in a personal sphere community that is bonded together and living together, it's much harder to function without some sort of economic accounting system to keep energy exchanges mutual in our personal relationships (friends, extended-family, coworkers, people in the same church, club, or team). Also, since most personal sphere relationships aren't sharing money, businesses, and major life decisions together, it is easier for peoples' needs to be lost in the shuffle without dependable ways to meet them. In the personal sphere in Domain 9 we might see friendly trade or barter mixed with simple giving and using money in a non- or minimally-profiting manner (providing goods and serves at, or near, cost).

In the local sphere, because of its size and diversity of beliefs, values, and lifestyle choices, it's even harder to function without an accounting system. However, it can be done if the foundation is there. It also depends on the nature of the local sphere. If the local sphere is a large eco-village, where people are sharing at many levels and identify as part of the eco-village, then it would be more realistic to have a larger-scale gifting/needs-based economy. In an unintentional and less bonded local sphere, which is much more common at this time, giving local people discounts, having a local currency, and using direct barter is a way to honor this sphere while moving towards a Domain 9 energy sharing system.

Obviously the collective is the trickiest place of all to bring in a gifting/need-based economy. This is especially true because unsustainable capitalism and profit are the driving force in economics at this time. Domain 9 comes out of the deep recognition that all human beings are part of one family, and that if we diminish one another to raise only ourselves up, as we often do in Domain 8, then eventually we all suffer for it. I have become fairly successful in ethically and ecologically participating with capitalism. I've chosen to do this because I see that capitalism has "the canopy" on the planet right now, and most human resources come through it. If I want to get GaiaYoga up into the canopy and establish it, I need to somehow take the energy of the current dominant system and use it to fuel this new system and consciousness. There is a risk of getting lost or poisoned by playing with this energy, and losing sight of my deeper goal of creating a Domain 9 container that transcends all of the Domain 8 issues. However, as long as Domain 8 dominates, then it's unrealistic to avoid using its economic system to harness necessary energy to grow GaiaYoga Culture.

Certainly we want our businesses to be ecologically sustainable, ethical, and supportive in creating our deeper dreams. This cuts out a lot of business possibilities, but it's a lot easier to sleep at night if one knows that the way they're gathering financial energy is in alignment with their values.

I want to emphasize: Ownership, currency, and entire economic systems do not exist, except as social agreement. This is very important to realize. How we set up these agreements has huge repercussions on our quality and experience of life. Most of us have accepted an agreement that is designed by the bankers and elite to serve the bankers and the elite. We can do something different, but it takes a lot of clarity and dedication to create new and functional agreements around these things, and to find people who want to experiment with these agreements.

In a Domain 9 culture, there is no illusion that we can own things, or people, or land. Yes, we can have long-term, dependable access to, and intimate relationships with things, people, and land; and these relationships can be supported and respected by other people. This quality of relationship, where everyone's needs matter and are met through natural giving, is the deeper reality underneath the social contract of ownership. As people's needs and inspirations to give shift, we can let situations and relationships change in an organic way, trusting that new, and probably "better," ways to meet ours and other's needs will unfold. A Domain 9 economic system is based on serving everyone involved in the system, including the natural, material, and social resources. As our economics reflect the deeper truths of human relatedness and human nature we will be able to enjoy life, being supported, and contributing to the world much more.

Spirituality within the Domains
(Practice, Realization, and Internal Experience)

Our connection to Spirit, God, Source, Higher Power, or whatever word(s) you prefer, is a very important part of most people's lives and most cultures. With GaiaYoga, spirituality is very important, and how a spiritual practice shows up can vary tremendously from person-to-person or various communities practicing GaiaYoga. The main litmus tests with spirituality and GaiaYoga are as follows: Does the dharma and the practice support true wholeness, does our practice support integration with Earth, self, and community, and does it support fluidity and empowerment through all the Domains?

From reading so far about the Domains, it's easy to grasp that there are general trends of how spirituality is expressed throughout the cultures of the different human Domains. In Domain 5 there isn't any spirituality, per se. In the same way animals don't particularly have a spiritual practice, Domain 5 people don't either. They are just being here/now in the mystery of life: Nothing more, nothing less. The Aborigines of Australia (who are a Domain 6 culture for the most part, but with strong Domain 5 elements) connect to the Dreamtime as a form of spirituality. Essentially the Dreamtime is connecting deeply with Domains 1 – 4 and 10 as Spirit-and-Earth unified; connecting the primal creation and natural energies of the world.

In Domain 6 cultures, spirituality has a few faces. One connects with archetypal energies through totem/power animals, nature spirits, and plant-spirit-medicines. There's a multitude of different ways that Domain 6 cultures connect with these energies and use these medicines. Usually connection to these archetypal energies occurs in the form of sacred ritual. Ritual is a significant spiritual practice in most tribal cultures. As I said before, ritual and shamanism are ways to step through the Domains, lowering the emotional/psychic/social contracts, thus dropping psychic and sensory limiters of day-to-day life, facilitating a "journey" to experience other aspects of life and our selves (including Domain 0 or 10). This is done through vision quests, various trance techniques, fasting, drumming, being buried alive, living with animals, etc. If you look at the sacred art of tribal cultures, it reveals what is learned and "brought back" from these journeys. A specific ritual that is a cornerstone of spirituality in most tribal cultures is the initiation process that their young men go through to transition from childhood to adulthood.

Most tribal cultures have a cosmology of different Spirits which might include the four directions, the Divine Feminine and Masculine, the sky, sun, moon, and the Earth, animal spirits, plant spirits, wind, water, and rock spirits, etc. Some have the sense of a single greater force/being, some don't.

Domain 7 spirituality often has more of a sense of The-One-Great-Other than Domain 6 cultures do. And often this great other is a punishing "God" like we see in Judaism, Christianity, Catholicism, and Islam. Paganism is often expressed as a Domain 7 sub-cultures' way of having a more Domain 6 rooted spiritual practice. Buddhism and Hinduism are other Domain 7 religions, but they have a whole different flavor than the Western religions.

Among the major Domain 7 religions, at least in the exoteric versions of them, God/Spirit is not really for the masses to directly experience. In the same way that there are many more social contracts in Domain 7 cultures, there are a lot more contracts with God. In the Eastern religions, one needs to purify one's self <u>a lot</u> to really know God. In the Western religions there's a gap between God/Allah/Heaven and humanity. While there can be some ecstatic communion, in general God is unreachable. This is very unlike Domain 6 spirituality. This gap is managed by the priesthood -- those who've somehow earned a little closer seat to God than the rest of us. And they are on payroll to help us out. Though many priests are sincere in their devotion to God and humanity, the orders they're in are usually corrupt and ultimately working to keep people obedient, god-fearing, productive citizens. They're not into liberating them. In Domain 6, shamans serve a similar cultural function, but there's a much mellower hierarchical power structure than in most Domain 7 priesthood orders. Priests tend to be a lot more attached to their jobs and political position than shamans, who are generally not as worried about job security, or maintaining the spiritual gap.

This dynamic is not active within the esoteric side of most of these religions. These esoteric schools differ in that there is direct access to high spiritual states and God. Sufism and the followers of Rumi are an example of this. The Essenes are an example of this in Christianity. Domain 8 has some of its own religions, but most of the big religions of the world were born in Domain 6/7 a few thousand years ago, got strong in Domain 7 and have continued into Domain 8. What has newly emerged in Domain 8, which could segue into Domain 9, are spiritual practices that have been created by spiritual leaders who didn't like the religious options they saw in the world. Some examples are Osho, Adi Da, Saniel Bonder's Waking Down teaching, and many teachers from the East who integrate Western ideas into their teachings. There's also Deepak Chopra, Ram Das, Drunvalo Melchizedek, modern Adviata gurus like Gangaji and Papaji, all the different channeled and new age teachings, Science of Mind, Neil Donald Walsh, The Seth Material, The Michael Teaching, Carlos Castaneda, The Way of the Peaceful Warrior, etc... There have been numerous modern spiritual teachings°°, teachers, and traditions created in the last 50 years.

What they all have in common is that they are attempting to address the issues that Domain 8 people struggle with. The expansiveness of technology and physical freedom to travel, combined with the degradation of our families and lack of cultural bonding, combined with our expanded minds, access to education and technology, and cross-cultural experience, has created a new "customer" for religion and spirituality. Thus the need for a new "product."

A big chunk of these newer teachings are in one way or another efforts to transcend or ascend the world. I'm very concerned about these teachings and would strongly caution people from buying into them because they don't produce the results they purport. They only "work" if we fragment ourselves, marginalize or deny some aspect of our total being. In this way they are violent towards self and unable to be maintained without constantly holding off the complexity of real life.

There are also a lot of new teachings that are about integrating with and accepting all of life and connecting to Spirit in-as-and-through this. I'm more in support of these teachings and practices. I support them because they generate wholeness in a person, they encourage integration with all aspects of life, and they can be maintained with less effort because one is embracing all of the complexity of life within the practice.

What is a Domain 9 culture's spiritual practice? Well, first we must really answer the question: What is spiritual practice?

The Spirit facet can be framed as the synthesis of The Divine Masculine and Feminine. The Divine Masculine is Consciousness, pure attention, free from matter, birth-death, and change (Domain 0).

The Divine Feminine is the Energy of Life, Death, Rebirth, Love, Light, the manifest, that which changes. It's also different qualities of subtle energy (auras, chakras, kundalini, chi, etc.), unseen spirits, archetypal forces of nature, connecting with peace and silence, loving other humans as we love ourselves, Tantra°°, etc. (aspects of Domains 1 – 5 and all of Domain 10). Another way to visualize it is that Spirit is Consciousness united with the spectrum of frequencies of Love/Energy.

Spiritual practice is about connecting with any and all of these energies/consciousnesses (not as some separate Great Other, but as Who I Am, an intrinsic part of my own beingness). Spiritual realization creates a sustaining and perpetual awareness or identification of the Divine Masculine and/or Divine Feminine. The strongest realizations are ones that integrate both of them and are stably maintained without effort.

It's important to realize that there's a big difference between spiritual practice and spiritual realization. Spiritual practice, the way most folks conceive of it, is doing some sort of activity in the hopes of increasing one's connection to God/Spirit/a guru/peace/harmony/love or increasing one's connection to and flow of their own subtle/spiritual energy. Practice could include a type of spiritual energy cultivation techniques°°, or spiritual study, contemplation, meditation, prayer, rituals, sacred music or movement, etc. Spiritual realization is a state of being or consciousness or awareness that once achieved (realized) is integrated into one's life and presence. A mundane example of this would be learning to ride a bike. When one can't ride a bike, it takes lots of "practice" to learn to ride, but once you "realize" how to ride you don't have to practice to maintain that realization. Sure, someone riding regularly over that same year will be in better biking shape than one who didn't, and a person who hasn't ridden might be a bit "rusty," but the fundamental capacity to ride will not be increased or decreased once the realization has occurred.

Spiritual practice, when done effectively, should be similar. Once you have a realization, it's yours for the rest of your life. Many people confuse spiritual practice with being spiritual. The irony is that it's likely that people who fill their lives with spiritual practice have less spiritual realization than one whose life does not contain a lot of "spiritual practice" because they have a stable and nourishing connection to Spirit without working on it all the time.

As a side note, the fact that some things are considered "spiritual" and some not, I believe, is an error in and of itself. I've always been a bit skeptical of how spirituality is framed in Domain 7 and 8. When one realizes the inherent Divinity in all matter and all beings, then it is apparent that just living ones life is as much of a spiritual act as doing particular "spiritual things." Yes, there are certain activities that really open people up, and it's a gift to know what those things are for oneself, and even more of a gift to have people to share that with, but this isn't an inherent measurement of how spiritual someone is.

To really be stable as an individual in the "higher planes" (Domain 10) requires a group consciousness (Domain 9). It requires community because consciousness is a social phenomenon as well as an individual one, and without the reflection and support of others, it's virtually impossible to maintain any "higher state." It also requires effective practice, based on an effective spiritual teaching. Again – Buddha, Dharma, Sangha, (the teacher, the teaching, and the community of practitioners). So, I believe that the next step for humanity is not to ascend to the higher planes, rather it's to integrate Domains 1 through 8 (which is Domain 9); and be present here on Earth living in Domain 9 cultures and families that integrate Spirit, self, community, and Earth in a sustainable and holistic manner. In other words, the next step is to practice GaiaYoga.

Again, in many ways it's a recapitulation of Domain 5, but with addition of consciousness and Consciousness (Domain 0). Domain 5 people didn't exactly have practices to be "more spiritual". Their spirituality, so to speak, was fully integrated into their daily life.

Currently, there isn't a Domain 9 culture on the planet that I know of, so what is obvious to me in my life is that my main spiritual practice *is* (co)creating a GaiaYoga Culture. I want to really emphasize this, mainly because a lot of people have seen my life practice and doubted my spirituality because I don't sit around and meditate and do yoga and chant the way most "spiritual" people do. For me, it's not prudent use of my time to dedicate to those kind of regular practices, as it would take away my precious time for incarnating GaiaYoga Culture, and doing all the work, research, maintenance (aka, karma yoga), and social work this endeavor requires.

The Domains have an outer expression in the world. While I think it's easier to understand the Domains in terms of their external characteristics (plant vs. animal, tribal family vs. nuclear family, etc.), the Domains are actually an internal experience. They are an inner landscape of energy, consciousness, and ways of relating to Spirit, self, community, and Earth. This means it's important for our understanding and for our spiritual practice to elucidate what the inner experiences are of the various Domains. GaiaYoga spirituality is a Tantric process of truly shifting consciousness into another Domain and having a completely different sense of what/who you are while you are there.

We are nourished internally by the energies of these different facets of consciousness. We can journey into a physical space that exemplifies one Domain or another, but it is how we internalize the Domains that really makes a difference to us. We can actually journey through all the Domains while sitting still and alone in meditation or unconsciously while asleep.

In this light, another way to frame spiritual realization is having the capacity to be fluid through all the Domains, both internally and externally. Having a spiritual practice or spiritual experience from the platform of Domain 9 is a journey through the Domains, whether individually, or in combination, or in total integration. Below is an articulation of the distinct inner and spiritual qualities of the different Domains.

A Journey through the Spiritual Qualities of the Domains:

Domain 0 is an experience of stillness, emptiness, pure attention, awareness, and unshakeable peacefulness. It's internally experiencing/realizing the Divine Masculine, that which is "outside" or "prior to" space, time, and manifestation.

Domain 1 is light/energy/forces. Being or experiencing Domain 1 is about being that pure energy of creation. It's about seeing the light, feeling energy, being in the light, and losing one's sense of humanness and individuality into pure energy. It's a highly energized, clean, radiant vibration. It's also about forces like magnetism, gravity, auras, and the like. It can also be an overwhelming experience of the pure Love of The Divine Feminine. There are many teachings/practices about being the light or being in the light or experiencing light beings. This is simply identifying with this Domain. As glorious as Domain 1 is, there can be a trap if someone attempts to identify with Domain 1 to the exclusion of other Domains. Eventually there's a "gravity" that will pull you out of it, and many spiritual seekers resist this pull. Consciousness wants to experience liberation in the other Domains as well, though obviously it's easier to do so "in the light."

Domain 2 is atoms/elements/molecules/minerals. So the spirituality of Domain 2 is about connecting to elements from gasses to heavy metals, the wind and air, the rocks, water, and other complex molecular combinations. In the same way each of us is pure light, each of us is pure atoms and pure molecules. We have a "mineral body" as much as we have a "light body," or an "emotional body," or an "astral body." Domain 2 can feel very different depending on the molecule/mineral one is identifying with and whether it is in gaseous, liquid, or solid form. Like with Domain 1, it is a letting go of sense of self and just vibrating at the frequency of molecular life. It's a very pure, stable, and mindless state. Domain 2 is also where DNA is rooted. There is a greater density in Domain 2 than 1, but it is no less spiritual.

Domain 3 is plant. Communing with plants is essential to our wholeness both physically and spiritually. Plants are a form of consciousness and an expression of Spirit. Plants are rooted, peaceful, intimately connected to Earth and Sun. They are the magical alchemists that can digest rock, water, air, and sunlight (Domains 1 and 2) and transform them into plant life (Domain 3). Internally, Domain 3 is the feeling of becoming one with a plant or a group of plants, communing with them, slowing and shrinking down to the consciousness of a plant. Plants move towards the sun with their leaves, stems, and branches, and towards the Earth with their roots. They are also mindless, but they are conscious, self-generating, and intentional. To be alive and awake in Domain 3 is to feel the life-force, the presence, and letting go of one's identity as a human being to experience being a plant.

Domain 4 is animal. Animals are also alchemists, in that they consume elements from Domains 1, 2, and 3 and generate animals and animal bodies out of those elements. Again, communion with animals, totem or spirit animals, and the power of our animal body is how we engage spiritually with Domain 4. One example of this is milking a cow as a form of meditation and experiencing the spirit of the relationship between cows and people. Other examples include bird watching, horseback riding, wrestling with a dog, communing with a cat, etc. Internally, Domain 4 is the experience of being an animal, either being simply one's animal self or communing with another animal - physical, breath, pumping blood, hunger, sexual, moving, sensory, instinctive. Be the dog, the wolf, the bee, the bird, and the fish, have their simpler mind and lose yours.

Domain 5 is aboriginal/nomadic. This is definitely the hardest Domain to access for a Domain 8 person. The main reason is that Domain 5 is more than individual consciousness; it is an intimate social consciousness (as experienced by the individual). In Domain 9 being able to commune with, and live from, Domain 5 is essential, since Domain 9 is also fundamentally an intimate social consciousness (as experienced by the individual). In this archetypal energy and consciousness there is only the present moment, all humans are of one family/people. There are no contracts between people, no ownership, sexual energy moves naturally (not in a naive or fantastic idea of what is natural, but in a holistically natural manner), senses are acute, and there's no awareness of Domains 6 through 8, just primal, human presence fluid with other humans and nature.

Internally, Domain 5 is a fully present, here-now, communal consciousness -- one that feels others, more than empathically, but as one group organism. It is a very grounded, gross, and Earthy kind of feeling, not a "higher" and subtle one. Examples of this include playing with a baby and getting into their consciousness, drumming in a circle and feeling the group energy, going on a group hunt, being one organism working together at a primitive level, having animalistic sex in nature, and being at a human birth in nature. It's about going into primal space together.

Domain 6 is tribal/territorial. To spiritually connect with Domain 6 is to get into the archetypal energy of tribal consciousness -- to feel the power, the intensity, and the Earthiness of tribal consciousness and tribal beingness. Internally, Domain 6 is a more cognitive state than Domain 5. It's a deep sense of connection with others and nature, but with the inclusion of more story, understanding and an identification with archetypal tribal roles (shaman, hunter, chief, warrior, healer, maiden, mother, crone, etc.).

Domain 7 is extended family/village. This is a very different consciousness than 5 and 6. Spiritually, it's about being connected to more people, but with a lower degree of intimacy. Linear time is present, as well as much more material and mental power. Internally, Domain 7 feels less whole and inter-connected than Domain 6. There's a much greater mental presence and more caution about who to be open with. For the most part, there's still a warm feeling towards others and a movement to cooperate with and trust one another. Village/extended-family consciousness is very sophisticated, thoughtful, aware of social taboos and norms, and has a fair amount of theoretical understanding of how life works. Compared to Domain 8, it is slower paced.

Domain 8 is nuclear family/cities. Spiritually it can be about connecting with fantasy, the vastness of the modern mind, with quantum physics, the art of Alex Grey, electronic music, etc. There are numerous events that have spiritual elements that have lots of Domain 8 consciousness and also the presence of other Domains woven in. For example, Burning Man°° or a Rainbow Gathering°° are Domain 8 crossed with Domain 6/5. A Grateful Dead show is Domain 8 crossed more so with Domain 7 and Domain 10. Internally, Domain 8 feels more fragmented, faster, digitized, and mental. There's a strong sense of the mind attempting to understand everything in terms of science or theories or mental structures. There's also a tension usually present, insecurity at a deep level, drive for experience and control over life. There's a lot of power in this consciousness. There's also a sense of disconnection from nature and Spirit, and often the sense of fending for one's self in relationship to others. There is more fear, more doubt, more (apparent) clarity in the mind, and more (experienced) confusion in the heart at the same time.

Domain 9 is experienced by individuals within sustainable-and-holistic community. Domain 9 feels very free, open, conscious, interconnected, expansive, clear, and turned on. There is a feeling of confidence with flowing through life and all of the other Domains. There's lots of love and empathy and the ability to identify with all peoples' feelings and positions. It's characterized by being psychically, emotionally, physically, and spiritually in tune, energized, and aware.

Domain 10 the transcendental/metaphysical. It is very "big!" The main experience of Domain 10 is being free of the physical body, free of the limits of Earth, less dense, more subtle. It includes expanded mind; seeing beneath, behind, between, over, and through what's normally opaque. It's the experience of being ecstatic, elevated, and liberated.

This completes the overview of how spirituality is practiced and understood by people in Domains 5 through 9 and in particular, how Domain 9 people can "move" through all the other Domains internally and spiritually. Obviously, there is a tremendous amount more to say about all of this. But for the purposes of this book, I just want to make some broad-stroke points to get the conversation going around spirituality, spiritual practice, and spiritual realization in relationship to the different Domains.

Sustenance within the Domains

The following is a dialogue I periodically engage in with interns at GYG or customers at my farmer's market booth where I sell coconuts. It's important to know that I free climb about 5 to 10 coconut trees a week, and have for over 20 years. Free climbing means I wear a pair of pants and a t-shirt, and scale trees up to 50 feet tall, barefoot, without the assistance of any other technology.

So the dialogue please...

Q: What's in a coconut?
Ano: I don't know, but it gets me back up the tree!

When most Domain 8 people consider sustenance or nourishment they think about vitamins, minerals, enzymes, protein, fats, calories, oxygen, etc. While this is a very popular and scientifically sound belief, I believe it misses the sublimity of what actually sustains our lives. I like to frame it this way: We are sustained primarily through intimate relationships. It is our intimate and indeed, sexual/sensual interactions and relationships with plants, animals, the atmosphere, the sun, other humans, and the Earth itself that actually keep us alive and enmeshed in the web of life. In many ways, GaiaYoga – unification with-and-as the living Earth - is about being sexual/sensual within all the Domains, particularly Domains 0 through 5. I believe it is by maintaining balanced relationships (particularly intimate ones) within all of the Domains that we generate health, integrity, and fullness of being.

Because they have lost connection with their instincts and their Domain 4 and 5 nature, people have looked to the mind to make sense of sustenance. In Domain 5, people only ate whole raw foods, there was no impetus to micro-analyze "what's in" a food. Bringing the mind to bear around sustenance is only "needed" because we're already confused and disconnected. Animals "know" where sustenance comes from; their instincts guide them to breathe, hunt, graze, forage, move towards the sun, drink or bathe, etc. They are sustained by both consuming whole foods, and also by engaging in the integrity of their natural, life-sustaining habitat. I argue that we are the same.

Let me demonstrate this by taking another journey through the Domains...

In many traditions, being realized, or having an intimate connection with Domain 0 is considered "enlightenment." When someone first "discovers" Domain 0 it is usually a profoundly nourishing experience, often satiating a person for days. It's a "food" that activates a part of our being that lies dormant in most people. This form of nourishment is very hard to quantify; still it is very real.

It is a fundamental fact that life on Earth would be impossible without the heat and light of the Sun, people are directly nourished by solar energy. Directly receiving solar energy feeds us emotionally, physically, and spiritually, primarily through our skin and eyes. Similarly communing with other forces and energies feed us, heal us, and enliven us. Intimately and perpetually connecting with Domain 1 is critical for our sustenance.

The primary nourishment of Domain 2 is breathing -- oxygen and other atoms and molecules enter our lungs and are exchanged with ones the body has already "used." I think of this of having oral/nasal sensual communion with the Earth. Ultimately, it's being sexual with the Earth, kissing it if you will. It is the most critical Earth-based relationship we have, in that we will cease to live if we go even a short time with out this intimate interaction. Beyond breathing we need intimacy with all sorts of other minerals. Hydration is our second most regularly required intimate interaction. After water, the degree of urgency decreases to intimate intake of salt, calcium, iron, and all sorts of other organic and inorganic minerals and elements. Entering into living bodies of water (rivers, ponds, lakes, oceans) is also extremely nourishing. This immersion makes the skin the active sexual organ, taking in all the wonderful living energy of Gaia's living water.

Obviously Domain 3 is a huge source of what most of us typically consider nourishment. Our intimate interactions with plants, both in the form of eating them, and communing with them while they're alive, are vital for our sustenance. Eating fruit is literally having sex with trees and plants. The fruit is their sex organ and we can experience great pleasure from the oral experience they provide. In some instances we kill the plant to eat the body of it; in other times we harvest the fruit, flowers, seeds, or leaves from and the plant continues to live. If we don't actually eat plants, (have sensual/sexual contact with them) we will not survive. Plants also provide much of the oxygen we breathe, so there's an interaction between them and Domain 2 that also sustains us. Other forms of nourishment that come from plants include smelling flowers and creating plant-spirit-medicines.

Domain 4 is a major source of sustenance for many people in the world in the form of meat, fish, poultry, eggs, dairy, bee products, insects, etc. Eating the body of an animal is also an intimate act, albeit, a sacrifice of the animal's life. There are thousands of carnivorous and omnivorous species in the world that hunt and eat other animal for their sustenance, so clearly it is part of the natural order for animals to eat other animals. While vegans and vegetarians choose not to eat meat and/or animal products for various reasons, they still need intimate interaction with Domain 4 to thrive, whether it's in the form of connecting with pets, wild animals, or benefitting from the soil web and the above ground web of interaction between plants, animals and the Earth that makes human life possible. For people who eat meat, it is obviously a very significant source of nourishment and one that people will go to great length to acquire. Another part of the nourishment that comes from Domain 4 is from sex and sensual touch that connects us with our primal, pre-human, animal nature. An infant nursing from their mother is included in this.

Our total human-to-human sexual sustenance also includes nourishment that comes from the human cultural Domains. Sustenance from other humans (Domains 5 - 9) comes in a qualitatively different form than the non-human Domains. The primary difference is that it mostly does not include the physical intake of matter into the body, except sharing "fluids" during sexual activity. While these fluids aren't a significant food source, they are actually perhaps the most powerful "thing" we can take into our bodies. Why? Because sharing these fluids is part of what creates deep emotional, physical, psychic, and spiritual bonds with those we share intimately with.

One way we feed through Domain 5 is via sex and touch from other people. Where in Domain 4 sexual/sensual nourishment is "animalistic," the Domain 5 aspects connect through primal emotions, pre-civilized human archetypes, and our primitive psyche. Besides overt sexuality, Domain 5 nourishment comes through primal emotional, familial and social bonds, and activities enjoyed within those bonded relationships. The deep communion a mother feels with her baby and that her baby feels from her is very much a Domain 5 form of nourishment. The father and other relations can also share in this nourishment with a baby.

The nourishment that comes through Domain 6 is anchored more in the personal sphere than in the intimate sphere. The nourishment of connecting with tribe-mates, communards, extended family, and close friends is very important for not only the emotional well being of a person, but also, at a practical level, their survival. The cooperation between people in our personal sphere, and even more so in an actual tribe or intentional community, is a very significant source of sustenance. There's a palpable energy amongst people who share this level of bonding even without anyone "doing" anything to or for someone else.

In the local sphere or a Domain 7 village we also get fed by important relationships both emotionally/socially and at a practical level. A whole village is often a survival unit, and each individual within is fed and sustained by its integrated cooperation. We are nourished by our locality via goods and services, via neighborly relationships, and providing those to others.

The most obvious nourishment that comes through Domain 8 is through the long distance cooperation of strangers who make goods and services available to each other. There is also a nourishment that comes from being part of a collective organization such as a nation, political group, religious or spiritual movement, fan base of a sports team or rock band, etc. It is energetically nourishing to participate in the collective, it helps to sustain an individual.

The nourishment that is gained by participating in Domain 9 is sublime, dynamic, and profoundly sustaining. My desire for this nourishment is a large part of what motivates me to write this book, to endure the process of community building, and to take huge risks in my intimate sphere to expand it and share deeply with multiple adults. Sometimes when I have a strong Domain 9 experience I barely need to sleep, I eat less, I have more patience and compassion with others, and I feel lighter in my body. I am powerfully sustained by participating in Domain 9, by ingesting that energy, and by connecting in that consciousness. To have Domain 9 as a one's stable home reality would be extremely powerful and sustaining.

Those fabled yogis who live in caves in the Himalayas are a testimony to the nourishment available through Domain 10. When a person connects with other "higher" planes, subtle energy activities and austerities that would otherwise be impossible become possible because of the quality of nourishment we can receive connecting to Domain 10. Some claim we can just live on Prana (which is a combination of Domain 1, 2, and 10). Others simply strengthen and nourish themselves through spiritual practice like Qi Gong, Tai Chi, EDGU, yoga, meditation, and the like. It's difficult to scientifically quantify this form of sustenance; and indeed many of the kinds of sustenance that come through social interaction are also difficult to quantify, but they are nonetheless very real and do truly sustain us.

As I said in the beginning of this section, I recognize the value in looking at nourishment in terms of calories, minerals, proteins, vitamins, etc. Nonetheless, I trust that you can see that it actually is more elegant, honoring, and ultimately, empowering to look at what nourishes and sustains us in terms of the living energy that is transmitted through relationship with whole beings -- primarily intimate sensual/sexual interaction with the Earth itself, the different species we consume or exchange with, and the particular people that we relate to and cooperate with. We are part of the web of life, and it is because of our participation in that living, dynamic, whole web that we find ourselves waking up every morning to enjoy life again.

The GaiaYoga Approach to Diet and Health

Since we've just taken an overall look at sustenance, lets zoom in and take a closer look directly at diet and how it interacts with our body's health and also the health of the world.

For a diet to fully serve a human being it must have integrity with Domain 4, our animal body, and Domain 5, our aboriginal nature. It also needs to be able to fuel a Domain 9 consciousness and lifestyle. Every wild animal eats an all-raw diet, without exception, so I think it's reasonable to assume that our animal organism wants to be fueled in the same way. For though our mind and consciousness have transcended Domain 4, <u>our bodies have not</u>. We're made of the same basic biology; human bodies function in the same fundamental manner as all other mammals.

In the mid-1990s I wrote and published the book, *Instinctive Eating: The Lost Knowledge Of Optimum Nutrition*, by Zephyr (my chosen name at the time). This book is primarily a re-expression of the discovery of Guy-Claude Burger, who discovered this natural way of eating in Europe decades earlier, and developed a community and retreat center in France, where this is practiced. The heart of this practice is using the senses, especially smell and taste, to guide us to what food will nourish our bodies and when to stop eating it. Sensual animal instincts (ours included) can only effectively function when foods are in their natural state, whole and raw. I would argue that we cannot consume foods without generating some kind of toxicity unless they are in their natural state. For much more about Instinctive Eating, you can read my book.

Now, I'm not claiming that if people don't eat only raw food by instinct that they will be unable to participate in Domain 9 and be short-lived and sick. What I'm saying is that if we want maximum health, power, and connection to nature, then we'll be most able to have it if we surrender to our species' natural limits and eat the way in which our animal body is genetically designed.

Our health is essentially a product of how well we (and our recent ancestors) eat, drink, breathe, express emotions, eliminate toxins through pooping, peeing, sweating, and the like, and how much we exercise. Our health is also impacted by the quality of our relationships, how much love we give and receive, and how much support we experience at both the survival level and at the level of fulfilling our dreams. Our health deteriorates when we don't take care of it. People don't just "get sick" out of the blue. For the most part, people slowly get sick from their lifestyle choices. I like to say that most people die by slow death from lifestyle. A perfect demonstration of what I'm saying is shown in the experiments run by Dr. Francis Pottenger Jr. (1901-1967) with multiple generations of cats being fed raw and cooked diets. This study is known as Pottenger's Cats.

I have an unorthodox way of understanding diseases and microbes. I don't see them as enemies that attack us randomly from the outside. Symptoms appear for good reasons, and from the instinctive eating perspective, symptoms are mostly attempts to heal and detoxify the body. These "diseases" are the agents of healing, moving the body towards deeper health, not some malevolent force out to "get us." Metaphorically, they help us clean out our closet, lift up the rug that we've been sweeping stuff under for decades, and do micro-surgery to remove toxicity.

The best way I know of to visualize this view of disease is with this analogy: Imagine you have a 50 lb. bag of grass seed and you spread them on four different ecologies: 1) a climax forest, 2) a suburban yard, 3) some freshly ploughed land, and 4) an asphalt parking lot. What will happen?

In the climax forest the grass seed will either sprout and then fail to take hold because of lack of sun, or more likely just rot and compost because there is no sun hitting the ground which would give the message to the grass to germinate. If they're hardy seeds, they might sit dormant for years waiting for a tree to fall down and let light in. In the suburban lot there would be places where the grass would grow and thrive, and places where it wouldn't. In the freshly ploughed area the grass would take off and take over. On the parking lot the grass seed might germinate, but it would quickly die for lack of soil.

In this analogy the climax forest is a truly healthy person with a dynamic immune system. The suburban lot is your average Dimension 8 person who's functional, but not truly healthy. The ploughed land is someone who is very ill, with a weak immune system. And the parking lot is a dead person. Dead people don't get sick or catch germs!

So the question is this… Are grass seeds contagious? Well, the answer is yes and no. They're contagious in that they blow in the wind and land all over the place, but they only have an effect if they land somewhere that has the conditions for them to thrive. So, in that way, they are not contagious. So, the confusion amongst people around disease is that most people in a particular culture and a locality all are taking care of themselves similarly, so when the wind blows and drops seeds or flu season comes around, they all "catch" grass or the flu. It appears that these things affect everyone equally, but in fact they don't.

So when people have a diet and overall health care practice that doesn't honor Domain 4 and 5, they are not able to have full health and have the resiliency of a climax forest. I lived fully and unconsciously entrenched in Domain 8 for my first 21 years, and have been doing my best to live in Domain 9 for about that long as well. I began eating 100% raw, organic food in 1990, which was my gateway into the life I have now. So I am a first generation person living this way and taking care of my health this way. While I have amazing health and a very powerful immune system, I still have issues from my early life (missing tonsils and adenoids, a persistent foot/skin fungus, weakened sinuses and nearsightedness). So, sometimes when the "winds blow," grass grows in/on me, but mostly it doesn't, and it doesn't impact me as much as it does most folks around me. It is very, very clear to me that my practice and diet is working and making me as healthy and whole and integrated with Gaia as possible, and I'm most grateful for this.

The main point I want to make is that most people eat a diet that was developed in Domain 6, 7, or 8. This includes all the ethnic diets of the world, all the vegetarian diets, and of course all the fast food, modern cuisine, and opportunistic omnivore diets, and even most of the "indigenous" diets. While these dietary practices are undoubtedly delicious and popular, some with millions upon millions of people, they all have some degree of (mostly unseen or ignored) negative impact on the integrity of our being, our health, and our consciousness.

While our personalities, clothes, and buildings might be of one ethnicity or another or of one country or another, our bodies and biology exist beneath and before all of that, so we are going to be most harmonious if we eat for our body and biology. To do this requires an apparent sacrifice of all sorts of flavor experiences, but as with everything, when one door closes, another opens, and I believe the door that opens when we eat in a way that's in harmony with our biology, is well worth missing out on some foods and flavors created by humans.

And why is the impact mostly unseen? There are two main reasons. One is that nearly everyone in the world is eating a cooked food diet, so like the fish that doesn't see the water it's swimming in, people don't see this or realize an impact is occurring. The other reason is that the impact doesn't happen all at once, like a punch in the face; it happens bit-by-bit, meal-by-meal, generation-by-generation. Until I made a clear break (back in 1990) and started eating 100% raw food by instinct, I had no clue what I had been doing to myself with food. Only with the perspective that came from stepping out of what literally everyone was doing could I start to see this humongous iceberg clearly. And as I got sober and began seeing what the real impact was, I became very passionate about staying outside of what is, unequivocally, the oldest and most popular human experiment of all – cooking food.

Besides impacting human health, cooked foods also have huge impacts on the health of the Earth. Just on the small scale, I suggest you look through your trashcan and see how much of the trash you create is directly or indirectly from cooked, processed, and/or packaged foods. I imagine it will be very sobering to see just your personal impact, let alone multiplying it by billions. On the other hand, a raw, instinctive diet generates essentially zero trash, except some cardboard boxes or plastic bags if you are purchasing food – as all the wrappers are biodegradable! Cooking itself is also a huge environmental impact, with the use of propane, natural gas, and other non-renewable resources to fire up or electrify stoves and ovens all over the planet. Even Domain 6 and 7 people have completely deforested their homelands and surrounding territories, cutting trees down to get firewood for cooking. So using wood is not a solution to lessen the impact of daily cooking.

Beyond cooking, the long-distance transportation and mass production of commercial food is also a huge environmental impact. Many Domain 8 people import water, beverages, and food from thousands of miles away. This means the food is less fresh, that it is delivered by petroleum-powered vehicles, often frozen or refrigerated (which requires more energy), and it also means everyone depending on this food is very disconnected from what actually sustains their life. It's really a quite vulnerable situation. When ones eats local, limiting the distance their food travels to under 100 miles, the freshness of the food increases, the energy needed to get it to you is dramatically reduced, and we are more connected to its source. To make my point more graphic, if the trucks with food and drink stopped coming into NYC, London, Tokyo, etc., everyone would be brought down to their knees, even the 1%ers. The whole party would stop.

Ultimately my motivation to eat a raw, local, organic diet is holistic. Doing so supports personal health, communion with nature, lightening my carbon foot print, reducing trash, enjoying deep pleasure (that's completely merged with nutrition), reducing the pollution and monotonous labor involved in the packaging and transportation of food, and creating more security and interdependence°° at a survival level by meeting my essential needs locally.

All other animals get their food raw, directly from their surrounding environment; and while doing something different has provided humans a very different experience than other species, I'm suggesting the overall result has too many hidden costs to warrant continuing with the experiment. Sure, it's been a big part of us getting to Domain 8 and made us what we are to (arguably evolved or mutated!) But I don't think it's helpful any more and the repercussions far out weigh the benefits at this point. Again, I am confident that we need to look to Domain 4 and 5 to find our natural and optimal diet, and that diet is inarguably a raw, organic, and local one.

Stuck In The Middle
(For Melekai)

Doc wants it out right now
Nurse wants to go home soon
Babe wants it safe and slow
Mom wants it sweet and smooth

Dad wants to run away
But he makes himself stay
All a midwife can say
Is I know a better way

Medical override
On a primal dance
Cultural imperatives
Put us in a twisted trance

Mothers' power was seized
Long long ago
I want her to have it
But where did it go

There's only a few hours
Before she waves into birth
Can't suddenly supply a tribe
To support this life's entry to Earth

> *I'm stuck in the middle*
> *'Tween nature and medical*
> *The Law says I'm liable if I "meddle"*
> *While doc decides he should earn*
> *One more costly cesarean medal*

> *Too much cold metal*
> *To welcome this life*
> *Need more Moon for the womb*
> *But they've eclipsed the midwife*

The feminine's final frontier
Been claimed and tamed by The Man
Women need more than tears
To restore our original plan

Birth is woman and her power
Birth is baby, a crowning flower
Birth is wild, how souls arrive
Birth is mystery, most alive

It's not about static power
It's about flowing life
De-throne the doctor
For a mature midwife

Who can step back, and let it be
Hold space, with empathy
Give care, where there's need
Be strong if she bleeds

> *I'm stuck in the middle*
> *'Tween nurture and mechanical*
> *M.D.'s say I'm merely menstrual*
> *They want me managed and manacled –*
> *Did birth trauma make them tyrannical?*

> *They're not the true authority*
> *Yet they wield the seniority*
> *This is our realm, our sovereignty*
> *Midwives revive births' dignity*

Birth is not a disease
We don't want your knife
Birth is the sacred conceived
For family, husband, and wife

> *So get the right woman for the job*
> *A mystic, mindful midwife*
> *Yes get the right hands for this soul*
> *A mystic, mindful midwife*

The GaiaYoga Perspective on Birth

Why is birth such a challenging experience for most women (and men)?

Birth is fundamentally a Domain 4/5 experience. If you've lived your whole life in Domain 8, with a smattering of experiences of connecting into the lower Domains or Domain 10, then you're probably very unprepared for the primal reality of birthing, which is the most intense experience an animal or human can have (the runner ups are sex, extreme sports, hunting or being hunted, and other threats to our bodies, like car accidents, tornados, rape, muggings, etc.) Birthing takes a "civilized" woman deep into her animal core, despite being so unfamiliar with it. It is no wonder women want drugs and choose cesareans. It is no wonder so many men are scared of the whole thing. Even though there's been trillions of natural human births over the course of humanity, for most people today it's outside of the limited "reality" they've lived in for their entire lives.

(On an intimate note: Even Melekai, the mother of my children, who's a certified nurse midwife, been to 100's of births, and is passionate about natural home birth, was so overwhelmed by the pain and rigors of her own first childbirth that after a day of labor at home with me, her midwife, and doula, she had us drive to the hospital to get "help!" It was way too late in the process for any help, except for the nurse and doctor to say, "You just got to push that baby out! We can't do anything for you now." With her last "escape route" closed off, Melekai went into the most intense physical "pain" of her life and pushed our son out within 20 minutes of being at the hospital. Even with all her training and experience she was unprepared for this radical Domain 4/5 experience.)

In order for birth (and then infant care and child care) to be an experience that can be done naturally and masterfully, women, men, and families need to open up to their animal and aboriginal selves. This needs to be done prior to birth and infant care, during less demanding times, so that when labor and childbirth occur it's not such a huge stretch into such unfamiliar territory at such an intense time. Ways to prepare for this include using plant-spirit-medicines, doing primal emotional therapy, vision quests in nature, group sex, hunting, coconut tree climbing, and in the other direction, connecting with the orgasmic and sublime energy of birthing.

When children are birthed to parents and cultures that don't identify with Domains 4 and 5, the newborns are not received and handled the way they truly need to be as primal social animals. These well meaning parents end up creating immense amounts of trauma and social and emotional wounding for their infants, babies, and children. But since they don't really understand their primal animal and social nature they can't parent that energy in their children. (Read *The Continuum Concept* for more about this.) Indeed, one of the biggest areas of growth and healing in creating Domain 9 culture is around birthing and parenting. If we have the consciousness and support we can birth and raise children who are rooted in this culture from the beginning, and can move forward with out so much healing work to do as adults.

The primary goal of parents and communities is to raise children in such a way that they are conscious and activated in all the Domains and able to have both acceptance and discrimination around all the aspects of life. Essentially, we have the same goal for adult "transplants." Many of these same skills are needed to "re-birth" Domain 8 adults into GaiaYoga Culture as the original birth. This is obviously a huge discussion, how to give birth and raise children in a GaiaYoga Culture. I just wanted to draw our attention here and plant some seeds.

Mono-Mom Imprint

Mono-mom imprint -- Don't know what to do with it
Single-source imprint -- We're all swimmin' in it
   So no one even sees it
   I guess I gotta live with it
   Got a lot to learn from it
   Maybe I can make peace with it

Mono-mom imprint
   Your absence has triggered it
   Like an infant in a closet
   The source has vanished
   Insecure and desperate

Mono-mom imprint
   A cause of co-dependence
   My mom had my only breasts
   So I've feared abandonment
   And that rejection meant death

Single-source imprint
   Can I ever get through it?
   It almost seems infinite

Oh, Acceptance   The feelings are there
Oh, Acceptance   From choosing to be unaware
Oh, Acceptance   That mother is everywhere
                  The source is everywhere
Oh, Acceptance   We're all learning to share
                  We're all learning to share
Oh, Acceptance   It's in me, not out there

Mono-mom imprint
   I'm no longer an infant
   Who'd die by abandonment
   I'm an adult creating kinship
   And vulnerability to re-imprint

Mono-mom imprint
   Make the monogamous myth
   Of prince-and-princess
   "Soulmates" who seem heaven sent
   To live in single-source limits

Single-source imprint
   Well, I'm not a victim of it
   I'm a source of this rift
   Yeah, I'm through blaming it
   I'm in a paradigm shift

Oh, Acceptance   The feelings are there
Oh, Acceptance   Resentment, rage, despair
Oh, Acceptance   To bond with you — I'm scared
                  When scared, be scared
Oh, Acceptance   That it's safe to fully care
                  We're all learning to share
Oh, Acceptance   It's in me, not out there

Mono-mom imprint -- We can live beyond it
Single-source imprint – But first we gotta see it
   Then feel, heal, and deal with it
   Or be doomed to make do with it
   And I really mean it
   So, I'm choosing to accept it

Explaining the Single-Source Imprint

Earlier I mentioned the single-source imprint. I didn't want to go into depth at that time, but now I want to elucidate on this as a concept and a phenomenon, and allow its effect to become clear and recognizable. First, let me define the word "source" in this concept. To think of what source is, visualize a newborn infant who is utterly dependent on its caregivers for food, cleanliness, protection, support for sleeping, elimination, and releasing emotions, warmth, closeness, and emotional and psychic connection. Obviously, when a baby is in the womb there is only one source of intimacy and nourishment -- the mother -- though she could be connected to many sources herself, depending on her cultural situation. When an infant emerges, its genetics and biology are "expecting" a Domain 5/6 culture that is integrated in nature (Domains 1 - 4) to be there to greet it and integrate it into the world (again see *The Continuum Concept*). An infant emerges needing a source, another person who provides primary-level care, bonding, emotional connection, security, and sense of home.

An infant is expecting to be born into a unified people, because it is the nature of humans to live as a unified people. In a Domain 5/6 culture there will be many "sources" to the infant; people to hold the infant, perhaps other women to nurse it besides the mother, children and men that know how to be with a baby and read its signals and respond caringly to its cues. This creates continuity and diversity of both experience and human connection. An infant experiences an integrated-multiple-source imprint as a child, which means that the infant learns at a core level that there are many people he/she can go to and be fully and compassionately met, cared for, and related to.

Adult intimate-sexual relationships are essentially the same quality and depth of bonding as the baby-parent relationship. In fact, many of the same functions and activities occur between lovers as between baby and parent: e.g. a person to share intimacy and closeness with, to sleep with, to release deep emotions with, to share bodily fluids with, and to freely receive support at the level of survival and home life. Lovers are just another point on the sexual cycle that flows between pregnancy, birth, and child-raising. It's not random that dysfunctional adults project their mother and father issues on their intimate-partners, husbands, and wives. This happens because they're sharing the same fundamental energy -- they are in the intimate sphere together.

If a child's intimate training is one of multiple sources, one of continuity, integration, and actually mostly getting one's needs met, then that is the training and consciousness that a grown child enters into the adult intimate/sexual dance with. They enter with fullness, looking to a diversity of people to connect with to get their intimate relationship needs met. The emotional/relational physics of this appear promising. By not having a huge backlog of unmet needs from childhood, an adult is able to flow among many strategies of getting needs met, through different people in different ways. Obviously, given equal circumstances, this person will have an easier experience as an adult because they're already more fulfilled and nourished, and they're not so fixated on one strategy, one person -- a single-source.

Now visualize a typical Domain 8 infant experience with a mother and father. Again, in the womb there is one source, the mother. This is natural and necessary. What isn't natural and necessary is the belief within the mother, and transmitted from her to her child, that there is not enough, there is lack in a fundamental way. She was raised with a single-source imprint herself, so it's easy to believe this and experience this lack. Currently, she probably only has one source for herself (the father of the child), and he's probably not always around. This stress and insecurity is transmitted to the child before and after birth. Even in the best of circumstances, where there is enough money, a comfortable home, and some connection to extended family, there is always the possibility that something will happen to "her man" and there will be no one to take care of her and her child. This leads to her clinging to that one man as the one strategy to meet her needs for protection, support, intimacy, and emotional and psychic connection. While this may sound beautiful in a romantic fantasy or a country song, it's really not a very secure situation in reality.

When this baby is born (probably in a hospital, but maybe at home), there might be extended family present for a little while, or maybe not. But soon there is only the mother (and hopefully the father and maybe some older siblings) to be the day-to-day care system for the infant. There isn't a bonded tribe of people to connect with and offer support. There isn't an extended family of people to relieve the mother so she can rejuvenate and maintain her sanity and self-care and not be in constant mother-mode. There aren't other nursing mothers for the baby to receive that deep nourishment and intimate connection from. There aren't other men to hold the baby, or to take the baby out and participate in activities together. Furthermore, there probably isn't a natural human habitat to connect with.

The baby doesn't experience that whoever has her is really happy to be with her, because when a lone mother is always being a source to a baby, there are times when she is burned out and resentful and wants space from the baby. However, she has no support system, so the baby is stuck with her (or left alone crying in a crib or another room) and the baby can erroneously come to believe that its needs are either a burden, because they're met with resentment and exhaustion, or that their needs are unimportant because the baby/child is neglected. In a Domain 5/6 culture, and even many Domain 7 cultures, there is almost always another member of the family to hand the baby to, so that no one adult is "stuck" with the baby when it would rather not be, and the baby can always experience that the adult he is with is truly joyful about being with him.

At the level of nursing, which is a very intimate and sensual dance, if there is only one mother, then sometimes that mother will not be available and the baby will suffer. Or the baby will be put on formula, which is a horrific Domain 8 pseudo-replacement for real food and human breast milk (there's loads of research on this if you need convincing). Furthermore, it's more than just nursing; the mother is usually the person the baby is brought to for soothing and empathy when the baby is crying. Not only do babies get trained to only nurse (which in adult relationships transforms into sexuality) with one other person, they become conditioned to believe that deep soothing and empathy only comes from one other person (or that one person is the best at it, and is dependable, and others might not be as good and aren't dependable). They don't just learn that there is only one physical intimate, they also learn there is only one emotional intimate as well.

So, not only is there a single source of food, intimate bonding, and co-sleeping, there is also a single source for empathy, soothing, and being held dependably. Now, in the best of situations in a nuclear family, the father is providing a lot of this (though of course not nursing) and this makes a difference, but it is a long way from the circle of highly-trained, exquisitely present, bonded, and integrated support that can come in Domain 5, 6, or 9.

Now this Domain 8 baby, who didn't get many of his core needs met, and moreover was trained to look for love/intimacy/emotional support all from one person, branches out into the world of adult relationships. The problem is that one other person can't meet all of another persons' needs in that way (certainly not over the long haul), so there is a fundamental "design error" at the core of how people pursue getting their intimate/sexual/emotional/family needs met. It's no wonder there are so many co-dependent relationships, dysfunctional families, divorces, and single-mothers, so much drug addiction, crime, violence, loneliness, pornography, prostitution, online gaming, and soap operas in the world.

There are a few other cultural patterns that add to this difficulty. In most Domain 8 cultures, public nursing is taboo. So, the very act that gives a baby life literally becomes shrouded in shame and embarrassment, tension, and stress when done outside of the home. This also communicates to the baby that there is something "wrong" with them for breastfeeding.

Ever notice in any documentary about any Domain 6 culture that the women are almost always bare-breasted? Ever notice that nudity is no big deal for the tribes' people? One of the main reasons for women being bare-breasted is ease in breastfeeding. There is no shame, taboo, or fixated sexual energy around breasts like you see in most Domain 7 and 8 cultures. This covering of breasts has big repercussions on adult sexuality and shame about our bodies and our sexuality. It also makes a lot of curiosity, secrecy, and confusion around breasts that has led to the demand for pornography and fantasy-based sexuality.

Instead of breasts being simply part of a woman's natural beauty, to be seen like a face, leg or, hand, and accessed as an open-free source for babies, breasts gets hidden and all sorts of extreme fascination, longing, and mystery gets attached to an otherwise simple part of the human body. A similar thing happens with penises, but they aren't part of a baby's daily life source, so the cultural impact is less.

I digress. Back to the main point about single-source vs. multiple-source nurturing of babies and how that impacts adult intimacy. I want to be clear that I'm not suggesting that having deep intimacy with one person (as a baby or an adult) is bad or wrong. Obviously, a single-source is better than no-source! However, when people aren't free to feed themselves how they want through their relationships it becomes an issue. While we might only have one source in our lives (even if we're open to having multiple sources), there's a huge energetic difference between wanting multiple sources and not having them, and having a contract to only have one source.

This becomes a profound difficulty when raising children. Being the father of two children who were born in 2011 and 2012, I can tell you that having only the skeleton of a community to raise them with makes things harder for them and for us. We would love to have more sources for them (and for us). In fact, that is one of the motivations for me in writing this – we want to give our children a thriving Domain 9 community to grow up in.

More Than One-And-Only

Was gonna write a love song 'bout my lover
Tell you how there's no other
Look like a man singin' to his lover
But sound like an infant whinin' for its mother

The radio plays 'em by the thousands:
"I need you baby" — "Be my man"
"You're the light" — "Air is you woman"
Don't cut the cord, I need you so bad

> See, I'm so lonely without my one-and-only
> It's what I imprinted as a baby
> It's time to mature and I don't mean maybe
> This single-sourcin' itches worse than scabies

Yoko, Priscilla, or Jackie O'
They could never ever let them go
Still, their men always wanted more
A mistress or more to spice up the show

I might feel wild
Having many lovers
But they feel war
When they don't love each other

That's what got me thinkin'
'Bout another way
All of us in one bed
Learnin' how to play

> I want more than just a one-and-only
> Want a clan, pod, community
> It's time to merge and I don't mean maybe
> More prime sources make more better babies

If we can love more than just one
We can have a lot more fun
But if we control with our jealousy
Competition ends expanded ecstasy

All these feelings
Are just tones to surf through
Be as the free kids
Untamed by taboos

Like wild wolf cubs
Rage, aggress, and fight
Laugh into a dog pile
Sleep as one all night

> But I'm controlled by my one-and-only
> (S)he says (s)he's my only baby
> (S)he won't share, and (s)he don't mean maybe
> Single-sourcin's more insane than rabies

See, I don't wanna dis you
Wanna life with you for life
And not get tamed in contracts:
I, your husband — You, my wife

And I want continuity
With people and the Earth
Not just "free love"
Like a 60's rebirth

You dig me and I dig you
And we sure each dig others too
Let's all live in one home, not in a few
Six in surrender is more than two

> Don't say you want just a one-and-only
> Say, "let's have the whole mandala, baby"
> It's not a harem, it's our home and haven
> We need "yeses," not "it could be, maybes"

See, infants need more than one-and-only
Birthright is tribal family
It's time to merge and I don't mean maybe
Six moms and dads can make a healthy baby

Come on babies, let's make healthy babies

Polyamory from a GaiaYoga Perspective

Polyamory is a way of expressing our sexuality in the world. It literally means 'loving many' but in today's world it is almost always done without a stable and ongoing Domain 9 container for it. I'm using the word "polyamory" as a catchall for several different forms of multiple-adult-intimacy (polygamy, polyfidelity°°, pan-sexuality, polyandry°°, etc.) Mostly it's practiced within a short term Domain 9 or 6 container (like a workshop, retreat, festival, or Network For New Cultures Camp), or as a way to spice up a Domain 8 lifestyle. There is nothing right or wrong with polyamory, I just want people to see the potential issues that can arise.

In Domain 5 or 6 cultures that integrate multiple-adult-intimacy in one form or other there is a container for it. The container IS the tribe, clan, or kinship group, their customs, their bondedness as a people, their long history with handling this energy together, and the fact that children of these cultures are raised with these practices going on from birth, and are well equipped to navigate this emotional/sexual/social territory when they become adults.

When adults raised in Domain 8 explore polyamory, outside of an effective container, they end up opening up a Pandora's Box that can lead to lots of undesirable and unexpected impacts. The sad part is people often go back, scarred and scared, to practicing monogamy or serial monogamy to avoid the painful side effects of stepping outside of the social contracts. (This has led to the funny and sobering phrase, "poly-agony.") While, having a container is no guarantee to avoid hardship, it certainly makes it much more likely that everyone can find their way through to a place of trust, happiness, and having their needs met. The container is the horse and polyamory is the cart.

One of my hopes in creating and living in GaiaYoga Culture is to have a container in which to enjoy the experience of integrated multiple-intimate-relationships in a way that is sane, healthy, sustainable, and harmonizes with child raising, the daily life rhythm of land stewardship, and doing our services in the world. We've coined a new term to distinguish this form of relationship: clan-based group-intimacy, or CBGI°°° There are many reasons I'm attracted to this, but the primary reason is that it creates a huge amount of power and aliveness in everyone involved as their life foundation. Contracts between people dissolve and a greater experience of self and relatedness is possible. It is certainly in alignment with Domain 9 culture and consciousness – separating security and sexuality – so folks can relate to each other from an authentic and empowered place.

To protect an intimate container, but also support its expansion I find the model of dating, going steady, engagement, and then marriage very useful. These represent four different levels of commitment and depth of connection within the intimate sphere. Dating is non-committed exploration of a connection. Going steady is a mutually dedicated exploration of a connection. Being engaged is a mutually dedicated exploration of whether or not to create a long-term committed connection. And marriage is mutually committing to a long-term connection.

I see that it's critical to learn to honor these differing levels, especially within CBGI or forms of multiple-adult-intimacy. If there's a couple (or other form of stable intimate sphere) and one of them is dating someone else, it's important to not suddenly treat the one being dated as part of the marriage (or committed member of the intimate sphere). It's also important to not discount someone being dated just because they're not part of the marriage. The "going steady" and "engaged" states are probably the trickiest to navigate when some of the people in the intimate sphere are already "married" (not necessary legally, but in heart, life, and Spirit). There's a real dynamic process of bringing people deeper into an expanded intimate sphere, and it is delicate and usually highly-triggering for those already involved (much like an older sibling receiving a new baby into the nuclear family home). Babies arrive into a family already fully committed to it for life (in most cases), whereas in a dating one may not decide to fully commit, so there's a lot more risk involved.

Melekai and I have been and are engaged in this process in a handful of relationships, and it is a challenging dance to master. We both agree that it creates more of what we want in the world and our home. This isn't where I will to go into all the dynamics involved in creating and practicing CBGI, as this isn't a how-to book about CBGI. (We're still doing the R&D on that one!) Though I will make discuss how CBGI supports creating and sustaining Domain 9 culture and look at the primary dynamics that arise and potentially undermine any form of multiple-adult intimacy.

Competition, Jealousy, Insecurity, and the Single-Source Imprint

If my argument is accurate I would suggest that opening to more sources of intimacy, primal bonding and sexuality would be relatively easy, as it is more aligned with our Domain 5 social nature, Domain 4 sexual desires and our Domain 10 spiritual potential. Some people find it fairly easy to directly share intimately and sexually with multiple adults (a.k.a. polyamory). They are able to enjoy the added attention, sex and closeness. Hopefully receiving that is the easy part! However, due to our conditioning some people struggle to actually enjoy the intimacy and sexuality they crave, and it almost goes without saying that most are profoundly triggered at the prospect of their intimate partner sharing intimately/sexually with others.

Changing our habits, even "change for the better," is often challenging for many reasons... There is the momentum of habits, both individual and cultural, the ease of the familiar, fear of the unknown, loyalty to our family systems, the learning curve in doing anything new, etc. Besides the obstacle of fear of change relative to poly-intimacy, issues arise in the other people involved, the one(s) that are also intimate with that person and are sharing them with the new/other lover(s). This is why one of the sadhanas (spiritual practice) in the Shivalila community was literally to make a bed for your lover and one of their other lovers to have sex (without you). One's ability to do this with compersion (see definition below), or not, is an effective way to get clarity about how much the energies of competition, jealousy and insecurity are affecting you.

First, let me define these terms and their opposites, particularly in regards to intimacy/sexuality:

Competition is both a psychic/emotional disposition and represents actions that are based on beliefs like "I'm alone;" "I have to fend for myself;" "I can't trust anyone;" and "there are limited resources and if I'm going to survive and enjoy the good life, I need to beat other humans to those resources." When we're *in competition*, we believe we will have more of our needs met for ourselves than if we work together and share with others. It's a very lonely place, and based on a fundamental lack of trust that other human beings care about our deep needs and want to help us meet them. Being born and raised in a culture that doesn't identify with or understand our core humanity can make it easy to hold these beliefs to be true. Relative to intimacy/sexuality, being in a state of competition there is no room for others' needs (except the object of my competition, "my beloved,") and any other presence in the intimate sphere is a threat to needs being met.

Cooperation is also a psychic/emotional disposition and represents actions that stem from beliefs. Cooperation is based on the belief that I'm interconnected to the world, people care about me, there's enough for everyone, and more needs are met by working things out with others rather than being self-focused. Relative to intimacy/sexuality, in a state of cooperation there is room for others (metaphorically and literally!) and their needs within an intimate sphere. There's room to come up with creative and mutually joyful strategies to meet everyone's needs in a given situation.

Jealousy is an emotion that can emerge when certain needs aren't met, e.g. inclusion, connection, to matter, to be seen, reassurance and intimacy. Jealousy usually follows a belief that I can't have access to "my source" because they are connecting with someone else. I want (intimate/sexual) access to that person and I believe I can't have it. I believe I am powerless to change the situation to a situation that meets my needs. Usually, a shadow belief that "I don't matter" and "I don't belong" is underneath jealousy as well. Jealousy is just another feeling to experience, emerging out of a beautiful need, but where it can "get ugly" is when it becomes what I call *a mood*. When it doesn't just cycle through like clouds in the sky but it lasts for hours, days, weeks, years. Then we become overwhelmed by a mood of jealousy and we become desperate to be free of it. Often acts of violence (emotional, verbal and/or physical) towards the person triggering our jealousy are an attempt to remove the trigger that is stimulating us with the hope of bringing back the peace we have when we're not being triggered, e.g. killing the person our spouse is having an affair with.

So you can see, jealousy turns into a mood based on the beliefs surrounding it, not because of the feeling itself per se. The beliefs allow for all sorts of highly ineffective behaviors that are designed to find peace and to meet needs. Again, I'm not saying jealousy is a bad feeling or that we should try to not feel it. It has a message we need to hear, so hear it and then take effective action to meet more needs for everyone involved (including the person triggering your jealousy!)

Compersion is a feeling we can have when we see a loved one get their needs met. In particular, it's associated with the joy we experience when we see people we're intimate with enjoying their bonds with other people. Compersion is at the heart of a healthy family or clan in which I have joy seeing my family members love each other and contribute to each other. As a parent, I often feel compersion watching my children play with other people whom they love and who love them.

Personally, I have felt compersion many times watching my lover be with another lover when I'm included in the situation – literally, when I'm in the same room with them. It's harder for me to access compersion when my lover is behind closed doors with another, though I have felt it. A lot of healing has come up for me around this dynamic. Beneath whatever "unbearable" pain that might be triggered, I've always found a wound from an earlier time in my life that is blocking my compersion and triggering my insecurity and jealousy.

So that leads us to ***insecurity***. The need for security, as I've said, is a powerful force in humans. As far as I can tell, most people raised in Domain 8 have well-founded insecurities around love and lovability, family, intimacy, beauty, self-worth, attractiveness and the ability to sustain intimate connection in the face of competition. Insecurity, like jealousy, is just a feeling that emerges out of a beautiful need, but it also can become a mood that inaccurately colors how we see the world,.

We need security deeply, but in our confusion and in our isolated nuclear family conditioning, we often place most of our security in the hands of our one-and-only beloved. This makes sense for a newborn, whose security lies in their connection to their mother and being nursed by her. However, as an adult this is not a very functional set up. In fact, it's a set up to be perpetually insecure! It breeds more insecurity, more jealousy, and more competition in a grasping attempt to get our security needs met through a single source. Yes, we can get security needs met through our lover/spouse, but not all of them, and not all of the time. To be secure, we need more strategies to meet our needs that are also effective.

Security is when we're fundamentally confident of our ability to survive, when we have emotional wellbeing, when we meet our sexual and intimate needs effectively and when we are at home or at peace in our body, and in our life as it is now. Connecting to our Self and to Spirit is essential to dependably meeting our need for security. Having access to a sufficient range of relationships makes feeling secure much easier. The foundational sense of security within a human being is designed to be transmitted to us by our clan/tribe in our youth. The daily experience of connection at the physical, emotional, psychic and spiritual levels is meant to fill a human being so that once they become an adult they're inherently solid within themselves. Think of the difference between a solid building with all the braces, high quality materials and the strong stable foundation it needs and a rickety building lacking braces, solid materials and a coherent foundation. Both buildings need security. One has it inherently. One desperately needs it.

That covers the basic terminology of competition, jealousy, insecurity and their counterparts. Now, before I go any further, I want to articulate....

The Four Core Archetypes Of Primary Intimate Relationships

1) Lovers (parent-parent) 2) Siblings (child-child) 3) Parent-Child 4) Child-Parent

The first two of these relationships are fundamentally equal in power (age, life-skills, capacity for responsibility and consciousness, etc.) and the second two are unequal. All four of these types of relationships are intimate and sexually bonded. They are based on sharing sexual energy (lovers); being born out of the other's sharing of sexual energy (child-parent); being born out of sharing my sexual energy (parent-child) or both being born from the same other adults sharing sexual energy (siblings). From this, you can see how deeply integrated sexuality, intimacy and family are. This isn't to say we can't have primary intimate relationships between grandparents/grandchildren, uncles/aunts/nephews/nieces, cousins and close friends. It means though, that if they are deeply bonded, the relationship will resonate with, and model after, one of the four core archetypes.

Those of us who have experience in adult intimate relationships know it's very common to project and act out any and all of these roles with other adults. Intimacy brings up unhealed wounds and unlearned lessons from our past intimacies (e.g. family of origin, past lives and our ancestors). This happens in monogamy to a large degree, but it happens even more with poly-intimacy.

Having another person enter an intimate sphere (as a lover) is akin to having a new sibling born into a family. Let me explain:

When an infant enters a family, it restructures the family system and alters the experience for everyone, including the parents, the older siblings, the entering infant, and possibly the extended family or community. In a Domain 8 nuclear family (and often Domain 7), where there are only two primary sources of attention and care (the parents), the arrival of a new baby (in general) means less time/attention for the other children in the nuclear family from these sources. It does not mean less love in and of itself, but possibly a less overt expression of it due to lack of resources. If the older siblings are old enough and have enough emotional maturity, they can often "have the baby" with their parents and get fed by nurturing/giving to the new sibling as an older brother/sister. However, if they aren't much older there is often competition, jealousy, and insecurity triggered by the infant entering the family. The redirection of attention from the parents to the infant can totally destabilize an older sibling's sense of security, wellbeing, place, power, lovability, etc. The pie gets sliced thinner. Sure, in the long run, a new sibling will be a playmate and life-long bond for the older sibling, but that doesn't matter to a child aged one to five who loses some of their parents' precious attention every day.

Structurally, this plays out quite differently in a Domain 5, 6, or 9 culture where there are typically more adult caregivers (sources) and also an alive children's culture born out of all the different-aged children from all the different co-parents in the tribe/clan. It's a much bigger pie and so each new baby shrinks the slices much less when they are born. There are so many more adults and older children caring for everyone, that parents can more gracefully ensure the care of their older kids when new ones come in. This helps breed cooperation, compersion and security in everyone.

Coming back to poly-intimacy and sexuality, it's easy to see that in a monogamous couple each person acts as the single parent for the other partner. I'll explain this in the first person so it doesn't get confusing. Say my lover, who I relate to like my single parent (read "source"), gets a new lover. If there's less than total integration and inclusion of me, the presence of the new lover either lands as a rift in my family (where I'm getting a new step-parent who doesn't include me and pulls my parent out of full presence in our intimacy) or it lands as a new baby who now gets most of my parents' attention – a competitor within the intimate sphere. Neither of these models works very well from my position.

What works better is if my partner and I hold the space of parents and welcome the new lover as a "new baby" whom we will "co-parent" into our family. It can also work if we act as siblings, receiving a new brother or sister into our family. This isn't meant to turn adults into children or create fixed hierarchies between people already in an intimate sphere and those entering it. It's meant to highlight how it lands in people, and what kind of projections and charges are going to be present when an intimate sphere grows. Our inner child's unmet needs are what can sabotage poly-intimacy and sexuality, not our adult consciousness. So this is where we need to be diligent.

To bring a new adult in as a lover successfully, the shifting dynamic must work for everyone in the intimate sphere or it won't work for anyone (for longer than a few hot dates!). This is why addressing competition, jealousy and insecurity is critical. This can be done on multiple levels. People can do inner work around it through co-counseling, clearings and other Light On Shadow processes. We can look at family system patterns through Family Constellations and unlock the family dynamics on the spiritual plane. Whatever we can do to focus our attention on the past and how it affects our inner workings of unconscious beliefs about our Self and the world will strongly support harmony and connection.

At a practical level, we can "go slow" in bringing people into deeper intimacy with us, taking the time to address the unseen shadows or beliefs step-by-step. This goes a long way in keeping the peace and making long-term success possible. What this means, practically, is a lot of NVC-based conversations with everyone involved to make sure people's needs are being met, that they're being met only through natural giving and that the strategies we use work for everyone. Working together and caring about everyone can maximize cooperation, compersion, security and trust.

Another way to address these issues is at the structural or "container" level. This is what Domain 9 culture and consciousness is about. I am very scared to engage polyamory in a Domain 8 container. I'm more open to engaging in a temporary container like a Tantra event, Network For New Cultures Camp or another kind of poly-friendly gathering or festival. But these containers have their limits. They certainly represent a way to meet people. But to make the relationship last will be very challenging without a long-term structure that supports it. This is what we are working on growing at GaiaYoga Gardens. It's a work in progress at this point!

So, why do competition, jealousy and insecurity exist? What causes them? Why is it so BIG in poly-intimacy-and-sexuality? And how can we cultivate the opposite?

Sadly, in Domain 8 (and in much of Domain 7) men are socially engineered/conditioned to be in competition with all other men, and women with all other women, especially at the level of sexuality and intimacy. On the surface, we might be friendly about it, but scratch the surface and we'll likely see a much "uglier" picture. If we have a monogamous model, then obviously there's only one winner in a competition for a particular person's love/sex/intimacy/attention. Even without a cultural meme, there is competition at the level of sperm in mammals (including humans) for the option to fertilize an egg and pass down one's genes. My understanding is that sperm of different human males will literally fight each other to the death in a woman's yoni!

In the collective sphere, men can conform and cooperate in armies, religions and businesses for the organization they belong to. In the local sphere, neighbors cooperate with each other in their local environment and view each other as assets. In the personal sphere, women often support each other emotionally and if there are women who have children of a similar age, they will create playgroups for mutual support in childrearing. And of course there are tons of services in all three spheres that we cooperate around and appreciate each other for, e.g. education, fire fighting, farming, entertainment, construction, health care, recreation and sports, etc. If we look around, there's a lot of cooperation in the human world.

But once we get into the intimate sphere, men and women typically don't cooperate or share with each other in remotely the same way. Yes, someone from the outside might come in and support your intimate sphere, e.g. a marriage and family counselor, a financial advisor, a midwife, a baby sitter, a maid, a healer, etc., but his support is usually on a short-term basis. Occasionally someone supports an intimate sphere on a long-term basis, but the actual relationship to that supporter is still only at the personal sphere level – they don't join the intimate sphere

Besides this lack of sharing in a two-adult intimate sphere with other adults, there's also lack of transparency. Most folks are very private about what goes on in their intimate sphere. For example: How much do people really talk about their sexuality in an open and sincere way with others? Men, how many times have you seen another man be sexual or have an erection in your life? Women, how often have you seen another woman all turned on and juicy or being sexual? How many of you have ever seen others being sexual (outside of pornography)? Unless you're gay or bisexual, the answer is often zero.

This most precious part of our life is completely hidden from those of the same sex if we're heterosexual. Is this really helping us? When I meditate on how life was/is in Domain 5, it seems clear to me that sex and intimacy occurred in public, in the big sleeping pile at night or during the day in nature. This is also what we see in Domain 4. Animals have sex in public. They don't have shame or secrecy issues (unless they're trying to sneak sex from an Alpha Male without getting caught - which I've seen on documentaries about chimpanzees). Sure, there's something to be said for the focus of being alone in an intimate event, but there are costs that go along with this privacy.

How many births have you been to other than your own children? How much do you know about your friends' finances? Do you have open sharing of your core emotions with others? Do we fully share the raising of children with anyone besides our spouse? Do we bond with more than one other person this deeply? Do we trust more than one other person this deeply?

I might seem crazy-naïve to ask such questions, like I don't understand "how it is." But I really don't think this is "how it is." I think it's how it has become over time due to a combination of the most shortsighted aspects of our genetics and widespread cultural conditioning. Yeah, I'm opening up a Pandora's Box when I suggest that how we handle privacy, sexuality, finances, child-raising and deep feelings in our intimate spheres is actually built upon a fundamental (unconscious) training around competition, jealousy and insecurity. Moreover, it's "a vicious cycle" breeding more of the same.

What exactly is competition relative to intimacy and sexuality? We (often) choose to compete when there is a limited resource that more than one person wants to access. We don't know another strategy in which everyone's needs matter and can be met. This last part is the important point. Competing is a <u>strategy</u> for dealing with limited resources. <u>It is not a necessary response</u>.

In the animal world there is clearly a lot of competition over mating -- deadly competition! The males often exhibit the active symptoms of the competition through displays or conflicts. Sometimes that competition is over a single female. Other times it's over a harem, depending on the species. In general, "might makes right" in these competitions, with the victor getting to have sex with the female(s) (now or indefinitely over time) while the loser does not. It's all about the individual animal ensuring his genes get passed on to the next generation no matter what the costs. Watch a nature video about animal sexuality and you will learn a lot. The loser in these competitions might be killed, expelled from the group, or at minimum subjugated and made submissive to some degree. Unfortunately for the group, the winner of the might makes right contest might not be the best for overall group stability and/or genetic diversity. This is certainly true in humans, where we want to encourage other qualities in future generations besides the ability to beat out other males in mating.

At this time I would like to differentiate between competition and self-assertion, which is directly related to cooperation. In the human cultural Domains, this difference is significant in regard to the effect on the whole of the group. Competition has a "zero sum" outcome. The term Zero Sum is an element of game theory in which the amount lost is always equal to the amount gained. In a situation (such as a game or relationship), a gain for one side entails a corresponding loss for the other side. That is One Winner, One Loser (or with multiple participants, second place is considered the first loser.) Zero Sum is the outcome of all competition.

Self-assertion, however, implies that each participant does their best, clearly knowing all will benefit. There are no "losers." There are no thoughts of revenge, no self-recrimination for failing, no one is expelled from the group and the group becomes stronger as each individual is inspired to do better. For example, take basketball: Two teams, each with five top notch players on the court, each player a stand out on their own, each player asserting themselves. However, one team's players hog the ball, competing with each other to be the mightiest on their team and score the most baskets, while the other team's players pass the ball to others to secure the benefits of group cooperation. In the long run the blend of cooperation with self-assertion creates many more needs to be met than competition. On the surface you will see the same level of effort towards accomplishing the goal, but the relationship amongst the participants is very different.

Competition around sexuality and food in Domain 4 is "natural," though in the case of bonobo apes competition is purposely mitigated through many strategies that include female leadership of the groups and lots of shared sexuality. For humans the questions are: Do we serve the cohesion of the collective when we fight over females (or males)? Do we create the kind of deep connection human males want with other human males? What are the costs of maintaining this "ownership" of females? What is the cost of a female "owning" a male? Perhaps there's a constant insecurity, knowing you could be ousted by another male at some point and lose your Alpha status? Or there will be a younger, sexier, better woman who will take "your" male? Perhaps there's insecurity wondering if the female wants you or is just submitting because you beat the other male(s)? These dynamics are present in both animals and humans, though I'm much more concerned about their expression in humans.

As humans we certainly have this competitive drive around sexuality and particularly reproductive sexuality and the passing down of genes. But sex for humans is about a lot more than passing down genes, so when we let this Domain 4 animal patterning around reproductive sex run our life, we are not honoring all of who we are as humans. (I'll talk more about all the functions sexuality serves in the Holistic Intimacy and Sexuality section later in the book.)

Competition isn't right or wrong. It's a strategy that produces results -- results that meet several needs in the short term for the winner, and doesn't meet hardly any needs for anyone else involved at all. Around reproductive sex, competition is a real force in animals that is not going away, but it can be re-expressed consciously as self-assertion in humans. My point is that the strategies we use around sharing and sexuality are not fixed. Even in the intimate sphere we can be our full expression and cooperate towards meeting everyone's needs in the situation. As I already said, this is what happens in a healthy family, teamwork. We can come up with much more intelligent, nuanced and effective strategies than the ones that have been passed down to us over the years -- based primarily on our blind desire to reproduce at all costs and the unconsciousness of Domain 7 and 8. The overall consciousness of Domain 9 IS this more effective strategy. It's the way through to sustainable functionality around sexuality, intimacy and family.

Let's consider how sexuality was expressed in Domain 5. Imagine a bunch of humans sleeping together in a large cave, staying together for warmth, safety, power, emotional connection, etc. Certainly sex occurred in and around sleep. It must have been a normal part of their communal life, along with eating, eliminating, hunting, gathering, sleeping, playing with children, etc. While this probably didn't mean daily orgies, it did mean than sexual energy flowed freely through the clan/band of humans and that we didn't lose fundamental access to others because of sex.

Competition wasn't the only force. There was also sharing and mutual caring. While only one man and one woman can have intercourse with each other at a particular time, this doesn't really speak to how competition around sex plays out. It's about openness of access to each other over time. It's the same as with parents who have multiple children. At any one time, a parent might only be giving their intimate parenting energy to one of their children, but that doesn't mean their other children don't have fundamental openness of access to that parent.

Hopefully, this choice to move attention around one's multiple children doesn't generate deep insecurity, competition and jealousy amongst siblings. Most successful parents are able to minimize this and maximize a sense of security, cooperation, shared joy, inter-connection and wholeness within their family. This is also possible amongst adults practicing polyamory.

What is the interplay between competition, jealousy and insecurity? Let's start with insecurity… Security is a very important need in humans -- security around home, food, raising children, emotional/sexual/intimacy needs, etc. As we discussed earlier, how we attempt to meet these needs has shifted through the Domains 5-8, and this has generated more and more insecurity over the generations. While there is no absolute security while we are mortals, there is a threshold above which our security needs are fundamentally met. We can have a strong living system that meets most of our needs most of the time. We can have the resources to maintain that system and improvise when it falls short.

Relative to intimacy and sexuality, security is very important. It's rather common, coming from Domain 8, to have wounds, shadow beliefs, trauma and doubts around our security in our intimate sphere. If this is left uninspected and unhealed, we engage in intimacy/sexuality from a place of behaving as if we are insecure. It's like a "mood" that colors all our interactions. If we have this mood of insecurity (which is not looked on as very sexy or attractive) we will probably feel shame around it as well and do our best to hide it from potential mates/lovers. The insecurity is still in us, so it will end up showing up in some unconscious way that will probably not produce very pleasant or effective results.

When one is insecure, one wants to become secure. Or to say it in NVC: when our needs for security are not being met, we want to get them met. In Domain 8 especially, most folks look to their mate and mating as the solution for much of their security needs. Of course, this strategy has serious limitations and design flaws, but people do it anyway. If I'm projecting my security needs onto my monogamous sex partner, then jealousy around and about what they do makes a lot of sense. Someone else "taking them away from me," even just for a little while, is a threat to my sense of security. So, this amps up the force behind the jealousy and it is almost certainly going to be unconsciously blended together with the feelings of underlying insecurity. Instead of just a passing feeling: "Oh, I'm jealous Mary is having a date with Bob because I was hoping to connect with Mary tonight. Oh, well, I'll just find something else to do tonight," the jealousy and underlying insecurity become this dominating mood that envelops a person and makes life utterly dysfunctional because our fundamental security appears to be at risk.

This level of insecurity probably emerged from ongoing neglect of many of our needs as a child, so if we're to effectively meet our security needs we need to turn our attention to the source of it, not just the trigger. If we don't heal the original wounds, no amount of apparent security in the present time will be able to really nourish us where we are hungry.

Whether we actively compete with the person who is triggering our jealousy, we are in a state of competition with them. If we don't engage in active competition with the person triggering us then our inner experience will likely be based on the belief that we have "lost" the competition and we might behave as if we will continue to lose indefinitely. This disconnects us from that person and breeds a sense of isolation, distrust and more insecurity. This insecurity leads to more energy behind the feelings of jealousy, which leads to more competition. And around and round we go, and where it stops nobody knows.

If we do actively compete with the person who's triggering our jealousy then many outcomes are possible, but in the end none of them feel very good to anyone involved. At worst, there is violence and at best a cold war with no real victor. Or perhaps the opposite - a single act of violence might do less damage than years of a cold war. But either way is not going to support the kind of consciousness and relationships we want.

At the heart of the "problem" is the use of strategies that just aren't effective. If our strategies around sexuality, intimacy and security were really effective -- in that they met most of our needs, most of the time, over the course of our life -- then we wouldn't be concerned about all of this. As I've said many times in this book, it's a design error. The strategies we've been using aren't designed to work consistently, that's why they don't! We can do much better!

While polyamory might seem like an over-stimulating nightmare to the part of us that is insecure, monogamy is not actually an effective strategy for truly addressing our issues around competition, jealousy, and insecurity. At best, we might mate with someone who really doesn't have attractions for others, and really digs us and we feel the same towards them. In this situation, we probably won't be triggered into feeling jealous or insecure, and there won't be any actual person to compete with. So we can look like Joe Cool (or Jane Cool). But even if we aren't triggering that latent material, nor actively feeling jealous or insecure, that doesn't mean we're actually secure deep inside. Ignorance may be bliss, but it's still ignoring and thus a very fragile bliss. Moreover, few people actually experience this kind of relationship lasting longer than a honeymoon phase.

This is why Shivalila dharma calls it "a monogamy contract." It's an agreement to avoid triggering each other with our real desires, longings, and needs for connection and experience with others outside the contract. This way neither involved gets their feathers ruffled and there can be the appearance of social harmony. The contract creates a domesticated relationship and it mutes the wildness and aliveness in people (hence the book entitled, *Mating In Captivity*, by Esther Perel). In fact, I argue that the contract is actually built directly out of insecurity, jealousy and competitiveness, and serves to generate more of all three of these.

Because we are insecure we choose to make rules in the hopes of preventing us from feeling insecure. Because we're competitive and afraid we'll lose, we don't want to have to compete. Because we're jealous and ashamed to admit it, and embarrassed to feel and show it, we make it so we aren't triggered into our jealousy. Jealousy and insecurity are really just feelings that emerge out of unmet needs. As I've said, most people turn these feelings into what I call "moods" where the feeling lasts much longer than some minutes, and instead become a long-term dominating filter on our life experience. No one wants to live in these moods. The monogamy contract does do the job of keeping that mood at bay most of the time.

The effective way to address these issues is two-fold. As I already indicated, the first is to engage in effective healing work beyond our present relationships. The second is to bring sober attention to these forces within us and within our relationships so we can create the content and context of our relationships to be based on the living energies of cooperation, compersion and true security.

(I want to re-affirm here that I'm not saying that monogamy is "bad" or "wrong" or that being sexually intimate with only one adult can't be part of a natural human social structure. There are many beautiful needs that are met by people using the strategy of monogamy. I support "natural" monogamy, where the people involved aren't in contracts or codependency and aren't avoiding competition, jealousy, and insecurity, and they feel free to engage intimacy how they're inspired and they're inspiration leads them to monogamy. I very rarely encounter what I would call "natural" monogamy, but I recognize it exists and I value it.)

Ok. Let's imagine that humans are primarily manifesting cooperation and compersion. Imagine they are deeply secure in relationship to their intimate sphere, sex, love, finances, deep emotional connection, etc. What might that look and feel like?

Here's a possibility from a child's perspective first and then an adult's perspective...

- - - - - - - - - - - - - -

I'm a child. I live in a multi-generational, integrated tribe where all ages of people and several clans all cooperate together. We share land, daily life, play and adult stuff. I usually sleep in a big bedroom with many adults and other kids. It's super fun! I have many adults who I can go to for connection, play, protection, and to learn stuff. I nurse off of three different women: my mother and two other women who have children around my age. I have more than a dozen kids to play with. We all spend time together through out the day and we do interesting and fun stuff.

I have lots of trees to climb, places to explore, and different homes where I hang out. Most of the time, I'm free to go anywhere in our community's land, unless the adults are doing something they don't want kids around for. People tell me they love me all the time, and watch me play games and celebrate all the small changes I go through. I'm overflowing with abundant love, connection, and clarity about who I am and who my people are. I'm fundamentally happy and grateful...

I'm an adult. I live with three other men, four other women and 6 young children in a large bedroom with 5 beds. We all love each other and take care of each other on all levels. We share finances, sexuality, intimacy, child-care and the flow of life. There is a comfortable ease of intimate connection between all of us. Sometimes we are sexual in pairs, sometimes in larger formations. We also have another sleeping hut that we go to when we want solitude or when two people want extra focus for their connection.

Over the years, we've addressed many issues around competition, jealousy, insecurity and the like. Many times we thought we might not get through to the other side. But when we did, we were always so relieved for the healing and the continuity of our group intimacy. We have the best of all worlds. We have the kind of stable security people want out of a monogamous marriage and the diversity of connection people enjoy when they are dating. Just like in any family, our relationships aren't all exactly equal with each other, but they are all valued. At the end of the day, we can look into each other's eyes and the eyes of our children, and experience immense gratitude for the quality of love, connection, joy and juiciness we have together.

Our pod of 8 adults and 6 children is part of a larger intentional community of about 40 adults and 20 children. We share a lot with those other people too, including 30 acres of land, a school, lots of creative projects, growing our own food, businesses, etc. We have a conflict resolution council that many of us sit on in rotation to help us through the challenges that arise in our relationships and within our own selves.

I'm thrilled to have four lovers whom I live with and connect with in a beautiful and integrated way. I'm also very close to my lovers' lovers - some of whom live in our pod's home and some whom are part of the greater community. I am fundamentally at peace with my lovers having other lovers. I realize that I continue to be loved and wanted even though my lovers have other sources of intimacy. (Just like I want connection with all my lovers even though I have multiple lovers.) In fact, there's even more turn on and desire because of the increase in people to be intimate with. I enjoy a profound amount of intimacy, connection, trust, pleasure, health and wellbeing. I can hardly describe how blessed I am and how wonderful it is to share this experience with so many other adults and to pass this abundance of love and connection on to our children. I'm stoked to wake up every day and give to my people, and to enjoy the nourishment I receive. What a miracle!

While this might seem naively fantastical, I totally trust this is a very possible and practical way to organize and live our lives. For sure, it takes a pioneering spirit and intentionality to go from a Domain 8 model of intimacy to a Domain 9 one, but look at how much we have to gain as lovers, parents and children!

In closing, I'm not saying that the only way to have a healthy dynamic around competition, jealousy and insecurity is to be polyamorous. But it's certainly a way to get sober about how competitive, jealous, and insecure we are around intimacy and sexuality! More than anything, I want to help people understand that if you run at the first sight of being triggered in and around polyamory and you blame your feelings on the form of relationship, you are missing something huge already in yourself. It's up to you to decide if poly-intimacy is a medicine you want to take, a meal you want to partake in. But I certainly hold that there is a distinct difference between causing new pain in present relationships and revealing old pain via the process of relationship. We can detox from our diet or make ourselves sick, but either way symptoms are produced. It takes real wisdom to tell the difference. Both monogamy and poly-intimacy can potentially be re-toxifying or de-toxifying.

Also, people can engage in any form of intimacy as an effort to avoid or go numb to their competition, jealousy, and insecurity or as an effort to heal it. We can also create the structures or agreements in our relationships based on being ruled by these energies or based on liberating ourselves from being ruled by them. Whatever intimate relationship form you engage, I encourage you to be honest with yourself and realize the repercussions of your choices. I encourage you to promote cooperation, self-assertion, compersion and security within yourself and all your connections. For that is what supports True Human Freedom and leads us to making choices that truly serve all of life.

••• OBSTACLES, INSIGHTS, & CONSIDERATIONS •••

The Great Obstacle: The Pursuit of False Human Freedom

One of the greatest obstacles to co-creating *True Human Freedom* is people investing their time, energy, hope, and identity into "false human freedom." False human freedom is an individual or cultural activity or belief that is "mis-marketed," and doesn't actually produce the result it purports. A classic example of this is individualism. In many Domain 8 cultures the "good life" is founded on individualism, individual freedom, and unchecked autonomy. For example, a person with money can buy any land they want and do whatever they want with it (with some state and federal limitations). They can be the worst land stewards in the world, but they have the freedom to do what they want because they have the money to do it. Any fool with money (the power to induce other humans to act on their will) has the freedom to make as a big a mess as they want.

But it's more than that. It's that the most popular Domain 8 visions of freedom are separated from Spirit, Community, and Earth. There are many examples; from business and political leaders acting without consideration of their impact on the environment, the masses or their employees, to a hippie "going with the flow," bouncing from place to place, either making no agreements or breaking agreements wherever they go, to a college student who is all about partying, being popular, and doing as little as possible to get by. They are all driven by this concept of individual freedom being the right-and-true bottom line.

In the wake of looking through the different Domains, it's quite apparent that this is a very short sighted and dysfunctional vision of freedom. The reality is that a life based fundamentally on individualism is very <u>not</u>-free. Why? Individualism blocks one's ability to engage in a natural human social structure (a Domain 5 or 9 community) or create bonded and dependable relationships (a stable intimate sphere) – which are two core aspects of being human. If we can't engage in these core aspects, then we can't manifest our fullest humanity, or enjoy the fruits of doing so in life. We're crippled and blocked to our greatest power and pleasure. If we can't be who we are, then how can we be "free?" There is a profound limitation to one's power when one is unable to deeply cooperate as equals and disconnected from the Earth, and Spirit. Remember "yoga" means "unification," thus GaiaYoga, unification with all of life on Earth.

There is so much more power and freedom to be had in this holistic yoga, but it means giving up this smaller vision of freedom. As the saying goes, "The good is the enemy of the great." To someone who is riding high in Domain 8, the requirements of Domain 9 can look like a huge cramp in one's style, but the fact is that just like strings woven together as rope are much stronger than all the individual strings on their own, so are people much stronger (and hence freer) when they are unified with each other.

When one's identity and sense of security is rooted in individualism, anything that might decrease one's personal freedom is easily perceived as a threat to one's security. This is, in part, why socialism has a stigma in a Domain 8 capitalistic society. There appears to be a loss of power and security in considering everyone equally. In most Domain 8 cultures, the most one will stretch their personal freedom and core security is to include an intimate-partner and your children.

The way I like to conceive of it, the American idea of freedom (which is quite popular beyond America!) is akin to a cancer cell in a human body. All the non-cancerous cells are "not free" to do what they want, they are "bound" to their orders from the managerial energy of the body, and told what to do and expected to do it. Whereas, cancer cells have "broken free" of that limitation and can do what they want. They have individual freedom. (I know this isn't exactly how cancer works, but I think it's an effective way to illustrate the point.)

Seen in this light, it's obvious that this vision of freedom is deadly. It leads to the whole body's death. Cancer leads to death in the human being, which ironically also kills the cancer cell. Human beings are well on their way to being the death of the world, other species, and ourselves. How is this cancerous version of "freedom" possible? Why is it so popular and successful?

Surpassing our Natural Limits:

It's possible because humans have this unique capacity to separate themselves from natural limits. No other species can do this. We don't just do it through tools and technology. We also do it through cooking food and through suppressing our emotions. I'll already discussed diet and health, but I want to elucidate on how suppressing our emotions makes it possible for us to live outside our natural limitations.

Years ago I was told, if an infant chimpanzee is separated from its mother it will die an emotional death. It will grieve to death and not accept nourishment because of emotional pain. I'm not sure to what extent this is true or where the cut off line is, but the corollary is what's important. In humans, at some point the infant will stop grieving, disassociate, and survive. I actually believe that this single quality, more than any other, distinguishes us from the other animals -- our ability to cutoff from our feelings (our core self), disassociate from the pain and cordon off part of our being, adapt to the disassociation and survive. This capacity is very powerful in terms of supporting survival through trauma and indeed repeated trauma, but the cost is huge.

The cost is that we become disconnected to our whole selves, disconnected from nature, crippled in our ability to bond with other humans, and fragmented by broken family bonds. We end up taking all this energy that's designed to be directed to our feelings, relationships, and connection to nature, and channeling it into our minds. In the extreme, we have heartless soldiers who will kill over ideology, emotionless scientists who will create weapons of mass destruction, business people who view the world as resources to extract without concern (oil, metal, forests, fish, coal, etc.), or bankers and politicians who act without care for their impacts on the citizens of the world.

This capacity to suppress pain, disassociate, and survive (albeit crippled and less sensitive) has allowed humans to dominate the planet and each other, and supported us in going way beyond the natural limits of our species. So we're now free to fly around the planet (even though we're without wings), live where it's too cold to be naked (even though we have no fur), live where none of our food is growing, manipulate almost everything, and create artificial environments in the form of cities and virtual reality. However, this apparent freedom is based on being very un-free. We're un-free to feel our pain and truly heal it. We're un-free to be sensitive to the natural world and to the world of human relationship. We're un-free to live without destroying the world in order to maintain short-term survival. We're un-free to live close to nature within a group of people in one place and just be earthlings. We're un-free to accept our natural limitations and live within them, experiencing the deep harmony, acceptance, and grace this brings. We're un-free to eat a diet that is in alignment with Domain 4/5 (raw, local, organic) and supports our full health. We're un-free to create businesses, lifestyles, political systems, and cultures that consider the whole, serve the whole, and are sustainable over time. We're un-free to create a much greater power that comes from people living and working together, functioning out of natural giving, making life much easier, and freeing individuals up to bring their souls' dreams to life.

But we are free to completely ruin the world for every other species and all future humans however we want, and for as long as we want, even if no one wants to play with us anymore. Indeed, we have the freedom of a toddler having tantrum when we are rooted in individualism. We can have it be mine, mine, mine, and we can beat up all the other toddlers too.

In the same way that every other species has natural limits, so do humans. These limits include a climate range they can live in easily; natural foods they are suited to eat, that they access directly within their territory; clean air and water; an organized family system; mating rituals; and child raising techniques. If you ever watch a nature show about an animal you see that each animal is living out its natural order in relationship with other creatures in their natural order.

There is something inherently beautiful about it; how they live out these natural limits is what makes the species what it is. Using a musical metaphor, there is a "key" that their life song is sung in, and it is in harmony with the Earth and Nature. Somehow most humans have stopped singing in tune with this greater harmony, and frame it as an assertion of our individual freedom. But to me this "freedom" is like a child banging on a piano, making a cacophony. Sure, it's fun for a bit, but who wants to listen to a concert of it? Who can play along with it? What makes a song beautiful and inspiring ARE its limits. The melody and chords define its limitations. You don't just hit every note at once and call it beautiful. We can be creative and play solos within the limits, there's plenty of room for spontaneity. When you learn a song, you learn its structural limitations, and create within it. This is what most humans have stopped doing in life. Most humans are out of tune, lost, and suffering in a fragmented and disassociated false human freedom.

The Not-So-Great Obstacle:
Creating Domain 9 While Loved Ones Recreate Domain 8

Speaking of "transplants," most every person who becomes part of GaiaYoga Culture will have a family-of-origin or "blood-family." This family will most likely be a Domain 8 family, where there are parents, grandparents, uncles, aunts, nieces, nephews, and cousins that live in separate households, probably sprinkled across the nation or even world. What is an appropriate way to relate to one's family-of-origin?

People who join intentional communities or communes often find their family of origin thinking they've "joined a cult." GaiaYoga Culture is not a cult. (Note that "cult" is just a shortening of the word "culture," a slur made by the "authorities," or "authors," those "in power.") As I see it, there is only one way to relate to the people in one's family-of-origin – with love, compassion, respect, and honor. We can be "critical" of the structure of our family, and we can be sober about dysfunctionality in our family, but neither are grounds for withdrawing love or denying our bonds. We are creating GaiaYoga Culture "on the shoulders" of our current family; we would not exist without them. Indeed, someone co-creating GaiaYoga Culture is an ally to the health and healing of their family.

Sure, many members of our family might not understand or appreciate our lifestyle and cultural choices. Some might even think, "We're going to hell." We probably can't change them, but our only hope for change is to remain in a loving and compassionate relationship with them, and do our best to see them for their feelings and needs by practicing Nonviolent Communication. If things go well, then we will be able to have conversations that allow them to see the beauty behind our choices. As one of my close friends says, "We are the answers to our parents prayers." But perhaps they need help in seeing that!

There isn't an inherent conflict between creating and living in a Domain 9 culture and having a Domain 8 blood family. In fact, if they see that we still love them and that we are intelligent in our lifestyle and choices and respectful of theirs, it's much more likely that we will find allies and supporters, rather than enemies and naysayers.

Creating a Community of Intention and Affection

I once met a man who had been in and around the intentional communities movement and he said he was no longer interested in communities of intention. He concluded that when people come together around ideas, or shared values, or shared vision, it ends up eroding into a stale and empty effort, because sharing at the level of the mind does not create the inspiration and connectivity that makes life worth living. He said he was now into "communities of affection" -- people who had natural chemistry between each other, and shared an affectionate loving energy.

I was really struck by this. I didn't agree with his conclusion to throw out intention. I saw intention as a masculine principle and affection as the feminine principle (in simplistic terms). For any endeavor to thrive, it requires both principles to be active and integrated. So, what I came to realize is that even if I share "intention" with someone, that's not enough to ensure it will feel good to live with them. On the other hand, it's not really enough to have chemistry with someone and live together based on that. That leads to a great "honeymoon" and a lousy "marriage."

If people share the same intention but only have some chemistry they could be in the same tribe, but not the same clan. If they have little chemistry they could in the same larger culture, but not in the same tribe. Chemistry creates closeness in terms of energy and love; intention creates closeness in terms of mind and cultural identity. Sharing of an intimate and/or personal sphere requires both to make it sustainable.

Sustaining Relationships through Polarity and Conflict

As I say in a song of mine, "humans are the toughest crop of all." Intentional communities rarely fall apart because people can't grow food or repair plumbing, or even because they can't generate income. Most communities and partnerships end because people do not know how to work through polarity and conflict and stay in relationship. More than any other skill and passion, this is what is necessary to create and sustain Domain 9 reality.

Many people are afraid that if they get angry with someone or get into a fight with someone that it will be the end of the relationship, but I completely disagree. To me this, in many ways, is the beginning of a relationship. It's the beginning of people taking off their masks, their nice acts, their social faces, and really showing up. It's an opportunity for greater intimacy and understanding – if anything it is a reason to celebrate. Not to celebrate that there is conflict, but that there is enough safety and trust in the connection that people are willing to open up and take risks.

I find it fascinating that people are more comfortable having sex with a virtual stranger than they are sharing anger or other strong emotions like shame, grief and fear. I believe this is because, in fact, sharing anger is actually more intimate than having sex. Now I'm not talking about being violent or verbally abusive; I'm talking about clean and honest expressions of strong emotions.

Most folks remain on one side of a polarity and can't harmonize with the other side. Often people in a polarity who are sharing living or workspace together find themselves cyclically in conflict. On the other side of conflict and polarity is the potential for deep bonding and the Tantric weaving together of apparent opposites, but this is only an attractive option if one sees the value in the work and has the support to get through it.

While doing this kind of work with emotions, communication, cooperation, and beliefs is necessary to sustain relationships, it doesn't have to "be our primary sport." In the same way we need to sweep the floor or weed the garden, we need to do work in our relationships and our personal shadow work. Yes, it's different work, and yes it's work most of us aren't well trained in, but it is necessary nonetheless.

Ultimately, most conflicts and polarities can be resolved inside one's self when one has the tools to do so. After the inner resolution occurs, often the external situation resolves without any additional effort. This resolution is connected to our ability to take 100% responsibility for our experience from an authentic place. There are numerous modalities that support this kind of work. They include Zegg Forums°°, Nonviolent Communication, processes from The ManKind Project, Re-evaluative Co-counseling°°, Family Constellations°°, Ho'oponopono, rituals of The Dagara people, and "Native American" talking circles, among many other techniques. These types of practices can bring us back to center and to a place where we can enjoy life, our relationships, and our communities. When executed effectively, they literally dissolve conflicts and polarities, and what is left is love and connectedness -- the juicy stuff we all really want!

Two Relationship Insights:

This is a good place to mention the two biggest lessons I learned from my first communication teacher. These insights have a lot of bearing on sustaining relationships and understanding why we create situations in life that we don't want or don't think we "need."

The first is: *relationship ends when you get to the conversation you cannot have.* It was odd for me to think of a relationship as a conversation, but in a lot of ways that is what a relationship is. So, if there's a tension that can't be talked about or a polarity°° that can't be addressed, that's pretty much the end of the relationship, or the beginning of a very dead relationship of politeness, or a very dysfunctional relationship of constant low-grade conflict.

To be able to have difficult conversations requires using an effective communication model (which NVC provides), the desire to maintain relationships, and often either an outside perspective, a "3rd sider," to mediate, or some kind of greater conscious container to support the conversation. It takes more than just will or wishful thinking. In order to have the kind of long-term relationships that Domain 9 generates, we certainly need to be able to navigate any conversation, and thus maintain continuity in our relationships.

The other lesson is: *that which we cannot verbalize, we dramatize.* In other words, one of the ways we grow and learn about aspects of life that we aren't conscious of is to generate a "drama" that enacts the energy and makes it a visible event in 3D. If a person intends to learn from their experiences, they can learn from what they dramatize, and become able to tell a story about it and obtain wisdom regarding it. Once you can verbalize your vulnerable experience of a situation then the soul doesn't need to create the dramatic lesson to be played out for understanding to be present. So, while I hear a lot of new age folks saying they don't want "drama" in their life, it's actually a necessary growth/learning process until the lesson is understood and integrated.

Part of what I hope to contribute to people through expressing this is to give people clarity so they don't have to make so many mistakes, or dramatize lessons that I've already learned. Hopefully, by my verbalizing, I can shorten the road for others and make it more likely they can manifest their dreams and visions.

Accepting our Genes, Re-assessing our Memes

In doing my second rewrite of *True Human Freedom*, I started to grok something that had eluded me until after I finished *Sex At Dusk*. I'd been exposed to the discussion of memes and genes earlier in my life, but only in tying this whole argument together did I see it in greater depth. For those who don't know, a meme is a cultural corollary to a gene. A meme is the information or patterning of a culture, and it has a life of its own, like a gene does.

How culture shows up in Domain 4 and 5 is purely gene-driven. Animals don't have much capacity to decide to change the way they live, particularly at the social level. When there is adaptation or a new species develops, there is a change, but it's not like penguins are going to intentionally re-design and adopt a new mating system. Species are guided by their genes, via their instincts, to food, to mating practices, to shelter, to family creation, to most everything. Early humans were the same. In other words, we didn't actually have a conscious choice; we simply lived out the dictates of our genetic imperatives.

A very important thing genes do is set up social/mating systems that avoid or minimize incest (which often leads to unhealthy children). In the dawn of humanity this was achieved somehow. There are various theories for how young women (who were newly fertile) and young men found their way to new genes outside of the circle of their brothers, sisters, fathers, mothers, and closest aunts, uncles, and cousins. One of the few advantages of the isolated nuclear family being around a lot of other isolated nuclear families (in Domain 8) is that there are lots of other genes out there to mate safely with. As we've stepped through the Domains, the strategies we've used to avoid incest have evolved. I bring this up because it's important to consider in how we develop Domain 9 cultures. If cultures get too insular, like the negative image of a "commune" or "cult," then they run the risk of heading into the cul-de-sac of incestual mating. This is not an effective way of doing what genes are driven to do – successfully pass themselves on to the next generation.

In fact, genes are so intent on surviving and passing themselves down through offspring they'll do almost anything. In many species, the male is so intent on this that he will kill the infants of other fathers just to eliminate the competition for his offspring. Genes, "at their worst," are completely self-serving, self-centered, and very shortsighted. Instead of cooperating with other genes to maximize survival, genes compete with other genes (particularly male-male competition at the level of sperm, mating competition, fighting, alpha-male social systems, and infanticide).

Memes came along later, in Domain 6, and then grew in power in Domain 7 and 8. As I previously stated, memes are cultural versions of genes -- patterns that have stability, create structure, shape experience, and are passed on from generation to generation. Indeed, memes grow out of genes. One can think of genes as the seeds of memes. The memes grow when they find fertile soil, and that soil is thousands and thousands of different genes (different people), and enough consciousness to create social agreements and patterns.

Differing memes (or absence of them) are a primary force in defining different Domains. They're the collection of social agreements that both limit and promote different consciousnesses and life-experiences. If you think of humanity in terms of a single human life span, Domain 5 is our infancy. Infants are very pure and connected to nature and unrepressed, but infants are also lacking understanding, wisdom, and the capacity to see the big picture.

Religions and nations represent a set of memes. Wars and conversions are ways memes conflict and compete with each other (just like genes do). People feel closest to those who share their genes, but they also feel close, safe, and secure with those who share memes with them (Christians like Christians, Republicans like Republicans, etc.). An intentional community is made up of people who share the same meme, and also do the work of releasing and healing the memes they previously lived by. When children are raised in-and-by a tribe in an (essentially) equal manner, it's because the adults recognize that the children in the tribe are all children of the same meme, and there is a drive in the adults to pass on "their" memes. To me, a sign of growth towards our human potential, is when the drive to pass down genes is outshined by the drive to pass on memes ("good" memes) regardless if they're one's particular genes or not.

As humanity has developed through the Domains, from 5 to 9, there have been two major forces at work. One is the force of increasing understanding, wisdom, and experience that yields emotional, spiritual, social, and psychic maturity and ultimately, mastery. The other is the force of forgetting and disconnecting from our primal (Domain 4 and 5) inner-nature and thus becoming more disassociated from outer nature (Domain 1 through 4). Presently, the force of disassociation seems to be dominating most people. There's a fringe minority that have worked to remember their inner-nature, connect more with outer nature, and have also grown their awareness of and connection to Domains 0 and 10.

So the Catch-22 here is that genes have given us the drive to survive and dominate the world, which has given us a lot of power, but as I said, like an infant, these same genes are short-sighted and don't see the big picture. Examples of this short-sightedness abound, from pollution, to using violence to get what we want, to nuclear power plants, to making cheap products that tax our natural resources but create more profit, to substance addiction, to junk food, etc. So, while the genes are very skilled biologically they're not very skilled sociologically, or aware of the humanities, sustainable resource acquisition, emotional connection, seeing beyond psychic projections, creating a sense of connection beyond the genetic family, spiritual growth, etc. This is where memes come in and where the maturity and wisdom that develops through aging comes in.

Part of the discrimination we need to do is to see what our genes are managing and see if they're managing them well. For example, our genes manage our respiration, digestion, and blood flow very well. They don't handle jealousy and insecurity well. They handle hunting and foraging well, but don't really know what to do with all the tools and technology our minds have made.

Most of the memes most folks live by were developed by shortsighted genes and have been naively passed down from generation to generation. Now we have a profound opportunity to create holistic and sustainable memes, pass those down, and also pass down the meme of re-evaluating memes and improving them. In many ways that's the promise of GaiaYoga Culture – a truly, holistic set of memes that considers all the Domains in how to set up culture and lifestyle.

So instead of our sense of self and continuity being linked to our genes (the nuclear family) and the extension of our genes (our extended family), our loyalty can expand to see those within our meme. This devotion to memes over genes is one of the biggest differences between Domain 5 and Domain 9. And it must be a big difference, as it's taken humanity and our pre-cursors tens of thousands or maybe millions of years to get this far!

Cultures of Preservation Versus Cultures of Acquisition

One of the biggest cultural memes that is blocking us from creating a sustainable-and-holistic Domain 9 culture is the meme of "acquisition" or "over-acquisition." Much of my thinking around this dynamic comes from the author Daniel Quinn's teaching about *leaver* and *taker* societies.

We are the descendants of the survivors -- those who had the good fortune and skills to reproduce and pass down their genes and memes to us. There's a momentum in us to recreate these genes and memes. But, as we've seen, much of what has gotten us here is not worth recreating. I'm highlighting this particular meme because it's so pervasive that it easily overlooked and recreated.

A culture of preservation is one that sustains and maintains the system that supports and generates its life. Think of a tribe in a South American jungle that has a low population density and uses the resources of the jungle (food, building materials, medicines, etc.) to survive without really "making a dent" on the jungle. They preserve the jungle while they sustain themselves.

A culture of acquisition is one that acquires resources at an unsustainable rate, without concern of the long term impact on the capacity for the system to support life, and uses those resources to gain great power along the way. Think of the British Empire, which cut down most of their oak trees to build war ships. They took over the world, but lost their forests in the process. Today, Domain 8 cultures acquire petroleum, metals, fish, forests, coal, minerals, whatever it wants to continue "the show," at a profoundly unsustainable rate, and we all enjoy "the good life" because of the comfort and ease this has allowed. Indeed, it's pretty hard to say no when we're drunk, stuffed, housed, traveling, and communicating because of all of this over-acquisition of natural resources (Domains 2 – 4).

The seduction is that cultures of acquisition have much more power in the short term. Tragically, they tend to wipe out cultures of preservation in their process of acquiring what feeds this power. Preservation will win out in the long haul, but those of us born in Domain 8 are children of the acquirers. We've been taught that it is the way to survive and win, and indeed it has been! So, for GaiaYoga Culture to work and thrive, we need to go beyond just preserving nature, and re-create new sustainable human habitats, out of what's left after all this acquiring, and then preserve those. We need to take the power we have as acquirers, and design, recreate, preserve, and sustain, the foundation that makes our lives possible -- a diverse, abundant, and healthy natural world.

Avoiding "Traps" with Gurus and Leaders

One danger in creating community around a charismatic leader or guru is having them become the unhealthy center of it. Unfortunately, it's hard to start a community or culture without a charismatic leader or guru. The trick, for whatever leadership generates a community, is to be able to make the community more about the greater values, vision, and network of relationships, than around the personality (strengths and weaknesses) of the leader or leaders.

"Cults" can form around individual leaders, but a culture can't. A culture must be something that has universality to it and is not dependent on the energy of the founder(s) to keep it alive and thriving. An effective founder is able to use their power to lead people into the shared vision and through obstacles to creating it, instead of leading people to him/her-self. To really do their job well, they make themselves obsolete in that role and become just another community member.

The Limitations of Eco-Villages

Eco-village is a popular model of living outside of mainstream Domain 8. In an eco-village people share a piece of land and have their own personal, self-contained home-site next to other people with whom they share similar values. This is basically combining Domains 7 and 8 (leaving out Domains 5 and 6) and handling Domains 3 and 4 in a sustainable and harmonious manner. While this is a vastly better way to live than the way most people do in Domain 8, it is insufficient for creating a container that honors all of our humanity, as it doesn't include Domains 5, 6, and 9 in its design. This means that these aspects in each of our beings don't get the conscious support or inclusion they need for us to be whole.

The main issue is that most people in eco-villages don't cooperate with each other nearly as much as they imagined they would, because they all have their separate households to maintain. This means they don't develop as much capacity for deep cooperation and group bonding. This lifestyle doesn't "force people to grow" from living so close together - for it's in close quarters cooperation, and by exploring family dynamics that our deepest learning, healing, and development can occur. Also, if we are still fundamentally slugging it out on our own as an individual or couple, we don't face our deep fears around trusting others beyond a spouse with our security and survival.

The intention behind an eco-village is not to create a deeply bonded and deeply cooperative Domain 9 culture, so I am skeptical of the ability for this model to satisfy all our needs. It's a huge step, as I said, but I don't think it's sufficient.

••• NOW WHAT? •••

The Foundational Social Agreements of GaiaYoga Culture

Alright! So we're in the home stretch now. Time to get more pragmatic. I've presented this immense and exquisite vision of how we can live that is almost certainly a long way from how you are living right now. And even though I'm writing this treatise, I want to be honest that I don't continuously manifest the consciousness necessary to live the way I'm talking about. I'm constantly living with my focus on my growing edge.

We all know how to live the way we've been living, but how do we actually live the way I'm articulating? And how do we even start?

While I've made clear the vision I'm suggesting we co-create, I actually haven't stated outright what our social agreements°° look like or made clear what holistic health or holistic intimacy and sexuality really looks like. After discussing those three topics, I'm going to get down to the nuts and bolts steps it takes to create GaiaYoga Culture at the material level. Before we do any of that, let's create clarity about what are the social agreements of GaiaYoga Culture.

Abralut articulated what he called "the covenants of Shivalila," which is a social structure designed to actualize and sustain Domain 9. In the beginning he had three covenants, but later expanded them to four. The first three are: 1) non-violence (ahimsa), 2) open-and-honest communication (transparency), and 3) non-ownership (relating to everything and everyone as simultaneously free and interdependent, and fundamentally unable to be possessed). Later, as the experiment developed, the community added Tantra as the fourth covenant. They considered Tantra to be a practice of both identifying with the various archetypal energies and roles in self and others (e.g. infant, baby, toddler, teenager, artist, leader, priestess, fierce mother, yogi, student, shaman, seductress, primal man, warrior, etc.) and also to address polarized energy within relationship to resolution. I agree with Abralut in theory about these four covenants. In practice, though, I believe these covenants were expressed ineffectively in either a hyper-masculine way or in superficial manner. Because of this, the two Shivalila experiments didn't produce the result they intended.

Abralut was looking for the most simple and minimal agreements that people would need to make in order to create a free and connected social space. His goal was to create a social order free of contracts, because contracts block the free movement of living energy. These include monogamy contracts, employee-boss contracts, nice contracts (avoiding topics that might disturb or upset another or oneself), private property, possessing ones children, and any other form of repression or hierarchical fixing of roles between people. Of course, without some social agreements, energy that we don't want to cultivate can arise and dominate. So that's where these covenants come in.

These four covenants are essential commitments/agreements to enact in order to create GaiaYoga Culture. We certainly need a safe space where there is no physical or emotional violence, or threats of violence, both among each other and also towards ourselves (this is not necessarily an agreement to not hunt or eat animals, this an agreement between people, particularly people who live together). It's also clear to me that if a community is lacking NVC and authentic transparency, then it has little chance of success. Those are the first two covenants.

Non-ownership, the third covenant, is more challenging to fully comprehend, and then practice gracefully. First off, it is important to realize that ownership itself is a social agreement - not an inherent reality - that the strategy of owning might, or might not, meet needs in a given situation. Moreover, it's pretty absurd to believe that a 150 pound human being that lives maybe 100 years can "own" a piece of the Earth. It's also pretty absurd to think we can own another person – like a lover or a child or an employee. Ultimately, we can't really own anything. How can someone "own" an atom and make it "mine?" We can't. What we can do is get other people to agree that we own something and then act and relate as if that agreement is the truth. When ownership agreements are about tooth brushes, shoes, prescription glasses, and the like it's not that big of a deal, but it can easily go beyond the mild kind of ease and security we experience around having dependable access to personal items.

Ironically, a bunch of people living the covenant of non-ownership together may look like they actually own things together. They share things freely with each other, as long as everyone is capable of caring for things well. For example, you don't share a power saw with a 2 year old, or a small tool with someone who loses things all the time. But this isn't out of owning the thing; it's out of protecting people and things with discrimination and caring. Think about a typical husband and wife that have one bank account – they co-own everything and share freely with each other. Expand that spirit of intimate sharing to include a whole community. That's non-ownership.

I think where the covenant of non-ownership is easy to understand is in relationship to having a needs-based or gifting economy. People realize that the joy in life is from giving to others and receiving what is given freely, and this consciousness naturally outshines the drive to possess things and people. On a practical level, in a particular Domain 9 kinship group, there is sharing of pretty much everything as communal (our land, our solar panels, our food, our toys, our tools, our cars, our debt, our mess, our children, etc.). This level of sharing isn't something to extend to another for philosophical reasons, but meant to emerge out of a bonded relationship°° of mutual commitment to each other and the community, and not out of ideology.

It's fairly easy to understand that philosophically I am incapable of owning anything and that there is only relationship. The challenge is at the day-to-day level, where it's very important to honor the difference between our intimate/personal sphere community, and the people who are outside of that circle. We are likely to use the social agreement of ownership with those we don't live with, especially if they don't exercise a natural respect for the connection other people have with the items they use on a regular basis. Living in this non-ownership consciousness with people who share it is fairly easy, but the trick is maintaining this consciousness with people who live in ownership consciousness, staying in integrity while also protecting your community's resources. If I visit someone's home and don't honor the intimate dance going on within it because "no one can own anything," then I'm missing out on the deeper truth of what it means to have a home on the Earth. It comes down to people respecting the relationship people have to each other, things, and land. We live in a delicate web of relatedness both with other people and with Domains 1 – 4, and it's only if the web is treated with skillful care can our quality of life be sustained.

So, for non-ownership to function effectively each of us must recognize that not only can no one else own anything, but also that I can't own anything either. We're all in the same boat. All that exists is relationship between interconnected beings (plants, animals, people, and eco-systems) that are all cells and organs in the body of Gaia.

Tantra, as the fourth covenant in Shivalila, is a commitment to dwell deep in one's authentic beingness, and relate to others from that place. It's about going to each person's depth (including ourselves) and honoring what is there – all the different archetypal, primal, and spiritual energies and roles that person embodies. It's about full expression of our vital energy in all its forms, which definitely includes sexual energy, and working through polarized energy in our relationships. Tantra is to be practiced with the intention of honoring the multiple-source nature of the world, rather than to reinforce the single-source imprint. This is essential to the stability of a community.

For GaiaYoga Culture to thrive over time another agreement/commitment that I believe is necessary is a commitment to organic and sustainably sourced food, fibers, fuels, fertilizers, fodder, farm-aceuticals, and building materials, (can't think of an "f" word for that one:-) This doesn't mean everyone must agree to be directly involved with food production or other resource production and acquisition. What it means is that each individual and each community as a whole takes responsibility to make sure that how they acquire resources is sustainable. Many people call this Permaculture. At a community level, it generally means that a community will grow all it's own food and use the most local resources it can for building materials, fertilizers, etc.

Directly related to the commitment to sustainability at an outward/material level is a commitment to personal health, balance, and wellbeing (internal sustainability). Every individual needs to discover what methods and practices actually work for them. There is certainly a range of diets and substances and daily life rhythms that are not going to support this commitment and a range of them that will. In other words, there's not just one way to support health, balance, and well being, but, on the other hand, there are many choices that simply will not support these qualities.

The last commitment that I think is critical for success is to do one's personal healing work (a.k.a. shadow work or de-conditioning work). This is something like the Tantra covenant, but it's a commitment to oneself as opposed to a relationship commitment. It's pretty simple, there's no way a bunch of emotionally traumatized, shadow-driven people who are living unconsciously out of their conditioning are going to have a chance of sustaining GaiaYoga Culture. This inner healing and growth work is essential.

In summary, I'd say there are seven agreements or commitments that are foundational to creating a lasting GaiaYoga Culture:

1) **Non-violence** (physical, emotional, psychic)
2) **Authentic, open, honest and compassionate communication** (essentially NVC)
3) **Non-ownership** (respecting everyone's sovereignty when relating to people, Earth, and things)
4) **Tantra** (resolving polarized energy in relationship to completion, relating holistically)
5) **Sustainable lifestyle** (at the individual and community level, aka external sustainability)
6) **Effective self-care** (diet, health, self-connection, inner peace, aka internal sustainability)
7) **Emotional and psychic integrity and healing** (light on shadow, healing childhood wounds, growing beyond one's conditioning, healing generational cultural wounds and patterns)

These are somewhat broad stroke agreements, and I imagine as GaiaYoga Culture and consciousness grows, different communities will refine this for themselves and find what kind of social agreements create the container they want and need.

What Is Holistic Health and Healing?

There's a lot of sincere intention and discussion around health and healing, particularly "holistic" health and healing, in the circles I move in. I've listened to a lot of peoples' ideas over the years and ultimately my "litmus test" is the actual health of the practitioner and the extent of the manifestation of wholeness in their life. I don't expect perfection out of people, but I do want to see that what they are doing is leading them towards their stated destination. To my chagrin, I've found most people are not actually on course to true holistic health, as much as they want to be and believe they are. The reason is that most people don't really understand what wholeness is for a human being. Another way to say it is this: people don't really get what the potential of human health, vitality and power is so they settle for much less than their full potential.

Using the language we've developed in this book, *wholeness is being fluid in consciousness and awake and empowered in dynamic, balanced activity through the Domains, Spheres of Community, and GaiaYoga Matrix.* Relative to the Self Facet, it means that our physical, emotional, mental and soul bodies are in full functionality, integrated with each other, and in alignment with their true nature. (A healthful Self Facet is where most "holistic health care" stops.) Relative to the Community Facet, it means we're living in intimate, personal, local and collective spheres that are well designed and, when implemented into life, support holistic sustainability (i.e. Domain 9). Relative to the Earth Facet, it means we enjoy a deep and full connection to Domains 1 - 4. And relative to the Spirit Facet, it means we are realized in and as Domain 0 and we are free to move about Domain 10 consciously and intentionally as needed or wanted.

Obviously, this is a tall order. What this means is that to enjoy true holistic health we need to be living in a holistic culture and cultural consciousness, connected to nature and Spirit. As I said, from my experience it seems that most people's ideas of holistic health end with the self (and don't usually include our aboriginal Domain 5 nature). For sure, it's an expanded view of the self from non-holistic health models, but it still only considers the individual, and not the individual's relationship to the rest of life and how those greater systems impact one's health.

So, I guess I'd say I have "high standards" for holistic health. I see it as being a healthful self, within a healthful family, within a healthful community, living out of a holistic cultural meme, fully connected to Spirit and Earth. That is, practicing GaiaYoga! Enjoying True Human Freedom.

So if that's what health is, then what is healing? *Healing, simply put, is the re-aligning of living systems to being in integrity with their inherent design in form and function.* Healing can be a bit of a trap, unless we are engaged in an approach that is truly holistic, because we'll never get our real longing satisfied. In other words, if our vision of health is incomplete or inaccurate, then even if we get there we still "won't be healthy" and we won't know why, because we'll have done what we believed was sufficient to create lasting health. This easily leads to a lot of confusion, low self-esteem, and resignation.

Also healing can be a goal or intention in and of itself, which can lead to ineffectiveness. Sometimes people have called GaiaYoga Gardens a healing center, but I actually don't like that concept. I call us a holistic health center: GYG is about health, not healing. Yes, everyone coming out of Domain 8 needs healing on many levels. We need to heal to be healthful. But I don't want my life to be about healing. I want it to be about enjoying my health and well being, and the health and well being of my relations, the world and the divine.

Understanding what holistic health truly looks like changes how we handle healing. Think about our previous discussions around diet. How can we actually be healthful if we are eating a diet that is not in alignment with our Domain 4 animal body? We can't. Similarly, how can we be healthful if we're not able to express our sexual energy authentically? How can we be healthy if our connection to the divine masculine or feminine is blocked? What if we're stressed out and in survival mode because we're all alone or just with one partner raising a family? What if our air, water or overall environment is polluted? The answer to all of these questions is that we can't.

Sure, it's not black and white. We can enjoy a lot of health without having an ideal situation internally and externally. Life isn't about perfection. But if we're going to take the time and effort to address health and healing we might as well intend our greatest potential and be effective at it.

I think about it with this metaphor. If my Self - which can be understood as a cell in the living body of Gaia - is diseased and out of balance, then I need to address this. White blood cells and other healing forces need to be supported to do their job and heal us. Once we've achieved and can maintain a certain amount of personal health, then we can act as a white blood cell within the greater body of Gaia and support other cells (individual people) to do their personal healing. This is moving outward within the spheres of community, from the Self towards the Collective.

Healthy people can achieve an even greater amount of health through deep cooperation together, essentially by sharing and expanding their health together. This builds even more health and balance. It allows for even more support of others and the growth of larger communities of health. It's a positive domino effect, so to speak. Health breeds more health!

Using myself as an example: I enjoy a lot of health, but there are areas that I fall short of my potential. During the first 21 years of my life, on a physical level, I ate no organic food and very little raw food. I had my tonsils and adenoids removed. My eyesight deteriorated so I don't see distance clearly. My teeth are highly susceptible to cavities. I got a fungus on my left foot that still affects me to this day. I've worked hard to rebuild the foundation of my body, and have accomplished miracles, but there are limits and "permanent scars." Other impacts on my health are from being raised in a fragmented family and having much neglect in my early childhood, which has led to a lot of shadow beliefs and patterns of ineffective behavior in adulthood.

I have stress in my current life because I haven't consistently had enough stable and skilled support to take care of GYG effectively (which is a central part of my life's mission) and have stretched myself thin keeping it all together. Other impacts on my holistic health include being surrounded by people who still hold a lot of Domain 8 consciousness and cultural patterns; not taking as much time as I really need for self-care; and spending way too much time staring at computer screens as I attempt to grow GYG through writing, building and managing websites, emailing, marketing our immersions, etc. (This is also building health and future support for me, but there is a day-to-day cost to doing it.)

Few of us actually realize how much health and vitality is affected "negatively" or "positively" by how connected we are to others, nature and Spirit. I am driven to develop Domain 9 because of how much power and vitality I experience when I'm in this consciousness and connected to others who are in it too. We have a lot of juice to share with each other, but when we live in bubbles of our own individuality, the nourishment doesn't flow between us, which diminishes our health.

If our vision of health is just "not being sick" then we're going to handle our lives in one way. If our vision of health is "holistic" but just considers our Self, then we'll handle our lives in another way. If our vision of health is truly holistic and looks at the whole GaiaYoga Matrix, and generates wholeness itself, balance itself and integration itself within the Matrix, then we will handle our lives in a whole different way. I see True Human Freedom as synonymous with "holistic health." Indeed, how can we have freedom without health? And how can we have health without freedom? They are two sides of the same coin.

That's the heart of what I want to say about holistic health and healing. Obviously, taking action towards holistic health is a big process. Like fixing a car or renovating a house, you got to start somewhere, and do specific repairs and upgrades in a specific order. You can't "do everything at once." But unless we start with a clear picture of the end product we're probably not going to achieve our goal or full potential -- the well-running car with a sustainable fuel source and roads to drive on; the finished house within a sustainable social and material environment; or an understanding of what human holistic health looks like, feels like, and is. So, it behooves us to set a goal that is actually going to provide us with what we yearn for, even if it ostensibly makes the goal harder to reach.

Holistic Intimacy and Sexuality

For years I've been interested in Tantra, conscious sexuality, intimacy and the like. The woman with whom I originally developed the GaiaYoga teaching and bought the land for GaiaYoga Gardens was a natural-born, and then trained, Tantra teacher. I co-led some workshops with her while we were together, but never really felt comfortable as a Tantra, teacher, per se. The way I want to communicate about sexuality does not quite fit under the umbrella of "Tantra."

It wasn't until after I originally published this book in 2016 that I became confident enough to comfortably stand in front of a room and teach about sexuality. One day, while Melekai and I were discussing how we might teach on this subject, I said the phrase "Holistic Intimacy and Sexuality" out loud, and immediately I felt this crystallization take place in me – I finally had an umbrella to teach under - one that met my needs for integrity, inspiration, and confidence. So with that as our title Melekai and I developed a curriculum with exercises and started teaching.

As we developed our curriculum, I started to see more clearly why I wasn't comfortable teaching "Tantra." The main reason is that Tantra doesn't meet my needs for holistic integration. This is true of all teachings specifically about sexuality. One of the biggest gaps in these teachings is that they don't directly address the overall cultural container that sexuality and intimacy occurs in. Further, they don't honor the impacts our intimate sphere activities have on our personal, local, and collective spheres and vice versa. These are issues that CBGI addresses and solves.

Let me explain: Our original human sexual experiences took place in Domain 5. So it follows that any practice of holistic intimacy and sexuality needs to honor our Domain 5 nature and nourish our foundation. In other words, if our current sexual expression isn't in alignment with our aboriginal nature it won't serve our whole humanity.

To reiterate, Domain 5 humans lived in clans, maybe small tribes, that were nomadic, following food, water and warmth. They didn't have permanent settlements, private property, walls, rooms, etc. In general, a clan would sleep together in a big pile like wolves. This setup met many needs: safety and protection for everyone, warmth and comfort, emotional connection and closeness, support for intimacy and sexuality, care for children, ease, order, etc. Presumably, sex occurred in and around sleep, not privately the way we are used to nowadays. Sex was just another part of daily life, which occurred harmoniously around other activities like eating, hunting/gathering, relaxing, playing with children, etc. I believe that that this type of clan-based sexuality (CBGI) is at the core of our humanity. As much as Domain 5 humans ate together or hunted and gathered together, they slept together and had sex together, or at least next to or near each other.

Living was integrated. Even if mates were monogamous, they were intimate and sexual in and around their people -- children, adults, elders, everyone. This meant that sexuality wasn't just emotional, psychic, and physical glue for mates, it was glue for the whole band/clan/tribe. Sexuality was woven into the fabric of our communal life. We were seen, (and heard and smelled) by our people while being sexual -- it wasn't a secret activity, it was public. There wasn't any other way it could be since there were no walls, buildings, or huts creating any privacy. Like animals, we were out in nature, and unless you and your sex partner went far away from your clan, people would have access through their senses to what you were doing and with whom.

The very public nature of sexuality and intimacy that I am describing in Domain 5 has huge ramifications for our consciousness and sociality. Transparency is very important for our aboriginal self -- it's normal. Secrecy within a clan is abnormal. In Domain 5 sex, fighting, play, strong emotions, birth, pooping, eating -- all of it -- was typically out in the open for all to be aware of. Our primal natures are open to the others we live with. This creates a lot of connection, bonding, honesty, trust, and clear awareness of each other. So, when we "have sex" in private in Domain 8, without the container of a clan and disconnected from nature, we are missing much of what was always present and integral to human sexuality -- clan bonding, connection to nature, lack of shame, transparency, etc.

I've been at Network For New Culture camps where there's rooms set aside for the free expression of sexual energy in a public setting. I don't find the rooms to be erotic, per se, but I always find it very soothing to be around others having sex, and to experience it as normal, natural and observable. I feel fed by this in a very deep and sweet place. I experience it as an opportunity for clan-bonding and group openness, a return to normalcy for a very nourishing human experience.

I remember one time in particular, a couple was having sex on a swing and having physical difficulty because the woman was swaying too much, so I got behind her and held her so they could effectively engage. I wasn't turned on, I just wanted to support them. They could have needed help lifting a large table and I would've had the same kind of motivation - though that wouldn't be as novel of an experience.

I am not so focused on the kinds of sex people or having, or how 'Tantric' it is, or even about techniques for increasing pleasure. I believe that those are all important things, but I trust individuals and sex partners to find out what works for them at those levels – there's already lots of books, teachings, and teachers out there on these subjects. I don't believe that these are the elements that create or undermine holistic intimacy.

What I believe generates real wholeness is how we communicate; how we hold power with each other; the social/cultural/family container we engage intimacy and sexuality in; the presence and infusion of Love and Spirit in our relationships and sexual occasions; and the overall intention to generate wholeness through intimacy.

While procreation and raising children are certainly critical functions of sexuality and intimacy, there are many other as well. Being aware of and honoring these purposes is critical to having a conscious practice of holistic intimacy and sexuality. These other purposes may include the merging of consciousness of the participants, support for clan bonding, support for mate bonding, support for bonding as animals, mutual connection to Spirit (sex as prayer), adult play (including BDSM, dressing up, playing roles, erotic dance and movement, acrobatic sexual positions, etc.), expression of turn-on, rejuvenation, relaxation, stress reduction, expression of love and desire, moving archetypal energy, playing out of unconscious core roles towards healing, healing emotional/psychic wounding (especially childhood family wounds), deep nourishment, dissolving of contracts between people, and transmission of consciousness. Not necessarily all at once!

Ok! That's the fun stuff, but what does it take to sustain the vibrancy of holistic intimacy and sexuality over time? I see that there are four elements that need to be present and integrated for relationships to really thrive.

1) <u>Love</u>: A living desire to be with another person, a sincere appreciation of who they are, and a deep nourishment in connecting with that person. The presence of love is important for everyone involved in an intimate sphere.

2) <u>Commitment</u>: Without commitment there is no container and no real safety or security to create real intimacy. There are several things to be committed to: commitment to one's integrity, commitment to staying connected to the other person, commitment to getting through polarities together, and commitment to go through life-challenges together. Without this there's no way to get through what emerges in the context of intimate relating, (especially in a dynamic process like CBGI). If we have one foot in one out the door nothing of any real depth can occur because we're not truly present. "Maybe" is really a "no."

3) <u>Skills</u>: I can't overstate how important real skills are around relationship, intimacy, healing, and communication. People can love each other and have a commitment to each other and spend their whole lives banging their heads against a wall because they lack the skills they need to engage intimacy and sexuality effectively and consciously. People wouldn't think to fly a plane without training, but people grab the wheel of an intimate relationship thinking they can just wing it and everything will work out. More often than not, this doesn't quite work out, especially for people coming out of Domain 8, who have massive wounds and cultural conditioning that is antithetical to enjoying thriving sustainable relationships. (You can look through the Appendix and Glossary of this book for teachings that provide an array of skills to support healthy holistic relationships.)

4) <u>Support</u>: Even relationship gurus need others to support them in their own relationships. Many, many of us benefit from the support of an outside perspective. We all need "3rd siders" to help us when we are stuck in relationship. Moreover, we also need a greater supportive container to have our relationships in. As I've been saying, historically our clan/tribe acted as that container. Outside of CBGI, at minimum we need some kind of local or personal sphere support system to contain our relationships -- whether it be a circle of other couples that support each other, men's

and women's groups, our extended family, or some other kind of conscious and compassionate organization of support. Naturally, skilled support in this realm tends to be the most effective.

If we don't have all of these elements in our lives, I think that it is highly unlikely we will be able to sustain holistic intimacy and sexuality over time, or have our relationships reach their potential.

When Melekai, Omya, and I teach classes in our immersions we go deeper into discussion and exercises around holistic intimacy and sexuality. To support the intention of this book, I mostly want to draw attention to the basic elements of holistic intimacy and sexuality and invite you to explore it further, realizing that if we are not consciously engaging intimacy and sexuality in a holistic manner, sooner or later we will produce results that we're not going to like. The consciousness behind our intimate interactions matters profoundly, and the container in which our sexuality and intimacy occur also matters profoundly. Sex is deeply affected by and deeply affects our intimate and personal sphere, and can be a force that helps cultivate True Human Freedom or a force leading us far, far away from it. We get to decide and re-decide day-by-day and moment-by-moment which direction we are heading.

How Do We Create GaiaYoga Culture?

Ok. So you're sitting at your desk or lounging in your favorite reading chair or wherever, and you're thinking, "Wow, Ano! That's pretty far out stuff you're saying. I agree with you, and I want this too. But my life is so far from what you are talking about. How on Earth am I going to do this? And even more-so, how on Earth am I going to get others to want to do this with me?"

Well, yes, that is the question. Certainly there's not just one right answer to this question, but I do have some suggestions. Obviously, the easiest route would be to come visit GaiaYoga Gardens, where we are devoted to bringing this vision to life and learn from/with us. Then you can either take those seeds back to your home or make your home with us. If you want to consider this, then look at our website www.gaiayoga.org and email us to ask for an application to stay with us.

If that isn't a viable option for you then I'd say other steps you can take are to work towards creating a container in your own life for GaiaYoga Culture to thrive in, develop the skills needed to live this way, and make personal changes so you can align yourself with this way of living. This might mean finding a piece of land, a large house, or somewhere that people can come together and live together and grow their connections and practice GaiaYoga together. At the individual, level it would mean studying and practicing the teachings I've presented around diet, personal healing, communication, projections, sustainability, etc. This might mean finding teachers, workshops, or support groups, or starting practice groups and support circles yourself.

Ultimately, the primary thing is to STOP what you're doing now and start steering your ship in this direction. As I said in *An Introduction To GaiaYoga*: "The journey of a thousand miles doesn't begin with a single footstep, it begins with stopping walking the way you are going and turning yourself in the direction you intend to go." This is actually the hardest thing for most people to do: to stop and change direction. This takes a lot of humility, trust, and courage; especially when most people you know are going to continue on the course you are leaving.

Another thing you can do is to share this book with people you might want to live with, and see if they resonate with this inspiration and argument. Maybe you can find a handful of friends that want to really go for it together and you can get started that way. You can start blogging about it and see if you pique people's interest. I'm sure there are other ways.

The thing not to do is to become a zealot about this and shame everyone who's not doing this -- it doesn't work... I've already tried☺. The other thing not to do is to engage people at a deeper level of intimacy than they are consciously choosing with you. Community, and especially GaiaYoga community, is a team sport, and everyone needs to be choosing to participate and stretch themselves from a free place. Another way to start might simply be to do a lot of crying. This moves your grief, grief at not having the community and cultural consciousness you want in your life, grief at how far you are from manifesting it, grief about all the work ahead, and grief about not knowing how to proceed. Grieving is an effective way to release blocks to creating what we want.

Those are some avenues that might work. If you're serious about GaiaYoga, I recommend you get into communication with us, and we can support you as much as is realistic.

Tying the Bow around the Gift

What really drives me to "create GaiaYoga Culture" is hunger. I have tasted Domain 9 and it is the most nourishing, energizing, sublime, fun, and delicious "food." I want more of it! I'm the most alive (energetically charged, open, and flowing) when I'm activated there (and also activated in a balanced way in Domains 0 and 10). But as I've said, culture is a team sport. I can't really play it by myself. I can hang out and practice by myself (like a basketball player working on their dribbling and shooting skills alone), but I can't play the game by myself, nor can I generate that energy and consciousness by myself.

It's something that WE have to give to each other and receive from each other, together. Melekai and I are personally committed to that energy and consciousness. I am ready to give my all to a team, but I am not a team, I am not a "we," a couple is not a "we," I am only an "I" and without a real team to devote myself to and with there's only so much of this vision that will manifest.

This living web of fullest connectivity between people is really already here, even if we're not aware of it. It doesn't need to be created, per se, rather we need to choose to engage in it and remove the obstacles that keep us from experiencing it both short and long term.

So, what is the inspiration and argument for GaiaYoga Culture? Why would you take the risk and step out of your comfort zone and into this learning zone, and maybe even your panic zone?

Well the inspiration is simple – it feels really gooooood. Unfortunately, that really gooooood feeling is often on the other side of a lot of letting go of our current lifestyle and cultural identity and strategies for generating security. It also means feeling icebergs of frozen fear, a well of repressed grief, a shit-storm of rage, and a thick shroud of shame. So, I guess I'm asking you to trust me when I say, there's a profoundly worthwhile experience in opening to and integrating, all the Domains in one's life. Go ahead, put a toe in the water…

The argument is simple too. I don't think anything else is really going to satisfy all of our humanity. If I saw an easier path I'd take it. So I invite you to consider my argument, test it, look for errors in it, and see where the process takes you.

If you want to engage in this process with me, or dialogue about it, let me know! This is a core part of my life mission and I'm happy to share it on whatever level is natural and mutually agreeable.

~~~~~~~~~~~

There is still more to the GaiaYoga teaching and practice than what I've presented in the body of this book. In 2001 I co-wrote *An Introduction to GaiaYoga: A Holistic Vision for Living Sustainably as Spirit, Self, Community, and Earth.* This teaching booklet expresses the difference between a holistic and fragmented cultural consciousness, the lifestyles that come out of them, a map (The GaiaYoga Matrix) to navigate in wholeness, and another map (The Spheres of Community) to bring clarity on how to navigate through the different, overlapping layers of human community. The booklet also includes a list of core teachings that fill out the vision of a sustainable and holistic culture. In the following appendix and glossary I'll review some of the original GaiaYoga teaching and highlight other core teachings that comprise the foundation of GaiaYoga Culture.

I believe, with the addition of this book, *True Human Freedom*, the essential map or template of GaiaYoga is complete and the full extent of the practice and vision is now clarified.

I started writing this (which was going to just be an essay!) in the beginning of 2013 when I realized how terrified I was to truly show up 100% with who I am (fear), what I want (shame), and why I want it (desire). I hope that sharing this is going to help manifest my prayers and dreams, create a more powerful and conscious connection between you and me, and spark a lot of inspiration and action towards manifesting True Human Freedom.

The "promise" of GaiaYoga Culture is to solve many of the long unresolved issues of humanity -- including issues around sexuality, competition, jealousy, insecurity, power-over politics, human settlement design, and sustainable and shared resource use (economics) for individuals, families, and cultures. I believe humanity has been wrestling with all these issues as best as it can for eons. There's been a lot of headway made over the generations, and also a lot more entanglement. We are at a beautiful point in human evolution where we can truly liberate ourselves from the momentum of our collective pasts and create what we want, and what truly, holistically works.

We get to choose if and how…

Let's see, how can I end this? Ah, I got it…

We're all learning to share!

Thank you for reading and considering what I'm saying.

Sincerely,

Ano Tarletz Hanamana

To Be Or Not To Be The True Me

Follow in their footsteps – do you see where they lead?
After generations the grooves a rut, but still, we each believe -
If we're good and step in line and do what "they" said
Life will be good enough from kid-time 'til we're dead

So role, role, role your self, politely down your stream
Maybe, maybe, maybe, maybe one day you'll live your dreams
Trade in your paradoxical core for a safe, stable ride
You've read the headlines about those who didn't - you do believe they died

So try one foot rusting in the rut and one foot swinging out restlessly
A sophisticated dance, that's not quite free – steadily

> *Melt your mold -- Be who you really are before you grow old*
> *Break your ice -- Let the primal waters flow, not damned to be nice*
> *Pierce your veil -- Behind your fear of loss your soul can set sail*
> *Drop your chains -- You wear them like jewelry, though they're really scars of pain*

Listen to the sound muffled inside, the one's you always stuff
Feel where you're deeply drawn, that desire you don't dare touch
Move from the magic born within your kaleidoscopic core
Living from your dreams revealed, ignoring them no more

Love, sex, dance, delight, health, hearth, heal
Hear, say, hold, help, walk, crawl, feel
Parent, serve, lead, follow, roam, chores, play
Rain, sun, moon, stars, sand, mulch, pray

> *Melt your mold -- Be who you really are before you grow old*
> *Break your ice -- Let the primal waters flow, not damned to be nice*
> *Pierce your veil -- Behind your fear of loss your soul can set sail*
> *Drop your chains -- You wear them like jewelry, though they're really scars of pain*

It's just you, it's just you, all you won't be is just you
It's just true, it's just true, all that's inside isn't wrong, it's you
You can be, you can be, honest and free responsibly
You can choose, you can choose, to be or not to be…

So lead with your footsteps – and play with those who follow
Generate a groove awake from the sleep so hollow
If you're true to what's inside, you'll be blessed with grace
Enough's enough, its not so tough, to reveal, your real face

> *Melted your mold -- Broke your ice – Pierced your veil*
> *Dropped your chains -- You wore them like jewelry…*

••• TRUE HUMAN FREEDOM APPENDIXES •••

What Is Instinctive Eating?

In 1990, I dramatically changed my diet and began to "eat instinctively," which is a way to eat raw foods using our inborn instincts. Later, in 1996, I published the book *Instinctive Eating: The Lost Knowledge of Optimum Nutrition,* under the name Zephyr and began to formally teach Instinctive Eating. I now believe that understanding how instincts relate to food and health is crucial knowledge for anyone who eats. So I'd like to share the essence of what I've discovered over the last 20+ years of happily eating by instinct...

All diets are based on fundamental principles or assumptions. These may be scientific, cultural, aesthetic, ethical, spiritual, or intuitive. And all diets have varying degrees of effectiveness and pleasure, for different people at different times. The reality is that there are a lot of diets to choose from—*if* you are a Homo sapiens. But if you are any other animal on this diverse Earth, there is only one diet to choose: instinctive eating! Let me explain.

Instinctive eating is not a new way to eat. It isn't the latest twist on vegetarianism, nutritional composition, body-typing, Eastern wisdom, or health-oriented diets. Rather, it's the inherent living system for harmoniously selecting, eating, and digesting foods within our native biology. The way it works is incredibly simple, yet exceedingly effective. Imagine it's 50,000 years ago. You are hungry, walking on the beach, looking for food. Essentially, the only foods available are raw, whole, organic, and wild—what I call an "original" food. Next to a salt-water pool, you find a pile of seaweed, a group of rocks, a cluster of clams, a maggot-covered fish, fifteen fallen crabapples, and a broken, evacuated beehive, laden with honey. How do you know what to eat *and* what not to eat?

Simply put: the nose knows. Like a dog, you smell the foods, look for the best smelling item, and put that one in your mouth. If it tastes good, you eat it, and then find more of that food. This is the most significant aspect. The smell of a food is valuable sensory data to the instincts. The pleasure within the smell indicates that it might be nourishing food. If after passing the nose test, it also passes the taste test, then you *know*, physiologically, that this is a good food for you at this moment. It's that uncomplicated and direct!

So, why would you stop eating? This is the most magical part. An original food's taste will actually change in your mouth as your body's nourishment needs are met by each particular food offers. In other words, the honey or seaweed that initially tasted exquisite becomes less and less delicious, until it is actually painful to continue to eat. Really! The sensory experience changes, even though the food remains the same. That's because the body is a most sophisticated signal-receiving and data-processing organism. It's perfectly designed to prevent overeating via the taste change. Even if you are still hungry, you will not be able to eat more of a particular food, as long as you are sensitive to your body's messages to stop. Why? It just won't taste good anymore (unless you use condiments to mask and extend the flavor of this now non-nourishing edible).

This basic process is effortless and present in all animals. Essentially, instinctive eating yields tremendous clarity, liberation, and the security that you're eating the best foods for you — and only in the quantities that you need — as well as generating profound, long-term health benefits. And it all happens by following your pleasure!

So what happens if you eat a non-original food that no longer accurately communicates to your instincts? Let's take a look: A crabapple's smell and taste clearly reveals the essence of what that crabapple is, what its "nutrient makeup" is, and what its subjective value *to you* is. However, apple pie is a different story. The smell (especially right out of the oven) no longer accurately represents the essence of the food. And because of the cooking process and the combining of many foods, the taste change is now either completely absent, muted, or blurred. But your body is genetically programmed to "believe" that if something smells good you might need it, and if it tastes good you *do* need it. So it's totally natural to want to eat apple pie! Your body is following its innate intelligence. But the food is no longer living up to its end of the relationship by telling you the truth. It's saying to your instincts, via the always-attractive smell and taste, that it is an always-needed food. Well, need I say, this isn't *always* the case. And tragically, the symptoms of this tiny misunderstanding between food and instincts manifest as immeasurable suffering worldwide.

Nowadays most of our dietary arts and sciences involve eating non-original food, in a non-instinctive way. And they're tragically unrelated to our bio-instinctual system, which has existed since long before all the overlaid culinary systems. Because of this, we've developed boundless techniques for deciding what to eat, when to stop, and, indeed, what is considered food. These include endless diets, cultural dictates, weight loss and weight gain programs, using willpower to control eating, gluttony, eating disorders, guilt, shame — the list goes on and on. These are all sadly ineffective and inferior approaches compared to our inborn instinctive system, which can be trusted to handle all our food-selecting, eating, and digesting processes with impeccable grace and effectiveness. It's the right tool for the job. What a relief!

So what's the cost for this relief? Basically, there is one primary discipline: Eat only foods whose smells and tastes accurately represent their essence and that also communicate an accurate taste change. Practically speaking, this means selecting only from <u>whole</u>, <u>raw</u>, and <u>organic foods</u>. This might sound like a frustrating limit, but there are many of us who have walked through this doorway and have been happily surprised to discover an oasis of deep pleasure, *combined* with sustainable health and Earth-intimacy.

There are also some secondary disciplines: Eat only one food at a time, so that the taste change (or stop) on that particular food can be most easily "heard." And provide yourself with a wide range of original foods to select from. Of course, having a bunch of other hairless apes to eat instinctively with immensely adds to the pleasure!

One final point... This instinctive system doesn't only work with raw fruits, vegetables, seeds, nuts, bee products, and water. It also works with free-ranging, raw, and organic fish, meats, eggs, and insects. This might concern folks with ethical or spiritual considerations around eating animals or animal products. These are valid concerns, and I honor the spirit from which they arise. Nonetheless, the instinctive process exists and functions prior to ethics and religion. This is shamelessly demonstrated in the natural world, where some animals are carnivores, some omnivores, and some herbivores. There are many schools proclaiming which kind of a "vore" humans are. But regardless of the opinions of these different schools, raw meats *do* smell and taste good to many humans, and are found to digest properly and nourish profoundly. Again, from an instinctive point of view, the fact that these foods are sensually attractive is important information that indicates the body truly needs them for health and well-being. So if you don't like the fact that raw animal foods function according to the same principles as other raw foods, you might have some soul-searching to do. (And yes, it's also true that some instinctive-eating humans find raw meat totally unnecessary for their particular bodies, and this, too, is fine. In fact, it validates the instinctive process: No two humans have the same dietary needs, and indeed, a particular human's dietary needs usually change as their age and circumstances change.)

Most of us have been trying to navigate the dietary maze in some form or other for quite some time. What I've found is that the body already knows the way, and as we follow its wisdom, the labyrinth becomes a delightful romp in the garden. I invite you to explore your own body and instincts, and see if this message is validated in you. It might herald the beginning of a whole new sensibility around food, diet, health, and life altogether. It certainly has for me, and I wish the same possibility for you.

If you're interested in exploring instinctive eating further, here are some suggestions:

- Read *Instinctive Eating: The Lost Knowledge of Optimum Nutrition*, by Zephyr (my prior chosen name). It's available for $15 (plus $3 shipping) from GaiaYoga, RR2 #3334, Pahoa, HI 96778.
- Contact me about Instinctive Eating/Raw Foods Diet Coaching at aloha@gaiayoga.org.
- Come stay at GaiaYoga Gardens, the intentional community and permaculture homestead I'm co-founding in Hawaii. See www.gaiayoga.org for details.

~~~~~~~~~~~~

Why We Choose to Eat Raw Meat?

Isn't it dangerous to eat raw meat?

I feel confident that eating raw meat is safe. I know dozens of people who've eaten raw animal foods for years (some for more than two decades — including myself), and they all have experienced feeling healthier and stronger from eating raw meat, as opposed to eating cooked meat or not eating meat at all. There are indigenous cultures that ate raw meat for generations (Inuit, Assai, etc.). And in the animal world, no meat-eating animal on the planet (with the exception of humans) cooks its meat!

I feel more trust in the healthfulness of eating raw meat than cooked meat. Why? Because cooking food reduces the life-force in the food. What's more, cooking destroys the enzymes that are needed to digest the food. Cooking changes a food's fundamental molecular structure to a pattern that is foreign to our body. So we're ingesting something that's lost its vitality and is harder to digest. This is confirmed by the fact that we feel energized and light from eating raw meat, whereas cooked meat often left us feeling tired and sluggish.

Also, when meat or fish is cooked (especially if it's seasoned with condiments), it no longer gives reliable messages to our senses as to whether it's good for us to eat. Whereas with raw animal foods, you can tell by the smell or taste if something is "off."

Doesn't cooking meat kill the micro-organisms that cause disease?

This is another commonly-held belief. But commonsense tells us that we would have to cook meat to the consistency of shoe leather to kill everything in it, and obviously most people don't do this. So if thoroughly cooking meat were necessary to avoid illness, everyone who ate meat that was at all pink in the middle would be at risk of getting sick.

We actually have a very different perspective on these little critters. We believe our bodies are designed to co-exist with all kinds of micro-organisms, both in our food and in our bodies. As a matter of fact, we think they often serve a positive function of keeping us healthy by helping us to purify and renew.

Do you take any special precautions in selecting meat or fish to eat raw?

Yes, there are certain guidelines we follow in selecting meat to insure that it's safe for us to eat. Meat or fish must be raised without hormones or antibiotics. It should be free-range, preferably eating it's natural, raw, organic diet (e.g. beef that is pasture-fed, or fish that eat other wild fish and wild water plants). Pork has even more stringent criteria for safety, which no commercial grower that we know of meets. It's important to talk to your butcher and ask detailed questions until you're satisfied that all these criteria are met. When hunting or fishing, we recommend taking similar precautions relative to the quality of the meat and its food supply and habitat.

We also use our senses to tell us whether a raw animal food is good, just like every other animal does. Through smell and taste, our instincts inform us as to whether our bodies find the food needed and safe.

Are you saying that people should just follow their cravings?

No. Eating by instinct only works dependably with whole, raw, organic foods — in other words, foods in their natural state. And the signals to start and stop eating are most clear when foods are eaten one at a time. As long as you're eating whole, raw, organic foods, it's healthful (and safe!) to eat as much of whatever you're desiring as much you want. I want to emphasize this — our instinctive attractions to foods *in their natural state* are accurate guides that lead us to health and well-being (and also deep pleasure☺).

This point of view is radically different than the disposition most of us have learned of distrusting and trying to curb our appetites for food. Imagine living in harmony with your body's desires, rested in the knowledge that following those desires actually generates health. Can you feel how liberating that could be?

But isn't it morally better to eat without killing animals?

Most people don't judge lions or dolphins for eating other animals, and I feel the same way towards human beings. Here on Earth, life and death are inextricably interwoven, and it's impossible to engage only life and avoid death. Whether we eat an animal, a carrot, or a peach, we're still taking a life-form to support our life. So for us it's not about avoiding death, it's about respectfully participating in the whole life-and-death cycle. Many spiritually-evolved, traditional cultures, such as the Native Americans or Tibetans have eaten animal-foods for centuries, in a disposition of gratitude and blessing towards the spirit of the animal that was sacrificed.

Don't you think it's better to eat without killing animals?

I think it's best to eat according to what our bodies communicate they need to be healthy, rather than leaving it to our thinking or beliefs to dictate what we should eat. That's what's so wonderful about eating according to instinct — our bodies clearly tell us what we need, so we don't have to figure it out with our minds. Again, this is commonsense. We couldn't have evolved over the eons if we needed a diet book in our hands to tell us what to eat.

If someone is truly a vegetarian, they will know it because animal foods won't be instinctively attractive to them (meaning those foods won't look, smell, or taste good to them). On the other hand, if someone *is* instinctively attracted to animal foods (meaning that those foods look, smell, and taste good to them), we trust that this is a communication of their body's authentic need for that food. Either way the process is the same — find out what *your* body is saying it needs, and eat that. We've found this to be a profound and deeply connecting practice of trust in nature.

Does eating meat stimulate violence?

In the wild, animals that are carnivores or omnivores almost only kill other animals for food, and only when they're hungry and feel the instinctive drive. They do not kill for sport or torture, as humans do. So eating meat does not seem to stimulate violence in them. Our experience tells us that the same is true for humans.

Many people experience a grounding and/or energizing effect from eating raw animal foods. This is not the same as becoming violent. It's simply vital strength in the body. Another common experience people have after eating raw animal foods is a feeling of peaceful satiation and a profound sense of "feeling fed." Thus, our observation is that, if anything, raw animal foods stimulate natural strength, peacefulness, and balance — the opposite of what we expected!

What about factory-farming of animals?

I absolutely want all animals to be treated humanely and allowed to live as close to their natural state as possible (including humans!). My personal goal is to raise our own livestock in a compassionate way and to be in relationship with them throughout their life and death or hunt wild animals. Even from a self-gratifying point of view, food from animals that were treated inhumanely tastes worse and is less satisfying. So our instincts, as well as our values, lead us away from factory farming.

Couldn't we end world hunger if everyone stopped eating animal foods?

I see this as a partial solution to a larger problem. Yes, there might be more food for the total world population if we all ate a plant-based diet. But since I don't believe this diet will support optimal health for all people, I don't see this as an acceptable solution.

The causes of world hunger are very far-reaching and involve much more than simply having enough food to prevent starvation. To really address world hunger, we must look at how things got out of balance to begin with and confront issues such as the politics of food distribution (and resource distribution altogether), overpopulation, and the destruction of our topsoil, forests, and oceans. Even if we were to feed everyone today using a plant-based diet, if we continue doing all the things that have lead us to the current moment, it would only be a matter of time until that, too, would be insufficient.

Furthermore, virtually all of the arguments opposing land and water use for raising meat are based on evaluating our current agricultural practices, which are unsustainable. In sustainable and integrated agriculture systems, animals often take up no extra space and actually give additional energy to the land in terms of labor and manure, thus increasing fertility and health. So the real issue here is not about meat-based diets versus plant-based diets — it's about sustainable versus unsustainable agriculture. Sustainable agriculture systems can definitely include animals raised for food.

OK, I'm curious about what you're saying. What should I do now?

- Read the books *Instinctive Eating: The Lost Knowledge of Optimum Nutrition*, by Zephyr (aka Ano) and *We Want To Live*, by Aajonus Vonderplanitz.
- Check out these websites: www.gaiayoga.org, www.beyondveg.com, www.westonaprice.org, or www.primaldiet.com
- Try some raw animal foods, if you're attracted to do so.
- Come to GaiaYoga Gardens in Hawaii and learn more about Instinctive Eating.

~~~~~~~~~~~~

GaiaYoga (The Vision and Introductory Teaching)

For those who don't know, Gaia is a Greek word that means Earth, particularly the Earth goddess. In the 1970s, James Lovelock's Gaia theory stated the Earth has it's own soul and identity as a planet, and that all the life forms on it are like cells of it's body. Yoga is a Sanskrit word that means unity or more commonly a practice that serves to generate experiencing unity. So GaiaYoga is about experiencing unity with the Earth, experiencing ourselves as a cell of the Earth, unifying with our total humanity, and experiencing a fundamental connectedness, cooperation, and shared identity with all the other cells of the Earth body.

Much like a cell in a body who serves a particular function, yet is first and foremost serving the overall will/needs of the body as a whole, the primary life focus of an individual GaiaYogi is *wholeness itself, balance itself, integration itself.* (As opposed to any particular area of life like communication, career, relationships, food growing, health, fun, politics, self-expression, service, spirituality, parenting, etc.) Making one or a few areas of life our primary focus creates an inherent imbalance and a fragmented culture, even they are wonderful things we are focusing on.

The initial GaiaYoga teaching booklet, *An Introduction To GaiaYoga: A Holistic Vision For Living Sustainably, As Spirit, Self, Community, And Earth,* came out in 2001. It contains two maps of holistic living and culture – the facets and edges of the GaiaYoga Matrix and the Five Spheres of Community – and is also an inspirational argument to choose to live sustainably and holistically in community. Following are diagrams of these two maps, more discussion about the Spheres of Community, and an essay that I turned into a flyer called "What Is GaiaYoga?"

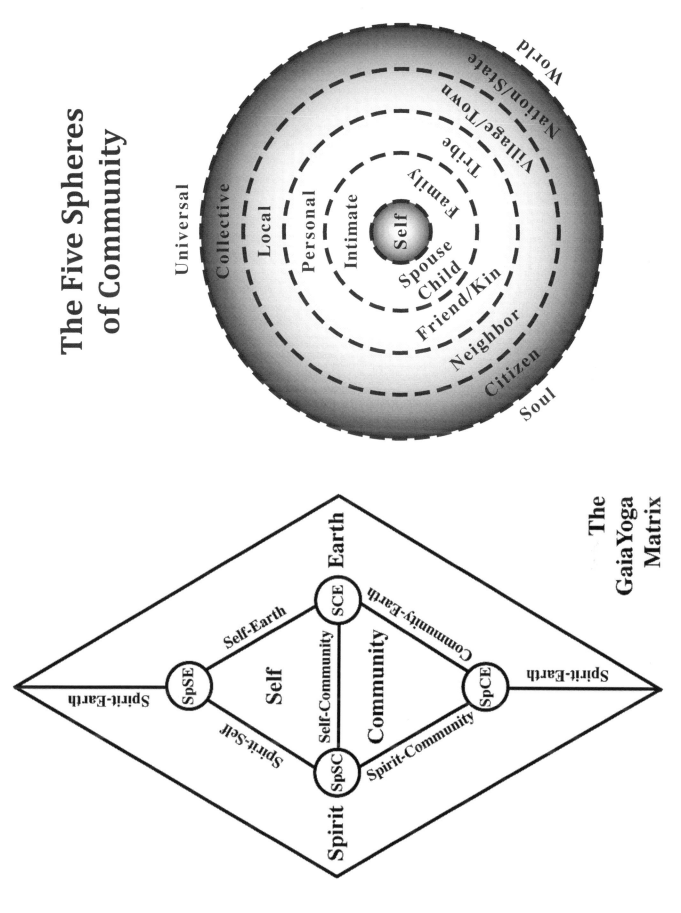

What Is GaiaYoga?

GaiaYoga is a vision and practice that is being pioneered at GaiaYoga Gardens (GYG) intentional community. It is the integration of many other teachings into a cohesive consciousness and lifestyle that is intended to support people in living from their deepest humanity. More than an individual practice, it includes developing bonded-human-social-structures (cultures, tribes, clans, and families) that express our true nature as human beings. GaiaYoga is in many ways the antidote for the predominant culture designed around unchecked capitalism, fantasy, car-and machine-based human settlements, dysfunctional family-systems, emotional illiteracy, fear and oppression of nature, chemical dependence, absence of integrity, and broken relationships.

GaiaYoga goes much broader and deeper than most "yogas" which primarily address an individuals' body-mind -- supporting inner peace and connection to Spirit. GaiaYoga is a dynamic and holistic "yoga" that addresses Spirit (realizing, integrating, and enjoying the Divine Masculine and the Divine Feminine), the Self (including the physical, emotional, spiritual, and mental bodies), Community (including the intimate, personal, local, collective, and Universal Spheres of Community), and Earth (developing strategies to sustainably live as an integrated "cell" of the Earth, individually and culturally).

GaiaYoga is a holistic practice that is modeled after the cultural and spiritual wisdom of many of the indigenous cultures of the world who lived sustainably for untold generations. Sadly, these indigenous cultures have mostly "lost their battles" (literally) with the current "beast" that is running the world. Most of us were raised by this beast and intentionally or not we continue the pattern. To change direction and make life work naturally and sustainably, we require a new vision, teaching, and daily practice that can heal and transform our lives and our cultures. GaiaYoga provides a way to emerge out of the world that we see now, and create something that has the beautiful elements of indigenous cultures, and knows how to wield the new power that's been found through technological and social evolution, without losing touch with our true humanity. It's a "take the best and leave the rest" approach.

What does it take for us have the kind of world we want, and be the kind of people we want to be? How can we grow through the huge pile of compost left by previous generations and find our way to the sunlight, creating both a healthy and full expression of our individuality, and a "container," a culture, a community for us to live in? For this we need a holistic cultural template. Truly, humans are no different than dolphins, or wolves, or bees, or ants, or giraffes, or apes, or even banana or bamboo: we are naturally "designed" to live in-and-as a bonded social organism. Our full human expression is to live as a unified multi-generational people. Call it a tribe, or a community, or a clan, or a kin, or whatever.

This is a huge aspect of the yoga we all need to do to create a beautiful, abundant, peaceful, and Spirit-filled world. *We need to take the energy of yoga – of unification – and bring it to culture.* This is a big "stretch" for someone who grew up in a city, or the suburbs, or a fragmented and dysfunctional family. There is lots of healing, lots of new skills, and lots of buttons to be pressed and worked through. How can we do it safely, directly, and effectively? This is part of what practicing GaiaYoga offers.

Using GaiaYoga as a "hub," we integrate particular practices, or "spokes," in dynamic relationship with each other and create a strong, balanced "wheel" that rolls well. GaiaYoga is also like a computer operating system (it works in the background) that's loaded with the finest programs (teachings). It integrates Marshall Rosenberg's *Nonviolent Communiation (NVC)*; Guy Claude Berger's Instinctive Nutrition; Aajonus Vonderplanitz' Primal Diet; Re-evaluative Co-counseling (RC); The ManKind Project (MKP); Permaculture, and other sustainable energy and agriculture teachings; The Tantric Transmission of the Shivalila Kinship Society; the rich wisdom of The Dagara people as shared by Malidoma and Sobonfu Somé; Saniel Bonder's Waking Down spiritual teaching and practice; Piankhy's Integral Science; The Michael Teaching; Taoist and Tantric sexuality teachings; as well an assortment of other new and old teachings and practices that grow sustainable-and-holistic consciousness and culture.

Wanna find out more? Ready to get started? Look over our website, read our booklet *An Introduction to GaiaYoga: A Holistic Vision for Living Sustainably as Spirit, Self, Community, and Earth*. Better yet, come visit or participate in one of our residential programs at GaiaYoga Gardens. GYG is a 17.75 acre, sustainably-designed homestead, holistic cultural experiment, and teaching and healing center located in Puna, on the East-side of the Big Island of Hawaii. We are pioneering this way of life and are looking for people to join us at many levels; as interns and students, as long-term residents, as permanent community members, and as cross-community teammates, spreading GaiaYoga and linking GaiaYoga Gardens to other places in the world.

GaiaYoga is the lifework of, me, Ano Tarletz Hanamana. I walked away from the culture I was born into in the early 1990s, when I was in my early 20s. Since then I've been healing myself, learning, practicing, and teachings skills that support GaiaYoga lifestyle, unlearning a whole lot, and bringing this vision to life! In 2001 I co-created the GaiaYoga teaching and in 2003, co-founded GYG. In 2009, I re-founded GYG with Melekai Matson. We now have two young children and are patiently co-creating sustainable-and-holistic culture at GYG. Our daily life is very beautiful, and still far from the mature, rich tapestry of multi-generational, Spirit-full, and Earth-rich tribal culture we envision.

One thing we've learned from Permaculture is that most problems, especially recurring ones, can be traced to design errors. In other words, if you start out with a bad design, no matter how much energy you put into tweaking it, you're still going to end up with problems. The same is true of lifestyles, teachings and cultures. The reason that most of us are stuck in various ways in our lives is due to poor design, not an inherent problem in us as humans. (We consider this good news!) It's about the seeds we planted. Plant a different seed - get a different result. GaiaYoga is a seed that can bring the results people are looking for, through all their hard work and seeking. It fundamentally re-designs and re-orients our lives for wholeness, balance, and sustainability, so that we can actually have all of our needs met.

Give us a Hallelujah!!!!

We hope you're inspired....

An Overview of the Five Spheres of Community

The Five Spheres of Community are in dynamic relationship to each other, they each serve different aspects of our humanity, they are all important, and they all can be lived in a highly functional and sustainable way, or a highly dysfunctional and unsustainable way, or anywhere in between. Each of the spheres has layers within them, and the edges between them aren't black and white. (Like a shoreline where there is a transition from ocean to land.) Nor do all relationships or situations fit like a cookie cutter into one of these five abstractions. Each sphere has an amorphous skin and flexible edges and differing depths. (Like human skin.) These can be understood as we explore the Spheres of Community consciously, but for purposes of just laying out this basic map, it's helpful to see their differences clearly and un-blur the lines between them.

While I chose the term and image of spheres, the diagram would more accurately look like a torus field where the center and the outside are the same. The diagram hints at this with the white in the center of the Self and the outside of the Universal Sphere.

The Intimate Sphere is primarily about our closest relationships and connections – spouses, lovers, children, and parents. When we are born, we come out of the Universal Sphere and come into an Intimate Sphere as a Self. For most Domain 8 people nuclear family is synonymous with intimate sphere, but in fact, it is only one form of intimate sphere. There are others, such as the various forms of poly-sexuality, and also very tight clans or kinship groups. Within the Intimate Sphere sex, finances, parenting, home, decision-making, and transparent communication are typically shared and integrated together. When children grow up and "leave the nest" they are usually no longer part of the Intimate Sphere, though there is almost always a life-long intimate bond between parents and children.

We can also have short term intimate experiences in personal growth workshops, retreats, therapy and counseling, on psychedelics, in rituals, during a one night stand, and the like, but I don't consider this the Intimate Sphere that is the foundation of a person's life. I call these kind of events intimate experiences or sharing intimacy.

Moving outward, **The Personal Sphere** is the next layer of connection. It includes close friends, co-workers, members of the same tribe or intentional community, people in the same weekly/monthly focus group (men's/women's group, bowling buddies, "stitch-and-bitch" friends, etc.), teachers and students, and extended family. In the classic human cultural form of mating pairs, within clans, within tribes, the intimate sphere includes the mating pair and depending on the particular culture also extend out into most or all of the clan. The Personal Sphere is the tribe and might extend down into the clan. There is overlapping in the clan between the personal and intimate spheres. In the Personal Sphere there can be sharing of some of the elements of the intimate sphere, but not total integration. Personal Sphere relationships often include shared survival (at the tribal or intentional community level), play, shared creativity, business ventures, working relationships, and emotional support.

The Local Sphere is a much newer phenomenon for humanity than the Intimate and Personal Spheres. It really wasn't until the development of villages (Domain 7) that the local sphere came into being. In the local sphere you are just another person in that locality; for instance, the local butcher, the teller at the bank, that woman who walks her dog every morning, another person in your high school, the guy who hangs out and reads a book at the same park bench, etc. Local sphere relationships are with your neighbors; you don't necessarily know their names, their stories, exactly where they live, but you know them and see them and have a level of safety and familiarity with them. A farmers' market or an elementary school are two great examples of a local sphere situation. Conversations in the local sphere are usually friendly and neighborly, about economic interactions, about the weather, local politics, who's getting married or having a baby, and things that matter to everyone in a locality.

The Collective Sphere is the most recent sphere to come into existence. In the collective each of us is just a citizen, with no personal or local identity per se. We are another Republican, another Jew, another member of Greenpeace, another postal worker, another resident of Florida, another European. The Collective Sphere is the home of states, nations, national and international corporations, airports, national elections, stock markets, television, Hollywood movies, websites, etc. Most of us receive a lot from the Collective Sphere in terms of goods and services, but most us don't noticeably influence it very much, unless we are rich, famous, or somehow influential and powerful at that level. In the collective most of us are pretty much anonymous members of the masses – another snowflake on the avalanche, another grain of sand on the beach.

The Universal Sphere is a different kind of expansion than we've been seeing from the intimate to the collective. The Universal Sphere is the realm of all being, of souls, of the things we can't see. When we say "Namaste" or pray for the welfare of all beings we are speaking within the Universal Sphere. The song *Imagine* by John Lennon is an expression of Universal Sphere consciousness. In the Universal Sphere race, religion, nationality, age, occupation, and whether or not we are incarnated is transcended. When we connect with our ancestors, angels, channeled spirits, or with The Divine, and when we die, we are participating in the Universal Sphere. The Universal Sphere and Domain 10 are essentially pointing to the same "thing."

And the cycle returns back to the Intimate Sphere if/when we are reborn...

~~~~~~~~~~~

What Is C.B.G.I.?

CBGI (pronounced kuh-bi-gee) is an acronym for Clan-Based Group Intimacy. It's a term we coined at GaiaYoga Gardens in the spring of 2019 to identify the particular form of intimacy and sexuality that many of us here are actively cultivating. GaiaYoga Gardens is pioneering holistic-and-sustainable culture -- we are re-evaluating all areas of life including diet, health, farming, child-raising, sexuality, family structure, communication, and more. Our intention is to sift through the myriad of cultures that have lived in the world and the consciousnesses that developed them, find understandings and practices that simultaneously reflect our primal human nature, our animal nature, our spiritual nature, our modern psyche, and our natural sociality, and integrate these into a whole cultural vision and consciousness. We often find that the most effective (need-meeting) way to live today deeply resonates with how we lived during the dawn of humanity - before we started altering our behavior from our inherent genetic expression. So, relative to intimacy and sexuality this begs the question, how did early humans handle intimacy and sexuality and how can we effectively re-integrate that into our current lives?

Let's explore… Using GaiaYoga® teaching terminology, there are five spheres of community: the intimate, personal, local, collective, and universal. Looking at the intimate sphere, let's strip away the "flesh" from all the various ways intimacy has been handled and get down to the bare "bones" -- what elements are inherent to any intimate sphere? What is shared that makes it an intimate sphere? The main elements are sexuality, bed, vulnerable emotional expression, sleeping, food and meal preparation, home, money and decision-making, child-raising, and the co-management of the fundamental direction of the family. (We can share some of these elements outside the intimate sphere – for instance, raising children in community, making a meal together, or living in a form of group housing beyond our nuclear family. And of course we can have intimate experiences at workshops or meet someone and have a "one-night stand," but these are not the same as an intimate sphere that is the core of one's life.)

In the dominant culture (what we call "Domain 8,") an intimate sphere is structured as two adults and their young children. But this isn't the only way to organize an intimate sphere. And based on our research and experience, the isolated nuclear family structure is not in alignment with our nature. For the bulk of human history people lived in clans – bonded, multi-generational groups of 15 - 40 people, living together in continuity. Prior to the taming of fire, clans slept together every night for warmth, protection, and connection. We assume that sex occurred in and around other clan members and all the other elements of the intimate sphere were present in the group. There was no privacy as we think of it today. People's intimacy was "clan-based." Our sexuality and intimacy held the clan together, supporting survival, childcare, elder care, and the clan's overall quality of life.

Just as bees live in hives, ants in colonies, or lions in prides, humans are designed to live in clans. We hold that it's the way we most effectively meet human needs providing intimacy, diversity, practical support, ease with childcare, support with aging and death, continuity of togetherness, fun, etc. Over time people formed larger groups, what we call tribes, which contain many clans. Out of our increased use of tools and taming of fire, over time, close-quarters human cooperation was replaced with more advanced tools, industrialization, long-distance cooperation of strangers, cooking, and general manipulation of nature. These experiments have had huge impacts on us. While many innovations met more needs at first – such as efficiency, ease, food stability, increased autonomy and material power - inevitably, moving away from our natural social structure and biological limits had hidden costs that weren't seen by the people at the time, (in the form of other unmet needs). The costs include more diseases from food manipulation, shame and subsequent perversion of our innate sexuality, externalized control, and increased technological dependence. This led to an ever-growing schism both from the natural world and between our fellow humans.

Relative to sexuality, in our history there has been a lot of deviation from the "norm" of heterosexual monogamy, with even more in the last few generation of humans. This includes homosexuality, bisexuality, transgender, androgyny, and all the forms of non-monogamy or multiple-adult intimacy, which includes serial monogamy, polygamy, polyandry, polyamory, and polyfidelity. These explorations are happening because many people are not content with the rigid structure of heterosexual monogamy. Monogamy doesn't dependably support the living of our natural, innate sexuality; it's led to the isolated nuclear family - which is a dysfunctional social foundation that includes contracts that prevent authentic expression of people's life-force energy. However, the various forms of poly-sexuality have their own flaws (consistently unmet needs) and this is why we've coined the term CBGI to distinguish the approach that we believe is in full alignment with our whole nature and all of our lives.

So what are the differences between monogamy, polyamory, polyfidelity, and CBGI?...

Monogamy has many systemic issues (especially practiced as an isolated nuclear family in a city or suburb. 1) Sexuality and security needs are merged so it can be very risky to be honest with our sexual needs and desires that don't align with monogamy. 2) The sharing of economics and childcare is limited primarily to the two adults in the marriage, which creates a sense of scarcity in meeting survival needs and is inherently inadequate at serving the many needs of children. 3) If divorce occurs, there is often no larger social reality that the mating pair can gracefully dissolve back into (a clan or tribe), so typically one or both lose a home, the children's parenting system is wounded or shattered, and there's general financial and emotional crisis and trauma for all involved. 4) We cannot meet all our intimate sphere needs reliably living with only one other adult, so we either suffer the unmet needs or engage ineffective or semi-effective strategies to fulfill ourselves. And 5) In old age we are not surrounded by a multi-generational community and typically end up in an "old folks home," instead of being a valued elder in a clan/tribe.

Polyamory, as it's practiced in an urban or suburban setting, is primarily just a model for multiple-adult sexuality; it doesn't intentionally address the care of children and elders or create greater stability and security through the container of a bonded personal sphere that the relationships are integrated in. Lovers might be spread around the country or world, which creates a split due to separation of intimacy and a hyper-focus on sexuality. We don't think it's possible for a human to sustainably participate in more than one intimate sphere at a time. Like an atom jumping between molecules, in order for intimacy to be sustainable, people need a single home/hearth. This dance between two intimate spheres or relationships can be done for a while, but eventually the atom needs to stand as a lone atom or become part of one molecule (either by merging all the involved atoms together into a single molecule or by giving up on including one of the atoms, settling for a smaller molecule.)

Polyfidelity (or group marriage) is about creating an expanded intimate sphere, where more than two adults are sexually fidelitous to each other. However, it doesn't explicitly include an integrated personal sphere - a larger group that lives together and supports the other social needs we have. Polyfidelity is more stable and more effectively addresses the needs of children than polyamory, but there is a huge gap in bondedness and life rhythm between those inside and outside of the fidelity, so it's much harder to enter or leave it gracefully. Moreover, if you get a group of similar age people to join up as a larger intimate sphere, they will lack a multi-generational support system to effectively handle support of children, elders, and overall life flow.

Clan-Based Group Intimacy is a design that holistically addresses all our human needs, not just our overtly sexual ones. This design is not some "new-fangled good idea," it's a recognition of our natural sociality that lives in our souls, bones, blood, and hearts. CBGI is inherently more stable, happy, and rich because... 1) We each have intimate home bonds with more than our sexual partner(s) and children. 2) Children have access to a multi-generational, integrated clan of parents. 3) There's real purpose and care for elders. 4) We don't have to choose between being authentic with our changing intimate/sexual desires and having security in our home and all that entails. Thus we can be intimate with whom we choose, transparently, with joy, and without shame or threat of huge repercussions. 5) There's greater ease and effectiveness at meeting our emotional, intimate, economic, and survival needs because more people are deeply cooperating together in a shared vision and life rhythm. This stably supports greater freedom, joy, pleasure, fulfillment, and power amongst the group of trusted and bonded adults (and children).

When we live in a clan we are living as one human molecule so to speak, so if we are intimate and/or sexual with more than one member of the clan the energy nourishes everyone in the clan and the clan nourishes everyone in it. So there isn't the fragmentation that is experienced in other forms of polyamory and certainly in affairs or divorce. The expanded intimacy is inclusive to those involved. It increases the well-being of the children because they have more mothers and fathers, it makes life easier to manage because there's more adults cooperating together for survival, the competition within genders and the polarities this generates can resolve, and there's more pleasure because we have more people to share juicy energy with.

Let's be clear, CBGI doesn't mean everyone has sex with everyone – it means there is a container that supports the natural expression of intimacy and desire that is larger than just a few people who want to have sex together. This larger social network meets the bulk of our social needs, so we don't need to over-focus on our sexual relationships as the main source of deep social interaction. Without CBGI, most of our other social interactions tend to be less authentic, intimate, and integrated as we might see in a school, work-place, single-focus social group that meets weekly or monthly, farmer's markets, social media, etc.

An example of CBGI might look like 30 adults and 10 children living together on a community-owned land. And amongst the adults there could be some people who are naturally monogamous, while others connect more fluidly, and other people in clusters of 4 to 8 in stable group intimacies. These group intimacies would do most everything together: sleep in the same room, care for the land, provide child-care, share finances and domestics, run communal businesses, share a kitchen and meal preparation, and all the major duties that running a household, business, and family entails. All that we're used to sharing in an isolated nuclear family are shared in a larger social unit, which is much more stable and sustainable. Again, in CBGI no one is required or forced to be intimate or sexual with anyone, and no one is required not to be intimate/sexual with someone within the clan because of social contracts, jealousy, or perceived threat to security. Everyone is living in their sovereignty and being supported emotionally and spiritually if any competition, jealousy, and insecurities arise. Also "divorces" are way less impactful because no one "has to" leave the CBGI just because they want to be less intimate with a particular person in it.

CBGI is a fundamental restructuring of how we meet our intimate, sexual, and primary social needs, and how we get our needs around security, survival, home, and childcare met. It provides the stability people seek in a monogamous marriage, with the diversity people seek in dating, affairs, and polyamory, with the other social needs we have that are often sought in men's and women's groups, workshops, festivals, and other short-term gatherings. It also provides greater economic ease and power from many people combining resources, a safe space for children to have a much larger circle of daily playmates, real "social security" in our elder years, people to play and make businesses with, and more.   WOW!!!   It's possible! If this essay inspires you…

- Explore (www.gaiayoga.org) -- learn more about our community and our whole cultural vision.
- Read *True Human Freedom: The Inspiration and Argument for GaiaYoga Culture*, by Ano.
- Participate in our 16-Day GaiaYoga Gardens Immersion Experience (offered 4x-6x/year)
- Set up a work-trade or eco-rental at GaiaYoga Gardens.

What Is Nonviolent Communication (NVC)?

Nonviolent Communication is the life work of the late Marshall Rosenberg, Ph.D. The intention behind NVC *is to create a quality of connection in which everyone's needs matter, and those needs are met through natural giving.* It is a way of thinking, speaking, listening, and a way of seeing the world. I consider it the single most important specific teaching for creating true and lasting peace in the world. Below is an essay I co-wrote years ago that I turned into a flyer called "What Is Nonviolent Communication?" Following that is a bit more explanation about the terms "strategy" and "needs," and following that are lists of feelings and needs as they are used in NVC.

For years, I've been searching for a consistently empowering yet honest way to communicate - one that promotes real connection between myself and others. Fortunately, I learned about *Nonviolent Communication (NVC)* a few years ago. Now I'm happy to report that my desire to consistently have compassionate verbal interactions — even in charged situations — has finally been fulfilled.

NVC is literally a different language. Even though English words are used, it's based on an entirely different understanding of life. In my old language, I focused on what was wrong with someone's logic or circumstances, countering with a response that demonstrated my ability to fix the other person. Even after the dialogue was over, I would continue the debate in my mind — concretizing my judgments, correcting the "other," and defending my position. Given the logic I used, it all made perfect sense (even though, when I really checked-in with myself, I was aware that doing this felt terrible and left me with unsatisfying relationships). Yet, to change this experience, I had a big hurdle to leap. *I needed to be willing to explore a new logic and language that could produce more enriching results for myself and those in my life.*

So what is so different about NVC? Let me give you a brief example. Let's say I passed a bulldozed lot. I might say, "God, what stupid people. They don't care a thing about the Earth! I wish they'd just disappear, because they're the real problem." (And that's an edited version!)

However, if I were to use NVC, I wouldn't communicate my evaluations and condemning thoughts. Instead, I'd communicate in the four parts of NVC — *observations, feelings, needs,* and *requests*, which clarify what's actually alive in me in this situation. Then the sentence might sound like:

> **OBSERVATION**: When I look at that bulldozed lot . . .
> **FEELING**: . . . I feel outraged and powerless . . .
> **NEED**: . . . because I want respect for the Earth and protection of ecosystems.
> **REQUEST**: Would you be willing to brainstorm with me about ways I can affect development on the island so that it's aligned with my values?

With NVC, there's no suppression of feelings or false niceness. There's also no blame, shame, or judging of others (or myself!). I can take the energy that I previously used in evaluating others and direct it instead towards identifying and expressing my own feelings and needs. Once I'm in touch with that, I can effectively ask for that which would enrich my life. For me, this is a profound breakthrough. By using this form, <u>I'm able to communicate any feeling, about any need, in a way that maximizes my chances of actually getting my needs met</u>. Whereas before, I spoke in a way that practically guaranteed my needs would NOT get met.

But this is only half of the equation. Perhaps even more unique to NVC is the practice of empathic listening, or *empathy*. When listening empathically, I again translate whatever is spoken into observations, feelings, needs, and requests. Let's say my partner comes up to me and says, "You're a lazy, messy bum, and I'm sick of putting up with your junk all over my house!!!" Using empathic listening, I can do something besides collapse, defend myself, or attack back. In this case, I might pause, reflect, and ask:

> **OBSERVATION**: When you came home and saw my slippers and towel on the floor . . .
> **FEELING**: . . . were you angry . . .
> **NEED**: . . . because you'd like to have order in the house?

Notice, I don't take on their condemnation, nor do I condemn back. Instead, I listen for feelings and needs, then make my best guess at what the other person is actually experiencing. *Empathy*.

Hearing this, she might say, "Yeah, but what I'm really angry about **[feeling]** is all the traffic and the fact that I had to work all day while you stayed home **[observation]**." Then I might say, "So are you really wanting peace and relaxation **[need]**, and you're angry **[feeling]** that being at work kept you busy all day **[observation]**?" "Yeah, what I'd love is to take the weekend off **[request]** so we can spend some intimate time together **[need]**." "I'm happy to hear that **[feeling]**, because I'm really wanting to connect **[need]**. I was actually bored **[feeling]** sitting around the house today **[observation]** because I was wanting company **[need]**." "Yeah, I can relate. Also, would you be willing to put your things away after you're done with them **[request]**?" "Yes." "Thanks."

This dialogue is an example of how NVC can take a potential fight and turn it into an intimate connection. And it only takes one person speaking this language to make it happen. For me, NVC is a way to address the complexities of being human in a truly nurturing and mutually beneficial manner. I've found it to be very valuable in creating sustainable relationships, families, and communities. And like any skill, it takes patience and practice to learn and incorporate consistently in day-to-day life.

Beyond its obvious merit in personal relationships, NVC has also been used successfully in organizations and conflict situations all over the world—in schools, businesses, prisons, and in volatile political arenas. It's helped bring peace to war-torn areas and turned around apparently hopeless circumstances. It seems to work for people of all races, classes, backgrounds, and situations. This excites me, because I want to be able to communicate with everyone in a way that is respectful and effective, while still being sincere and passionate. Prior to NVC, I didn't see how that was possible. Now I see it as natural!

If you're interested in learning more about NVC, here are a few avenues you can explore:

- Read *Nonviolent Communication: A Language of Life,* by Marshall Rosenberg, which completely explains the basics of this practice with many excellent examples.
- Look for Marshall's lectures on YouTube.
- Surf to www.cnvc.org to learn about the Center For Nonviolent Communication
- Attend a workshop or class in *Compassionate Communication*, which I offer in Hawaii
- Join a *Compassionate Communication* practice group and practice, practice, practice!

Strategy Versus Needs

Needs, in NVC, are the core energy of our being, the primary force that motivates us to do everything we do in life. Needs include love, meaning, respect, contribution, growth, fun, ease, connection, physical nourishment, and to be heard, seen, and understood. They steer our ship. They are what get us to initiate action. An example of this I often give when I'm teaching is of my deceased dog, Pilipili. When she was ages two through seven she used to get into any open car in our carport and sit in it so that if the car went anywhere she was in on the trip. The needs that caused this behavior were inclusion and adventure. Her strategy was to sit in the car. Now it was only a somewhat effective strategy because often no one would go anywhere and so she kind of "wasted her time." Or even though she was there we would still make her get out and not take her. Nonetheless, she used the strategy for years, and sometimes got her needs for inclusion and adventure met because of it.

Most people don't have any consciousness around needs. Why? For one, needs are invisible, so they can't be pointed to. They're not located in some particular spot in the world or in the body. (It's not like my need for love is in my chest and my need to matter is in my elbow.) But moreover, there's no language for it (except in NVC) and need consciousness is hardly taught in schools. Without any words to point to our invisible core energy and primary motivators, people logically place the energy of needs in a realm they can see... in the realm of the strategies that meet the needs. Most people blur the lines between a living energy in us and an action that satisfies it. When our awareness is only on strategies, people tend to cling to their strategies as if they were their needs. This misunderstanding can create endless problems for individuals, couples, families, clubs, governments, corporations, etc.

One of the biggest parts of NVC consciousness is separating needs from strategies. When needs are held independently from strategies we are able to connect directly to that living energy without having to associate it with anyone doing anything about it. For example, if I need rejuvenation I might take a nap, or get a massage, or go to a classical music performance, or meditate, or go to a yoga class, or hire someone to watch my children, or call my travel agent to book me a three-day vacation. But the need for rejuvenation lives in me independent of any of these strategies I might choose to attempt to satisfy this living energy in me.

If I connect with my needs (the core energy of my being) directly, not mitigated by any strategies to satisfy it, I meet my need for self-connection, which is incredibly nourishing in-and-of itself. Just dwelling in the connection to my needs often releases 90% of the angst or sense of urgency surrounding the unmet need because I become self-connected and I'm not lost in a desperate search to scratch this ineffable itch. I'm self-connected first and then I move out into the world consciously looking to get my known need(s) met.

Besides self-connection, connecting directly to our needs also supports clarity about what we need, which in turn supports us in more intelligently designing strategies to meet our needs. This consciousness allows us to be less attached to strategies, as we realize that the first strategy that pops into our brain is just one of the many possible ways to meet our needs. We can be open and flexible in our exploration to hone in on a course of action (a strategy). This can literally be the difference between war and peace.

Feelings/Emotions List

The following are words we can use when we want to express a combination of mental states, physical sensations, and levels and types of energy, that, when integrated, "add up" to a feeling/emotion. Feelings/emotions can be expressed through various combinations of words (including tone and volume of voice), non-verbal sounds, facial expressions, bodily movements, music, art, and sexuality., Being able to consciously and accurately name a feeling is a very important practice/skill for self-connection, other-connection, and it supports the *energy* to *move*: (e)motion. A "successful" expression of feelings leads to a new moment with the energy of that feeling resolved and completed. The four basic feelings are sad, mad, glad, and "'frad" (afraid).

Original list by Marshall Rosenberg, further added to by Inbal and Miki Kashtan of Bay NVC, Ano, Ürbāh, and others.

Group 1: Feelings we experience when our needs are being met

AFFECTIONATE
compassionate
compersion
friendly
loving
openhearted
sympathetic
tender
warm

CONFIDENT
empowered
open
proud
safe
secure

ENGAGED
absorbed
alert
curious
engrossed
enchanted
entranced
fascinated
interested
intrigued
involved
spellbound
stimulated

EXCITED
amazed
animated
ardent
aroused
bubbly
dazzled
eager
energetic
enthusiastic
giddy
invigorated
lively
passionate
stoked
surprised
turned on
vibrant

EXHILARATED
blissful
ecstatic
elated
enthralled
radiant
rapturous
thrilled

GLAD
amused
delighted
happy
joyful
jubilant
pleased
tickled

GRATEFUL
appreciative
moved
thankful
touched

HOPEFUL
expectant
encouraged
optimistic

INSPIRED
amazed
awed
wonder

PEACEFUL
calm
clearheaded
comfortable
centered
content
equanimity
fulfilled
gruntled
mellow
quiet
relaxed
relieved
satisfied
serene
still
tranquil
trusting

REFRESHED
enlivened
rejuvenated
renewed
rested
restored
revived

Group 2: Feelings we experience when our needs are NOT being met

AFRAID ("FRAD")
apprehensive
daunted
dread
foreboding
freaked out
frightened
mistrustful
panicked
petrified
scared
suspicious
terrified
wary
worried

ANNOYED
aggravated
dismayed
disgruntled
displeased
exasperated
frustrated
impatient
irritated
irked

ASHAMED
chagrined
embarrassed
flustered
guilt
mortified
self-conscious

AVERSION
animosity
appalled
contempt
daunted
disgusted
dislike
hate
horrified
hostile
repulsed

CONFUSED
ambivalent
baffled
bewildered
dazed
hesitant
lost
mystified
perplexed
puzzled
torn
tripped out

DISCONNECTED
alienated
aloof
apathetic
bored
cold
detached
distant
distracted
indifferent
numb
removed
withdrawn

FATIGUE
beat
burnt out
depleted
exhausted
lethargic
listless
sleepy
tired
weary
worn out

MAD
angry
enraged
furious
incensed
indignant
irate
livid
outraged
pissed
resentful

PAIN
agony
anguish
bereaved
devastated
grief
heartbroken
hurt
lonely
miserable
regretful
remorseful

SAD
bummed
depressed
dejected
despair
despondent
disappointed
discouraged
disheartened
forlorn
gloomy
heavy-hearted
hopeless
melancholy
somber
unhappy
wretched

TENSE
anxious
cranky
daunted
distressed
distraught
edgy
fidgety
frazzled
irritable
jittery
nervous
overwhelmed
restless
stressed out

UPSET
agitated
alarmed
discombobulated
disconcerted
disquiet
disturbed
perturbed
rattled
restless
shocked
startled
surprised
troubled
turbulent
turmoil
uncomfortable
uneasy
unnerved
unsettled

VULNERABLE
fragile
guarded
helpless
insecure
leery
reserved
sensitive
shaky

YEARNING
envious
jealous
longing
nostalgic
pining
wistful

Beloved Divine Energies
Universal Motivators or Needs

CONNECTION
Acceptance
Appreciation, Acknowledgment, To Be Valued
Belonging, Inclusion, Community
Care, To Care For
Communication
Companionship, Friendship, Closeness
Compassion
Consideration, To Consider
Empathy
To Hear and Be Heard,
To Know and Be Known,
To Meet and To Be Met,
To See and Be Seen,
To Understand and Be Understood
Love, Intimacy, Affection
Nurturing, Warmth, Kindness
Respect/Self-Respect
Stability, Security, Safety, Trust, Reassurance, Emotional Safety
Support, Cooperation Mutuality, Protection

AUTONOMY
Choice
Exercise of Will
Freedom
Independence
Space
Spontaneity

HONESTY
Authenticity
Congruency
Integrity
Presence
Transparency

PEACE (Internal & External)
Balance
Beauty
Communion (with Nature or Spirit)
Dignity
Ease
Equality
Harmony
Inspiration
Order
Orientation
Self-Connection
Wholeness

PHYSICAL WELL-BEING
Comfort
Health/Vitality
Hydration
Movement/Exercise
Nutrition, Elimination
Respiration, Circulation
Rest/Sleep/Rejuvenation
Safety (protection from physical harm & danger)
Sexual Expression
Shelter (from elements)
Touch

MEANING
Awareness, Consciousness
Clarity, Understanding
Celebration (of needs met), Mourning (of needs not met)
Continuity (of life and relationship)
Contribution, Engagement, Participation
Creativity
Competence, Efficacy, Effectiveness, Efficiency, Productivity
Growth, Learning, Evolution
Hope, Confidence
Integration (of new input)
Making Sense of Life
Power (the ability to marshal resources to meet needs)
Purpose
Self-Expression
Stimulation, Discovery, Exploration, Adventure, Challenge
To Matter

PLAY
Fun
Humor
Joy
Pleasure

Original list by Marshall Rosenberg. Modified by Bay NVC, then by Mercedes Kirkel, later by Ano and Ūrbāh.

NVC Grammar Summary and Reference Guide

Expression	Empathy (Listening)
Observation "When I see/hear/etc..."	**Observation** "When you see/hear/etc..."
Feeling "...I feel (present tense)..."	**Feeling** "...Are you feeling..."
Need "...Because I need..."	**Need** "...Because you need..."
Request "Would be willing to...?"	**Request** "Would you like...?"

Observations: Description of what is seen, heard, smelled, touched, tasted, sensed in/on the body, remembered or thought without added interpretations. For example, instead of saying "She's having a temper tantrum," you would say "I see her lying on the floor kicking and hear her crying." If referring to what someone said, quote as much as possible instead of paraphrasing.

Feelings: Our emotions, rather than our story or thoughts about what our self or others are doing. For example, instead of saying, "I feel manipulated," which includes interpretation of another's behavior, you would say "I feel uncomfortable" or "I feel scared." Avoid the following phrasing: "I feel like...", "I feel that...", or "I feel you/he/she/they..." These phrases are almost always followed by thoughts, not feelings.

Needs: Feelings are caused by needs (while triggered by observations). Needs are universal, the ongoing invisible living energy that is the core of our being. They are not dependent on a particular person taking a particular action. State your need rather than the other person's actions as the cause. For example, "I feel annoyed *because* I need support" rather than "I feel annoyed *because you* didn't do the dishes."

Requests/Strategy: Asking concretely and clearly for how to make life more wonderful, meet needs, get what we want (instead of what we don't want). For example, "Would you be willing to come back tonight at the time we've agreed?" rather than "Would you make sure not to be late again?" By definition, when we make requests we are open to hearing a "no," taking it as an opportunity for further dialogue.

Empathy: In NVC, we empathize with others by guessing their feelings and needs. Instead of trying "to get it right" we aim to understand. The observation and request are often dropped. When words are not wanted or are hard to offer, empathy can be offered silently.

Self-Empathy: In self-empathy, we listen inwardly to connect with our own feelings and needs (and observations and requests when appropriate). This supports self-connection and clarity for what our next step might be.

This chart is a slight modification of a chart made by Inbal and Miki Kashtan of Bay NVC.

••• TRUE HUMAN FREEDOM GLOSSARY •••

There are a lot of concepts, practices, teachings, and philosophies that I refer to in *True Human Freedom* that might not be familiar to many readers. This glossary is intended to provide clarity so that you can read this book without getting confused, as well as give you direction if you want to research any of these topics further.

There are some other teachings that are covered in The Appendixes because they are longer, more detailed entries.

The Glossary is in alphabetical order, and some concepts are nested within the greater teaching or category that they are a part of.

Bonded Relationship:

A bonded relationship is a connection with someone that remains alive over time and distance. A bond is created by sharing time with another person, in an open-hearted way, that includes more intimate and intense experiences. There are people who we feel connected to even after years of being apart. That's a sign of a bonded relationship. Now there are lots of old friends we have that we might keep up with over the years, but that's not necessarily the same. Most people have bonds with their parents, grandparents, children, siblings, spouses, lovers, close family members, and close friends.

Relative to creating GaiaYoga Culture, we want to have deep and strong bonds with people in our lives, but have them be able to be fluid – able to grow, adapt, change orbit, and allow for other bonded relationships as well.

Buddha, Dharma, Sangha:

This is a core teaching from Buddhism, which states that for a practitioner to achieve enlightenment/awakening it requires the support of these three aspects. Buddha: the teacher who knows and can effectively transmit the teaching. Dharma: "the truth" or the teaching itself – the spoken or written knowledge and techniques. Sangha: the community, or often understood more specifically as the spiritual community, that is practicing the teaching together. If any of these elements are lacking it is much harder to accomplish the growth, learning, and spiritual development one seeks. The power of Buddha, Dharma, and Sangha is universal and applies in many situations.

This same dynamic is also present in 12 Step Programs (Alcoholics Anonymous, etc.) In these programs, Buddha is the sponsor, the dharma is the 12 steps and 12 traditions, and Sangha is the meeting. In terms of GaiaYoga, Gaia is Buddha and to a certain degree I, function in that role. The teaching in this book and the other teachings that GaiaYoga integrates (like NVC, permaculture, Instinctive Eating, etc.) are the Dharma, and the community of people at GaiaYoga Gardens and anywhere else that people are seriously practicing GaiaYoga are the Sangha.

Burning Man:

Burning Man is a one week long annual gathering that takes place in the desert of Nevada in "the middle of nowhere" during August/September. It is a gathering of artists, free thinkers, radicals, cultural-creatives, hippies, seekers, partiers, and more. The gathering began in 1986 with 20 people in a much smaller and less intentional form than it is now. Since 2010 there have been 50,000 attendees or more each year.

The principals of Burning Man and its culture are: radical inclusion, gifting, de-commodification, radical self-reliance, radical self-expression, communal effort, civic responsibility, leaving no trace, participation, and immediacy.

Charge (also see Projection):

A charge is a strong emotional energy that's held in a person's body that gets stimulated by an event in the world and/or a thought or memory. Unconsciously, people often act as if the charge is caused by the stimulating event in the world. But, in fact, the charge is caused by a previous event, and that long-held charge is projected onto the current situation. E.g., let's say your mother was often late picking you up as a child and you had a lot of pain around it. Now, as an adult, your intimate partner shows up late to pick you up and you get super angry with them about it. While there are needs not being met in the current moment, and there is "reason" to have feelings about being picked up late, they don't explain the intensity of emotional response. This is because the charge is not caused by the current event; it stems from a well of pain that is tapped into by the similar circumstance and then that pain is transferred or projected onto the current experience.

The "problem" with projecting a charge is multi-faceted. One, the emotional energy can't actually be resolved in the current situation, because it's not what is causing the pain. So even if your intimate partner promises on a stack of *True Human Freedoms* to never be late again, it's not going to actually address the source of the pain (which is a childhood incident or series of incidents that is held as trauma). Thus any change by the person triggering you in the current time is going to be ineffective at dealing with the real charge. Two, it often hurts the person that is projected on, which generates new pain in the world and often leads to distancing between the projector and the projected upon. Three, since the person with the charge doesn't actually handle the true source of their pain, they actually build up another layer of emotional energy on the situation – including, probably, shame for misdirecting the charge, and confusion about why one is so upset.

There are many modalities that deal with projections and charges. Discussed herein are processes from the ManKind Project, Re-evaluative Co-counseling, Family Constellations, and Nonviolent Communication. I'm sure there are also other effective modalities that I'm not as familiar with.

Container:

A container is an intentional psychic/emotional field or context created by a group of people to allow a certain experience to occur within it; e.g., a circle of people who call in directions to create sacred space for a ritual, a gender circle, or a community meeting. Other types of containers include concerts, plays, large gatherings, schools, and 12-step meetings. Without a container -- a safe, conscious, and supportive social setting -- it's very hard for people to open up, be vulnerable, learn, go deep, or give support. Within a strong container, whatever work people do goes almost effortlessly, and without excessive acts of will by any one person. It's almost like the container itself does almost all of the work.

Contracts:

A contract, the way I'm using it, is a term from the Shivalila dharma. Contracts are agreements between people (usually unconscious) to constrain one's energy in relationship with another person. This is not the same as a conscious cooperative agreement, like "I'll meet you at 4pm to see a movie" or "you weed the garden and I'll clean the kitchen and then we can eat lunch together."

Examples of the kinds of contracts I'm talking about are nice contracts, monogamy contracts, brotherhood or sisterhood contracts, and guru-devotee contracts.

A nice contract is an unspoken agreement to only talk about superficial or non-conflictual topics, to ingratiate oneself for the sake of apparent acceptance and harmony. Being nice means avoiding or denying polarities in relationship; it's a mutual agreement to not ruffle each other's feathers. While a nice contract might be appropriate with the clerk at a retail store or a police officer, it certainly does not support creating the quality of authenticity we want in our close relationships.

A monogamy contract is an agreement to hide, deny, repress, or transform any desire you might have for another intimately/sexually and to funnel all sexual energy into one person. While there is nothing "wrong" with this, it does have a real impacts that are often unseen, most notably a feeling of shame whenever we strongly want something outside of this contract, and the requisite repression of those feelings/desires.

A brotherhood or sisterhood contract is an agreement (sometimes conscious, but usually not) to back up one's friend of the same sex even if they are out of integrity. Another part of the contract is to not to broach topics that might make them "look bad" or undermine their efforts. The military and "good 'ol boy" politics are two classic examples of where there are brotherhood contracts. Sisterhood contracts might be telling your girlfriend she looks beautiful when it's not your truth, being in a women's circle where you don't challenge each other with your real truth and keep things light and easy.

Contribute:

Marshall Rosenberg says that the greatest need a person has, once their survival needs are handled, is to contribute, to give, and to help meet the needs of other people. Marshall argues that we are hard wired to actually get our greatest fulfillment through giving; thus when we give, we do it for "self-full" (not self-ish) reasons because it fulfills us deeply to give. Over the years of considering this, I've also come to share this understanding.

Often, the need to contribute is obscured by trying to make money to survive, paying our bills, and generally be responsible for ourselves. People can easily lose track of the fact that they take action to give to other people as individuals, and as community and culture. That's where our inspiration comes from--giving. We also give to ourselves, which feels good, and interestingly, when we receive from others we are giving them the opportunity to contribute, which feels good too.

While it's easy enough to look through a judgmental lens and see that people are selfish, self-centered, greedy, and the like, underneath all of that is just someone attempting to contribute and probably missing the mark.

Co-Parenting:

Co-parenting, as it sounds, is the process of sharing parenting with others. It is used when the biological mother and father are no longer a couple, but choose to cooperatively parent their children. However, the definition I'm highlighting is when a community or clan share parenting as a group. Specifically, it indicates that more people than the biological parents are stepping up to be in a mother or father role (not merely an uncle or aunt role). Most co-parents have clear agreements and clear communication with each other to make the process work effectively.

Cultural Consciousness:

By cultural consciousness, I mean the consciousness at the root of a culture and its design. It's like a seed: it is the "blueprint" of information, patterns, and forms that manifest as a particular culture. It's the operating system within each member of a culture that makes the culture function and maintains social accord within it. It's the different values, beliefs, agreements, and ways of seeing the world that synthesize into a particular culture. It's the tune everyone in it is marching to. Examples of cultural consciousness include: seeing the world as an object for us to own and then manage all of its resources, believing in good and evil, functioning with the meta-concept of nation, objectifying women, or assuming that most large emotional charges we have as adults our caused by our childhood wounds (not from the current situation that's triggering us). Right now a pseudo-Christian, violent, distracted, media-formed cultural consciousness is one that dominates the United States. GaiaYoga cultural consciousness is one that fiercely values sustainability, integration, balance, wholeness, connection to self, others, Earth, and Spirit, and re-evaluating our social agreements on a regular basis to be sure they are working for everyone involved.

The Dagara (Malidoma and Sobonfu Some'):

The Dagara are a Domain 6/7 culture from Burkina Faso, West Africa. As a people, they are considered to be the strongest mystics and shamans in their region. Of the handful of indigenous teachings I have more deeply exposed myself to, I have found some of the greatest wisdom and inspiration from the Dagara.

Malidoma Some' was the grandson of the chief of his village. Dagara people are named using a process in which elders connect with the unborn soul when the baby is in utero, and the baby tells them its life purpose. For the Dagara, one's name is a way to remind the person of their life purpose. Malidoma means he who makes friends with the stranger. When he was 5 years old, he was stolen from his people by Christian missionaries and, along with many other young Dagara boys and girls, held against their will and oppressively re-educated with Western values.

When Malidoma was 17 he escaped back to his people, but his soul had been deeply wounded by his education and exile. Crippled in this way, his elders thought the only hope for him was to go through their people's initiation process that boys go through when they are 12 or 13 years old. They feared that he would not make it through the initiation because of the poisoning that occurred to his indigenous mind, but they saw no other hope.

Malidoma made it through the initiation, reclaiming many lost parts of his soul, went on to become a full-member of his people, and got further education in the West. He is one of the few people who truly has a foot in each world, and has written several books aimed at Westerners to help them understand the ways of his people, and other indigenous people in general. His now ex-wife, Sobonfu, also wrote books, speaking on other aspects of their people's wisdom, particularly about intimate relationships and Spirit. Their books have strongly influenced me and have given me a lot of validation around the accuracy of the GaiaYoga teaching since I first developed it in 2001.

Dietary Teachings:

There are a lot of diets out there to choose from. Some are obviously not health promoting or sustainably grown, some claim to be health-givng, and a few dietary approaches actually promote real human health. It can be hard to wade through all of this and find clarity.

Some diets are new, developed in the 19th, 20th, and 21st century, and based on scientific research of one kind or another (e.g. the Blood Type Diet, the Atkin's diet, the McDougal Plan, the candida diet, the 80/10/10 diet, etc.) Some diets are based on ethical or spiritual teachings, like veganism, vegetarianism, the Ayurvedic diet, or a Kosher diet. Some diets are cultural, developed over time by various Domain 6/7 cultures (e.g. Chinese food, Japanese food, Mexican food, Greek food, French food, etc.) Some diets are based on re-connecting to a more "primitive" time (Domain 5/6) in humanity and copying that diet (e.g. the Paleolithic diet, the Primal diet, the Weston Price diet, and other indigenous diets.) Finally, there is one diet that is based on recognizing our innate pre-cultural system (Domain 4/5) for handling food, Instinctive Eating.

For the function of this glossary, I'm going to take extra time to discuss the diets I respect and trust the most besides Instinctive Eating, which are The Primal Diet and The Weston Price Diet. Instinctive Eating is presented in The Appendix, prior to this Glossary.

> **Primal Diet:** An all-raw diet that emphasizes raw meat (beef, lamb, pork, chicken, seafood, etc.), raw dairy, raw eggs, and vegetable juices, with other foods such as fruits, whole vegetables, nuts, and honey included as well. The focus lies on what deeply nourishes and heals the body for people living in polluted modern culture rather than on what was historically eaten by prehistoric peoples. Foods can be combined according to certain rules, and recipes can be created that resemble conventional cuisine to some extent, or foods can be eaten one at a time. The creator of the diet, the late Aajonus Vonderplanitz (who tragically died in 2013 due to an accident) would recommend particular foods based on a client's state of health as determined by iridology and palm readings, and compiled an extensive list of food remedies for chronic and acute health problems (see his books *We Want to Live* and also *The Recipe for Living Without Disease*) which helped many people (including himself) make miraculous recoveries.

Weston Price Diet: A set of dietary guidelines based on the work of Weston A. Price.

Weston Price was a dentist who traveled the world in the 1930s to visit indigenous cultures in various stages of being converted to modern ways, examining the state of their general and dental health, and compiling their dietary practices. He found that the closer to a traditional diet being eaten by the people of an indigenous culture, the better the people's health. He demonstrated this with ample photographic evidence of people with perfectly aligned, cavity-free teeth despite no access to dental or orthodontic care. See his seminal work *Nutrition and Physical Degeneration*.

Concurrently, he found that all traditional indigenous diets included at least some raw animal products and that the most nutrient-dense raw animal products were revered by the culture, and were reserved especially for children, the very old, and pregnant women. His findings would later be taken as examples of phenomena explainable by epigenetics, a now-burgeoning field of scientific inquiry which holds that the presence of certain nutrients in the diets of parents and other ancestors can affect the degree of the full expression of genes in offspring (these effects persist for generations) even though no change to the DNA has occurred.

The foods recommended are not necessarily all raw (perhaps due to compromise with the sensibilities of modern conventional palates), but emphasize nutrient-dense animal products such as organ meats and unpasteurized dairy as well as other foods prepared in traditional ways such as fermented grains and vegetables. See the book *Nourishing Traditions* by Sally Fallon and the work of the Weston A. Price Foundation.

Egoscue Method:

Named after its founder Pete Egoscue, the Egoscue Method is a revolutionary approach to both understanding the design of the human muscular/skeletal system and to bringing true balance and health to it. The Egosuce Method is based on accepting that there is an inherent design to the human body, particularly the muscular/skeletal system, and if that design is not adhered to in how we move (or lack of movement) that over time the integrity/health of the body will deteriorate and lead to mis-alignment of bones as well as muscles not doing the job they were designed to. This has huge repercussions. Through simple exercises and a clear vision of how the human body is designed to move, stand, sit, walk, work, etc., the Egoscue Method, especially when combined with quality chiropractic and integral deep-tissue massage, is a deeply effective way to re-align our bodies with their natural, pain-free design, and avoid much illness and physical degeneration.

Ensoulment:

This is the concept that at some point in human history, the human species began to be a vehicle for souls to have a long cycle of learning, experience, and growth that span many lifetimes. According to The Michael Teaching, humans and dolphins and whales are ensouled creatures. Other creatures, though certainly deserving of care and compassion and respect, do not have that kind of process going on in them. This cycle of a soul growing from lifetime to lifetime, incarnating in new bodies after death, is one that takes a long time (like 100 or more lives) to complete. The empowerment that ensoulment brought could be a primary factor in what made humans step out of their natural, gene-defined, limitations and become this super-natural force that we are now.

Family Constellations:

An uncannily powerful, experiential, group therapeutic process developed by Bert Hellinger, a German man who was a Jesuit Priest, psychotherapist and lived with the Zulu for 15 years, that is designed to bring awareness to and heal recurring unwanted patterns in our lives. It's done by helping us clearly see dysfunctionality in our family systems due to blocked energy and love, and then transform that (internalized) system and open ourselves to the flow of ancestral love for us.

Participants are chosen to represent a particular seeker's family members or other aspects of their life; the configuration they form is known as a "family constellation" (metaphorically referring to how a larger system emerges from relationships between separate individuals just as a picture can be drawn between stars). This system has "a life of it's own" and deeply impacts individuals. The representatives feel emotions, sensations, and get information about the situation and relationships (without consciously knowing anything about them), elucidating past and present dynamics. The facilitator guides a timeless shifting of these family dynamics through the generations so that the seeker can experience - in a new way, on a bodily and emotional level - the nurturing support of the universe's divine feminine and masculine love for us through our mother, father, and "all my relations." It is a uniquely effective, dynamic, and healing modality.

Integral Science:

Integral Science is a teaching probably no one reading this has heard of, unless they've visited Twin Oaks community in Virginia, and met Pianky (Pi) Thompson. I met Pianky in 2000 at Pangaia, the permaculture, raw food homestead I co-founded and lived at for many years (which is now defunct.) It was a few miles from where GaiaYoga Gardens is now. Pianky was, and probably still is, the vastest mind I've ever conversed with. My head hurt after discussions with him, and that is very, very rare for me. Pianky was very critical of the lifestyle and underlying vision that we were living at Pangaia, which very much confused me as I thought our combination of raw food, permaculture, open-and-honest communication, and community living was pretty far out.

I argued with Pianky at great length, telling him I understood him and for him to just drop it. He would tell me I didn't understand him, and I would secretly think he was wrong... until one day after maybe a month of arguing with him I had a profound breakthrough, and realized that, in fact, I didn't understand him. Once I turned this corner I started to take him very seriously and became a student of his teaching. I consider his teaching, Integral Science, to be the seed energy that gestated inside of me and was born as the original GaiaYoga teaching that I articulated in the booklet, *An Introduction to GaiaYoga*.

The core of Pianky's message was this: There is only one life focus that actually works to produce the results people say they want, and that focus is wholeness itself, balance itself, integration itself. He had a map of wholeness that's foundation was the personal, local, collective, and transcendental. He was critical of teachings that only focused on one aspect of life, or were a patchwork of several aspects of life (what we were doing at Pangaia). He saw that at a structural level they were flawed and unable to generate real wholeness.

His way of expressing this was unbelievably scholarly and difficult to penetrate for most minds. That is why I took on the task of translating the heart of what he was saying by using concepts that spoke to me, and which I had confidence would speak to others. Pianky did not really bless me in what I did, but I believe I've done the world a service by gestating his ideas and putting them within the core of the GaiaYoga teaching.

Intentional Community:

The intentional communities movement took off in the early 1970s. It came out of the relative failure on the communes of the 1960s. "Communes" were the first attempt by people to live outside of the mainstream. The people who ran these experiments were relatively unskilled and unprepared to do what they were attempting. The next wave of people realized they needed a lot more skills and began to amass them over the decades since then. "Communes" got a lot of bad press and as a word it holds a negative stigma in mainstream society. Intentional community is a phrase that more or less means the same thing, but it doesn't have that same stigma.

There are hundreds of intentional communities in the world and there is a collective organization who can be found at www.ic.org that helps connect people with the intentional community that is right for them. There are many different "intentions" out there, and some are more functional than others. GaiaYoga Gardens is an intentional community based on the GaiaYoga teaching.

Interdependence (Dependence/Independence):

When 4th of July comes around I celebrate Interdependence Day. To me, that is the middle road that reflects a balanced reality. Interdependence is the recognition that while to some degree we can be independent (self-sufficient), it is not really sustainable over time. Dependence (or the ever so toxic "co-dependence") is dictated by and inability to function and thrive without a particular person doing x, y, and z.

People often pendulum swing between dependence and independence, without finding stability. Interdependence is that stable ground, that includes self-care, care for others, and being cared for.

The ManKind Project (MKP):

I've been an active member of MKP since April 2010, when I went through their weekend initiation known as the New Warrior Training Adventure (NWTA). MKP is an international organization that started in Wisconsin in 1985 by three men who noticed the disparity in how many men were engaging in personal growth work compared to woman. This drove them to develop an initiation weekend. They recognized that most indigenous and traditional cultures have an initiation process for their young men, that typically involves the uncles, fathers, and grandfathers taking boys between ages of 12 to 14 into nature, outside of the familiar domain of the village or tribes camp, and bringing them out of boyhood and into manhood through several days of rituals, challenges, and processes.

MKP recognized that Western men were lacking this initiation by elder men into the world of manhood and that instead they were stumbling into adulthood without mentorship, integrity, vision, mission, and accountability to core values or one's relationships. Thirty years later, over 50,000 men have gone through this initiation, and MKP has refined all that it does based on the investments of thousands of men and millions of hours of engaging in this kind of deep work as individuals and as an organization. I consider MKP the Mercedes Benz of men's group -- very well designed, sleek, effective, and powerful. Besides the initiation weekend, MKP supports weekly meetings, called integration-groups or i-groups -- autonomous groups that support men in integrating the energy, values, and skills, started by the NWTA, into their lives. MKP also offers many other trainings, and has a whole leadership track to grow men ever further.

The core values of MKP include personal responsibility in the form of integrity and accountability, identifying and living one's mission, community service, doing shadow work so we can live in alignment with our real values, effective and honest communication, emotional authenticity, multi-cultural awareness, and mastery of leadership. I can say with total certainty that my life would not be working anywhere near as well as it is without MKP. I encourage all men to check it out and see if it's good medicine for them.

The Michael Teaching:

The Michael Teaching is a channeled teaching of self-understanding. Michael was first channeled in the 1970s through a Ouija board by a group of friends in the San Francisco Bay area. The core of the teaching is a system that articulates or maps out the qualities of human personality and essence, somewhat like astrology, but quite different in it's structure and lexicon. Other parts of the teaching are about the nature of soul development beyond the physical plane, how to be a more loving and conscious person, and giving clarity around other aspects of metaphysical reality. I've found that the teaching has helped make sense out of a lot of aspects of life. Even though much of the teaching cannot be "proven," when I look at the world through this lens I feel much more relaxed, clear, and connected. So that makes me "believe" that this teaching is an accurate expression of the nature of the world.

There are several dozen Michael channels, and many of them have published books on the subject and offer channeling services to people. My favorite overview book is *The Michael Handbook: A Channeled System for Self Understanding*, by Jose Stevens and Simon Warwick-Smith. I've had dozens of charts channeled for me, and my friends, which explain in clear language the nature of one's soul and personality. These charts are very useful in helping a person develop themselves to their highest potential. I've gotten all my charts from a channel named Shepherd Hoodwin.

Modern Spiritual Teachings and Teachers:

Without going into great detail about these different teachings and teachers, I just want to draw attention to a handful of various gurus, authors, and channeled beings that have emerged in

Domain 8. The list includes the radical guru Adi Da; the visionary artist Alex Grey; Adviata gurus like Gangaji and Papaji; the author Carlos Castaneda; spiritual teacher and author Deepak Chopra; spiritual teacher Drunvalo Melchizedek; integral philosopher and author Ken Wilber; the channeled system of self-understanding called The Michael Teaching; the guru Osho; the author of Be Here Now, Ram Das; the developer of Waking Down, Saniel Bonder; The Seth Material; and Dan Millman's The Way of the Peaceful Warrior. There are many other teachings and teachers out there, though these are some of the more famous ones. The teachers/teachings that I still strongly resonate with on this list and recommend people explore are Alex Grey's art, The Michael Teaching, and the Waking Down process. This isn't to discourage people from these other teachings and teachers, these are just the one's I've found most valuable over time.

Natural Giving:

Natural giving is a phrase coined by Marshall Rosenberg, the originator of Nonviolent Communication (NVC). Marshall argues that our strongest need (after survival needs are handled) is to contribute, to give in an effective and meaningful way. Essentially, we are hard-wired to get our greatest fulfillment from giving. It is out of the recognition of this quality in humanity that natural giving emerges. It's natural to give, because it's what makes us feel good and we are driven to do it. Natural giving is in contrast to giving out of a sense of duty, obligation, fear of punishment, hope for reward (like money), or because one "should." The analogy from NVC is to only do something if you can do so with the joy of a young child feeding a hungry duck. In other words, only giving for the pure joy of the experience of the moment.

Network For New Culture (NFNC):

The Network For New Culture is a loose and evolving organization whose primary function is to put on "camps" for adults to get together and explore new cultural values. These values include polyamory, conscious communication, conscious sensuality and sexuality, communal living, and personal growth and healing. The original NFNC event is Summer Camp, which takes place in Oregon every year for around 2 weeks. Now there are East and West coast summer camps, as well as a Winter Camp in Hawaii and more camps sprouting up as the network expands. The camps are great places to meet new people and gain skills for creating a more loving and connected world.

Nuclear Family System (Isolated):

The foundation of Domain 8 culture is not simply the nuclear family (father, mother, and children) it is the isolated nuclear family -- a family that lives independently from the clan and extended family (grandparents, aunts, uncles, cousins, nieces, nephews). While it is biologically obvious that it takes one man and woman to fertilize an egg and make a baby, and that this triad creates a nuclear family, this does not need to lead to this family being isolated from the rest of their kin. In Domain 5, 6, and 7 cultures, nuclear families are an integrated part of a larger social unit (kinship group, clan and tribe, or extended family within a village). The social dynamics of a nuclear family integrated into one of these greater social bodies is significantly different from an isolated nuclear family living in a single-family home in a city or suburb. I consider living this way a fundamental design error, and a huge source of emotional, physical, mental, spiritual, and ecological disease.

Permaculture and Other Sustainable Agriculture Teachings:

Permaculture is a teaching developed by Australians Bill Mollison and David Holmgren in the early 1970s. They coined the word "Permaculture" because they couldn't find a word to describe the type of agricultural and homestead systems they were wanting to design, create, and share with others. Permaculture is now taught and implemented worldwide and has become the proprietary eponym of sustainable agriculture teaching. As defined in the primary permaculture teaching book, *The Permaculture Designer's Manual*, by Mollison and Holmgren: "Permaculture is the conscious design and maintenance of agriculturally productive systems, which have the diversity, stability, and resilience of natural ecosystems. It is the harmonious integration of the landscape with people, providing their food, energy, shelter and other material and non-material needs in a sustainable way." Permaculture leverages the power of design to generate solutions. This dedication to solid, well-considered designs sets permaculture apart from other approaches.

There are several other world-level sustainable agriculture teachings. John Jeavons' **Bio-Intensive Mini-Farming (aka Grow Bio-Intensive)**. John was a Stanford graduate in statistics, who brought his methodical way of thinking to the process of small-scale sustainable gardening. The primary book for this teaching is *How To Grow More Vegetables Than You Ever Thought Possible on Less Land Than You Can Imagine,* by John Jeavons. John's teaching, which also came out in the early 70s, and leverages the power of highly effective and efficient human labor and micro-design to generate it's solutions.

The man who most influenced Mollison was a curmudgeonly Japanese farmer named Masunoba Fukuoka. Fukuoka's teaching, know as **The Natural Way of Farming**, was a radical approach to growing food without the use of tilling or many other popular food growing techniques. His manifesto *The One Straw Revolution*, also came out in the early 1970s and chronicled his experiments with growing food by primarily leveraging the power of seeds. His second book, *The Natural Way of Farming* is a formal teaching book. His teaching is all about trusting in the way nature grows and is a very different consciousness than Permaculture, which is all about sculpting nature with human design.

The last major sustainable agriculture teaching is **The Korean Natural Farming** system, which was pioneered by Han Kyu Cho in the 1960s and 70s. More recently books have been published in English that explain his findings and techniques. One of the more popular ones is *Cho's Global Natural Farming* by Rohini Reddy. There's also a newer book by his son, Youngsang Cho, called *Jadam Organic Farming,* which continues his father's teaching and also simplifies it. Cho's techniques were originally centered on piggeries, and developing ways to make them odorless and healthier. This system leverages the power of micro-organisms, focusing on the proliferation of indigenous micro-organisms (IMOs), using bio-char (a form of specially made charcoal that creates "homes" for IMOs), and other materials and techniques to maximize microbial life.

Interestingly, all of these teachings came out right around 1970. I believe this is because of the converging of several global factors. One is the realization of the impact of a generation of chemical agriculture practice, which started in the 1940s and 50s. Two is the population increase from the baby boomers, and three is the consciousness experimentation of the 1960s. Necessity is the mother of invention, and until this time, there wasn't really a need for sustainable agriculture teachings, per se, as there had never been so much unsustainable farming and so many people.

Plant Spirit Medicines:

Plant spirit medicines are a whole category of psychedelic "drugs" made from various plants and plant combinations (including fungi which aren't technically plants). These medicines were all originally used in a shamanic way by various indigenous cultures that had relationships with psychotropic plants or fungi. Some of the more common plant spirit medicines include peyote, ayahuasca, and psychedelic mushrooms. These medicines help people shift the Domain their conscious is centered in and put them in touch with other Domains. Plant spirit medicines are a potent way to see/feel a bigger portion of the world and ourselves than we are used to in daily life.

Polarity/Polarized Energy

Polarity and polarized energy are terms from the Shivalila dharma that bring awareness to relationship dynamics that occur when two people (or two groups) have opposing positions or habits in a particular area of life. Common polarities include neatniks vs. slobs, intellectuals vs. emotionals, vegetarians vs. omnivores, practical vs. idealistic people, masculine vs. feminine, quiet vs. loud, agreement makers vs. go with the flow-ers, people who work out their issues in relationship vs. people who do it on their own, etc. Polarities can wreak havoc on a relationship or a community if they are not able to be resolved. Polarized energy is palpable to those sensitive to it, and most conflicts stem from some sort of polarity. The closer people are to each other the more urgency there may be to resolve polarities and create either a common strategy or a way to maintain a container that holds both sides peacefully. There are many ways to deal with polarities, using Nonviolent Communication principles to get below the strategies and down to the deeper needs in each person is one of the most effective ways.

Projection (also see Charge):

Projection is an activity done by one's mind. How it works is that an event happens in life that is somehow similar to an event from the past (usually childhood or possibly a previous lifetime). Instead of being fully present with the current event and responding to it, you respond to the event as if it was the earlier event – in the way you did in the past (usually as a child) with the same essential emotion and sense of self. The same emotional energy (charge) is present and the same beliefs you created about yourself and the original situation arise. The real problem with projections is that the person doing the projecting (and usually those projected upon) doesn't know they're doing this and may think that the charge is actually about the current moment, and that resolution to the charge can be found in the current moment. But neither of these is accurate. The source of the charge is the past and the still-held beliefs, and even if the current issue is resolved the actual source of the pain won't be addressed, so it will almost certainly arise again when another similar situation occurs. The pain from the original incident needs to be identified and felt and the beliefs need to be transformed into accurate, life-serving ones.

There are several ways to deal with projections so that they don't run and ruin our lives. MKP's Clearing Process, Re-evaluative Co-counseling sessions, and Family Constellations are ways to intentionally unearth the source of trauma and heal it so we can hold healthy beliefs about ourselves and the world. Practicing NVC and receiving empathy can also help us see projections.

Rainbow Gathering:

Rainbow gatherings began in 1972 as an annual event held in US national parks by "hippies." Besides this annual event there are many other gatherings that occur throughout the US and also Canada, Mexico, several countries in Europe, and a few other countries around the world. The gathering is a way for the "rainbow family" to stay connected and to celebrate life together. Some say it's the largest non-organization of non-members in the world. They have no leaders, and no organization. The Rainbow Family means different things to different people. Most Rainbow Family people are into intentional community building, non-violence, and alternative lifestyles.

The gatherings are a place where values like love, peace, non-violence, environmentalism, non-consumerism, non-commercialism, volunteerism, respect for others, consensus process, and multicultural diversity are promoted, taught, and modeled. Gatherings range in size from dozens of people to thousands.

Re-evaluative Co-counseling (RC):

Re-evaluative co-counseling is a powerful tool that lay people can use to help each other discover, explore, and heal the sources of their negative beliefs and stuck trauma. This leads to releasing the initial wound, unraveling the habits of mind and action that grew out of the initial traumatic experience, and thereby freeing the person from repeating the painful and ineffective pattern. RC is taught all over the US. There is an offshoot of RC called Wholistic Peer Counseling (WPC), which many people use here in Hawaii.

RC is usually practiced in reciprocal sessions of equal time spans. Typically one person will take the role of the counselor and the other will take the roll of the client. RC training teaches people how to be in both roles, how to give effective support and how to be supported in healing. People might set aside an hour for each person to be in one role, and then switch and spend a second hour with the roles reversed. This is the "co" part of co-counseling. The advantages of peer counseling are that no money is exchanged, people learn to give and receive healing energy, and that there is usually a large circle of trained people one can access for support, rather than just one professional counselor. While there are some things that professionals are better at dealing with than RC people, many participants find they can get superior support through this modality.

Rituals:

Rituals are a powerful way to shift a people's consciousness out of their "home" Domain and into another one. Rituals can also shift awareness within a Domain into another aspect or level of that Domain. Historically, rituals were developed by the early Domain 6 cultures to help the individuals within them "get back" to Domain 5 consciousness and find fluidity through Domains 1 – 4. There are many versions of rituals born out of thousands of different tribes and indigenous cultures. They include sweats, Sundances, fasting, vision quests, initiations into manhood for young teens, ingesting plant spirit medicines like peyote, mescaline, mushrooms, ayahuasca, or other psychedelic substances, pagan holiday celebrations, and many other rituals.

Most rituals that are effective are holistic, in that they include and integrate Spirit, self, community, and Earth. All rituals originate out of a particular culture; even so, many of them "work" for people outside of that original cultural container. There is a danger in becoming addicted to rituals if they are used ineffectively. This can happen if one maintains a Domain 8 lifestyle, but habitually uses rituals to find balance, rather than use ritual to create a more stable consciousness (Domain 9), that maintains its fluidity and vitality without the constant need of rituals.

There's a lot of healing and growth to do for most of us, so years or decades of rituals might be quite necessary to get us to a stable GaiaYoga cultural consciousness. But I think it's important that we have a goal of getting to a place where we need less ritual in our life and are simply dwelling in the consciousness we want without effort.

Sexuality-Intimacy Styles:

Most people in the 21st century are aware that not everyone "is" heterosexual. People "are" homosexual, bisexual, and the new orientations like homoflexible, heteroflexible, skoliosexual, and pan-sexual. These sexual orientations are almost exclusively practiced in the form of monogamy or serial monogamy. In mainstream Domain 8 culture there's some non-monogamy, especially when people are "young and dating," but for the most part the issue isn't quantity, but what gender one considers themselves and what gender one is being intimate/sexual with. Even less people are aware of the various forms of poly intimate-sexual relationship.

There are several forms of relationships that highlight more than two people participating in an intimate sphere:

> **Polygamy:** This is the most well-known form of "poly." Polygamy is when one man has many lovers or wives. The classic Arab harem is probably the most extreme example of this. There are many Domain 6 and even some Domain 7 cultures which support polygamy, particularly for wealthy and powerful men. While it certainly has its allure if you are a man, ultimately, the man practicing polygamy never develops the capacity to share with other men and probably never has to deal with his own insecurity, jealousy, competition, and childhood wounding around love and mother issues.
>
> **Polyandry:** This is the rarest form of "poly." Polyandry is when a woman has many husbands and the husbands are only with that one woman. There have been cultures that have polyandry as part of their relationship systems. Many of them existed when brothers married the same woman. Sometimes it is practiced as a sign of power for the woman, but more often out of increasing survival in harsh conditions or to prevent land from being overly divided.
>
> **Polyamory:** Polyamory, though it existed historically, is more of a modern movement born in the later part of the 20th century. Polyamory is practiced in numerous ways, mainly by "conscious" people who want to explore "alternative" relationship styles. In general, polyamory is about individuals having multiple lovers and those lovers having (or being able to have) other lovers. In general there are no commitments or marriages amongst

people practicing polyamory, though sometimes a married couple will have an open relationship and be sexual with people outside of their marriage.

Polyamory literally means loving many. Polyamory opens up a lot of energy and issues when it is practiced, and because there is often an amorphousness to people sharing polyamorously, these issues are often not thoroughly addressed. Polyamory can be practiced by sharing sexuality with many people or it could be practiced by having more holistic bonds with an open circle of people. Polyamory can work for adults who are emotionally strong, but for people who are emotionally "weaker" or for adults raising children, polyamory might not be a form of relationship that meets enough needs.

Polyfidelity: Polyfidelity can also be called "group marriage." Monogamy could be called mono-fidelity or fidelity to one other person. Polyfidelity is about having integrated marriage-level commitments with many people. This means sharing money, land, parenting, sexuality, intimacy, and all of life with a group of men and women. Most group marriages are open to expanding, but they approach people outside of the group with the intention to integrate them into the whole group, not just have them "date" one person in the group.

Obviously polyfidelity and polyamory require a lot of emotional and spiritual maturity amongst the people practicing it, and the practice itself matures people rapidly! I personally believe CBGI, the new term we've coined at GYG (see Appendix essay *What is CBGI?*), is the cutting edge of human development, and certainly a much better way to raise children (when done "successfully").

Shadow Work (Light on Shadow):

Shadow work, or as I prefer to call it, *Light on Shadow*, is a general term for any number of techniques and processes that support a person in looking into their "shadow." I like Mankind Project's definition of shadow: "a negative belief that I hold about myself that I habitually repress, deny, or hide." Common shadows include "I don't matter," "I'm worthless," "I'm not good enough," "I'm unlovable," and "I'm alone in the world." Sometimes these shadows appear to be aggrandized beliefs like "I'm better than others," "I'm more important," "I'm smarter than everyone," etc.

Out of these shadows people take actions that are not in alignment with their conscious values. The shadow "takes control of the ship" without the person realizing it is happening. Most people act out of their shadows numerous times a day, if not most of the time. If a person's life isn't going the way they want, it's likely it's because their shadows are running the show.

Light On Shadow is about bringing awareness to our shadows, taking them out of the shadows and bringing them into the light to be seen. Usually this is enough to create a change and to lessen the power and control of the shadow, because their power comes from acting below the level of awareness, once seen (like the Wizard of Oz behind the curtain) it's easy to see the dysfunctionality in the action and make conscious changes. There are many ways to effectively and consistently bring light to our shadows, some of which I've discussed in this glossary.

Shivalila:

Shivalila Community is the vision of Gridley Lorimer Wright ("Abralut") for creating liberated consciousness and culture. The term is taken from the Hindu language. *Shiva*, the Hindu God of Destruction or Transformation, is one of the triumvirate Hindu Gods that includes Brahma, the Creator and Vishnu, the Preserver. Shiva's power of destruction opens the path for new creation. This includes the shedding of unconscious behaviors, old habits, attachments, and the false self in order to create new opportunity. *Lila* is the Sanskrit term for free play or spontaneity. So *Shivalila* is the free play or theater of transformation and change.

The original Shivalila Kinship Society that Abralut founded was together during the early 1970s through the late 80s. The community was based on four covenants (non-ownership, open-and-honest communication, nonviolence, and Tantra) and the nine dimensional map of consciousness (that I have re-expressed as the 11 Domains of GaiaYoga). They also used psychedelic substances as a tool to liberate people from their cultural imprinting and conditioning. Because the relationship between Mother and child is the foundation of all cultural imprinting, it became the focal point of community endeavor. Identification with the egoless consciousness of infants, the spontaneous play of children and focusing on their well-being served as the basis of their community. The term "Mother" was expanded to include anyone regardless of gender or blood affiliation, who actively participated in the group focus. It was through this focus that the members of the community had the best chance at balancing themselves individually and as a group. In this way, guided by the covenants, co-parenting (including shared nursing) could neutralize the neuroses of the adults and sustain the basic compassionate nature of children.

Abralut published two books, *The Book of the Mother* and *The Tantric Transmission of the Shivalila Kinship Society*, during the late 1970s. He died in 1979 in India. When the Shivalila Kinship Society disbanded in the 1980s, several of the members relocated to the Kapoho area of Hawaii, which is where I encountered this teaching in 1992. A second generation of the Shivalila community lived in Hawaii from 1994 to 2003 at a homestead near Gaia Yoga Gardens. The Shivalila teaching, along with Instinctive Eating, Integral Science, Nonviolent Communication, Waking Down, and Permaculture make up the core lineages from which Gaia Yoga was developed.

Social Agreements:

People live by social agreements. Many of these are held in the unconscious. Of course laws represent a huge body of social agreements, but laws are at the collective and local sphere level. There aren't laws, as it were, in the personal and intimate spheres, and this is where most of our day-to-day life is centered. In many ways, the quality and effectiveness of our social agreements define the quality and effectiveness of our life.

Some examples of social agreements are what to talk about or not talk about, how power is held in a family, how are people "punished" or "rewarded," how children are supposed to behave, when is it OK to lie, do we clean up after ourselves, are some people more important than others, how do we act during holidays with our extended family, etc.

A big part of creating GaiaYoga Culture is bringing all of our social agreements to consciousness, so they can be re-evaluated and then either changed or adopted consciously.

Spiritual Energy Cultivation Techniques:

There are many practices from many traditions that serve to cultivate "spiritual energy." By spiritual energy I mean subtle (mostly invisible) energy that moves in our bodies and in all bodies. In terms of popular culture, "The Force" in the Star Wars movies is spiritual energy, and The Jedi cultivate it through their personal and communal disciplines. Most of the traditions of cultivating this energy come from The East, but there are also ones developed in other areas of the world. Some of the most popular ones are Tai Chi, Qi Gong, and Kundalini Yoga. People also use martial arts, EDGU, meditation, dance, sound, chakra work, and breathwork to cultivate spiritual energy. Tantric and Taoist sexuality are other approaches. These practices can also be done for other reasons besides cultivating spiritual energy. For example, people can meditate to quiet their mind, or dance for self-expression, or do martial arts for primarily physical strength and protection.

It's important for most people to have techniques to practice that nourish our subtle body. Not everyone is drawn to an overt and articulated spiritual practice like the ones I've mentioned, but this doesn't mean they are not cultivating their spiritual energy. Sometimes practicing these techniques lead to experiences in Domain 10, sometimes they just increase and connect us to one's personal energy flow, though it could be argued this is really two sides of the same coin.

Survival Needs:

Survival needs (in terms of NVC) are a category of needs that are essential for maintaining physical life. These include hydration, nutrition, elimination, respiration, circulation, safety (protection from physical harm), shelter (from elements), rest/sleep/rejuvenation, and health. Without these needs being satisfied, it is nearly impossible to have energy for fulfilling other needs, especially our need to contribute. Domain 5 and 6 cultures were much more interconnected in meeting their survival needs than Domain 8 cultures. This estrangement from the humanness of meeting these needs together is actually a significant loss many people don't realize they suffer.

Tantra/Tantric:

Tantra is a topic that is filled with confusion, controversy, intrigue, and many different (mis)understandings of what it means and doesn't mean. Tantra is a Sanskrit word which means "to weave." It's about weaving together apparent opposites (male/female, consciousness/matter, sacred/profane, life/death, sexuality/spirituality, etc.); weaving them together in consciousness, in culture, in our relationships, and in our bodies.

Tantra, in 21st century America, is generally thought to be about sex and sexuality, and while this is a valid perception, Tantra is really more about dissolving polarities between people and within one's self, and connecting with archetypal energies in relationship. There's a parable that I love that captures Tantra for me...

There are 3 monks walking down a path headed from one monastery to another monastery. There's a practicing monk, a Rinpoche (or leader monk) and a Tantric monk. While walking down the trail they come upon a huge bramble of poison oak blocking the way. The first monk says, "I must maintain my peacefulness and my practice, so I will return back to monastery we just came from." The second monk says, "I am committed to serving my students and the other monks where I'm headed. I must find a way to get there." So he walks for hours to get around the poison oak and gets back on the road on the far side of the blockade. The Tantric monk looks at the poison oak and says, "Ah, this is the way, and he jumps into the poison oak." The Tantric embraces all of life and turns it all in spiritual practice, and sees the divine in all areas of life, including sexuality, pleasure, power, and death.

Tantric sexuality which often includes connecting with energy, refraining from ejaculation, moving sexual energy into the higher chakras, and merging spiritually with one's partner. But Tantra is also an overall approach to life and relationship that is very direct, real, sublime, and juicy. GaiaYoga is very much a Tantric practice. The expansion and inclusion of consciousness into all the Domains is exactly what Tantra is about.

Transparency:

Transparency is about being honest and vulnerable in our relationships and expression. To be transparent means to remove blockages, to be seen. Essentially it means that we let our selves be seen all the way into our core. It means participating in relationship while revealing all your cards instead of keeping them hidden. Transparency requires a container to support it. It's probably not appropriate to be transparent in the middle of a retail store or a government building! Transparency is essential in creating bonded relationships and is a powerful practice that supports self-connection, connection with others, and group trust and cohesiveness.

Triggered:

"Being triggered" occurs when something re-activates a traumatic experience from earlier in your life (usually childhood). The traumatic memory, including any associated mental, emotional, physical, and spiritual distress and pain, gets brought to the surface by the present time event. This typically happens without conscious awareness. Usually we are not aware of the already-existing pain inside us; so instead we believe the person(s) who triggered us is generating the pain we're experiencing. (See Projection earlier in the Glossary.)

It supports connection, more effective communication, and deeper self-understanding to learn to recognize when you are triggered, and to realize that the person(s) or event that's triggering you is not the cause of your feelings. One of the best ways to identify when you're triggered is if your reaction seems more intense than what would be normal for the present situation? Being triggered can be medicine if you use the reaction as an indicator to feel your emotions, and follow them deeper into your being to locate the original trauma and heal it at the source (as is done in Re-Evaluative Co-counseling and other modalities). One of the most ineffective patterns in human relating is to project, get triggered, and blame the person who is triggering you. When we do this we avoid our feelings and needs and don't take responsibility for our experience.

There is a relationship between the cause of our feelings and the stimulus that triggers our feelings that is often misunderstood. The cause of our feelings, in Nonviolent Communication terms, is our needs – either as present time needs or long held repressed trauma (from unmet needs) from earlier in our life (usually childhood). These are called "frozen needs." If we believe the cause of our feelings is an event in the world (the trigger or stimulus) then we project our feelings onto the situation. And since the stimulus is not the cause, the emotional charge can never resolve as long we direct our energy at the stimulus as if it were the cause. It becomes a perpetual loop unless we can look within to find the source of the emotional pain.

A simple way to remember all this is to imagine you have a tender spot on your arm and if someone touches it, even lightly, you might scream out in pain. But if the same person touched another spot on your body that wasn't already tender you'd have no pain or screaming. So the same stimulus triggers a different response based on the condition of the body where it was poked. The touch is not the cause of the pain, the tender spot on the body is. If you spend all your time focused on the finger that poked you, you won't be able to really care for and heal the sore spot on you. Of course, you don't want it poked, but that's a small part of the process compared to dealing with the wound that was already there.

Waking Down (Beyond Hypermasculine Dharmas):

Waking Down is a spiritual teaching developed by Saniel Bonder. Waking Down, as the name implies, is a poetic way to distinguish the intention of this spiritual process from spiritual schools that promote transcending the body, mind, emotions, and relationships. Waking Down is a process of fully realizing Consciousness (the Divine Masculine principal) and simultaneously fully descending into our human personhood with all its messiness and mundaneness, including: birth, life, change, death, and Love and Energy (the Divine Feminine). While most spiritual schools suggest a path of purification leading to realization, Waking Down is about claiming a fully-embodied spiritual realization of Consciousness, merged with matter, exactly how one is right now. It's a different paradigm of spiritual practice and realization than most folks are used to.

Saniel was a long time devotee of Adi Da (aka, Franklin Jones or Da Free John) who was in many people's opinions the greatest spiritual realizer that has ever lived. Saniel left Adi Da in the early 1990s, deeply disappointed that after about two decades of spiritual work that he still hadn't achieved the awakening he had worked so hard to get. In his despair, hopelessness, and longing over the next year or so he stumbled into his own equivalent realization and finally got what he had been wanting in his years with Adi Da. But more significantly he saw <u>how</u> he achieved his realization and the errors in Adi Da's teaching methods (not what he taught, per se, but how he taught) that prevented his devotees from getting the spiritual realization they wanted.

Waking Down is one of the few spiritual teachings that I fully resonate with and integrates smoothly with GaiaYoga. I achieved what they call a Witness Awakening in 1998/99 while working with the community in Marin, CA. This is the tacit realization of Witness Consciousness, the aspect of being that is free from birth/life/death/change, abiding outside of space/time and simply witnessing manifestation. It's nothing "special" as every one of us "has the The Witness within us," but to actually become awake/aware/realized to it takes focus and support.

> **Hypermasculine:** is a term that Saniel coined which is a fundamental criticism of how many spiritual approaches function. This criticism can also extend beyond spiritual teachings into almost all aspects of how people approach life. In simple terms, a

hypermasculine dharma/teaching is one that purports that if you do a certain spiritual practice, (like worship the guru in a certain way, or stand on your head this long, or meditate this way everyday, or eat this certain way, or say this mantra, or don't have sex, or have sex like this, etc.) that you will produce a certain desired level of enlightenment or spiritual development.

The guru, or enlightened teacher, offers these disciplines to help aspirants become more spiritual, or to help them purify their body, mind, or emotions. Often, the disciplines are what worked for the guru to achieve their enlightenment, so they are offering their students a clear path to where they are. While this is a wonderful intention, it mostly doesn't work. It doesn't work, because each person's realization process is unique and what works for one person probably won't for another. According to Waking Down, the main thing a person needs to do is to "fall" into oneself while at the same time realizing Consciousness and the seamlessness between Consciousness and manifestation. Each person has their own unique self, so each person's "fall" is different. Adi Da wrestled his way into his realization on his own terms, but instead of supporting his devotee's in their own unique wrestling with the Divine, he told them to follow his way.

Another real simple hypermasculine dharma is vegetarianism. Many people think they need to be vegetarians to be enlightened, so they become vegetarians. Now while there's certainly nothing wrong with being a vegetarian, if you are truly an omnivore then you will be trying to be something you're not. This is where the problem comes in. Sure, there are some souls that are aesthetic-types, and living an austere life is true for them, but not everyone. Some people really are devotional types and thrive on a guru-devotee relationship, but just because that speaks to some people doesn't mean it should speak to you. So, in the Waking Down process, a person is supported in finding out what is true for them and what works for them, making that their practice. So instead of some great outside authority telling you how to become enlightened, you have people supporting you in opening up to your authentic process and then helping you stay on it.

Waking Down is more like a computer operating system than a computer program. It's not saying you must do this or that; it's a behind and under the scenes process that informs what programs to use and how they operate. I took inspiration from this aspect of how the Waking Down process functions as I developed GaiaYoga.

ZEGG Forum:

ZEGG is a community from Germany that supports polyamory, conscious communication, and conscious sexuality, among other things. ZEGG is directly responsible for the birth of the Network For New Culture (NFNC) in America. The ZEGG forum is a communication process that is done in community. Everyone get into a circle, there are one or more facilitators, and when a person shares they get out of the circle and stand in the middle of it and share with the community with the help of the facilitators. One of the main rules of the forum is that the person must keep moving and not talk directly to any one person. It's a process designed to promote transparency in community and grease the wheels of connection and keeping emotional energy moving. ZEGG forums are a mainstay of NFNC events.

Elate
(The True Human Freedom Song)
[Based on Escape (The Pina Colada Song) by Rupert Holmes]

I wasn't tired of my lady
Though we been together so long
We keep juicy and growing
Our hearth burning strong

Still we want to be sleepin'
With other lovers in bed
So we expanded our vision
Of what it means to be wed

>'Cuz we like true human freedom
>And tropic forests of rain
>Our dream's GaiaYoga
>And that our hearts rule our brains
>
>We like making love at midnight
>And to deeply relate
>And there's even more love in store
>Come with us and elate

See I want other people
To share with intimately
And so does my dear lady
Don't want the same ol' dull routine

So we prayed for more lovers
And for all involved to be glad
And though we felt lots of fear
We knew this wasn't a fad…

>So, if you like true human freedom
>And tantric tribe in the rain
>To grow lots of fresh food
>While our hearts rule our brains
>
>We want to meet with you really soon
>And be real and relate
>At our bar we'll drink cocos
>Discussin' how to elate

So we waited with high hopes
And 'e walked in with grace
I loved e's smile in an instant
And the curves of e's face

And my own lovely lady
Said, I like this one too
Then we laughed for a moment
And said, we never knew

>That you like true human freedom
>And tantric tribe in the rain
>And to feel all your feelings
>So you're not ruled by old pain
>
>That you like making love with more than one
>And you'll dare to create
>An intimate sphere so abundant
>Come with us and elate

———

Do you like true human freedom
And growing tribe in the rain
And to love whom you want to
And to together be sane

Do you like making love at midday
And to do what it takes
To have the life that you've yearned for
Let's evolve and elate…

———

Yeah, I live true human freedom
And tantric tribe in the rain
I feel all my feelings
I heal my old pain

I make love with more than one
And I dare to create
The life that I've yearned for…

>All together elate

Recommended Reading and Viewing List

This is a list of books, movies, and organizations that express a vision and/or practice that directly supports creating GaiaYoga Culture and/or healing from being raised in Domain 8. Entries are organized by the primary part of the GaiaYoga matrix they address. This is not an exhaustive list, but altogether this list contains much of the wisdom and practices people need to venture forth, with enough clarity, to effectively co-create and participate in a sustainable-and-holistic culture.

Entries marked with an * are books and movies we ask people to read or watch when they first come to GaiaYoga Gardens. (This book is included in this list.)

Holistic Wisdom
   A Brief History Of Everything, by Ken Wilber, 1996
* *An Introduction to GaiaYoga: A Holistic Vision for Living Sustainably as Spirit, Self, Community, and Earth,* by Ano Hanamama, 2001
* *The Emerald Forest* [movie], 1985

  The Fifth Sacred Thing, by Starhawk, 1993

  The Healing Wisdom Of Africa: Finding Life Purpose through Nature, Ritual, and Community, by Malidoma Somé, 1998
* *The Kin Of Ata Are Waiting For You,* by Dorothy Bryant [novel], 1976
* *The Matrix* [movie], 1999

  The More Beautiful World Our Hearts Know Is Possible, by Charles Eisenstein, 2013
* *The Last Samurai* [movie], 2003

  Voices Of The First Day: Awakening in the Aboriginal Dreamtime, by Robert Lawlor, 1991

Self Facet
I Don't Want To Talk About It: Overcoming The Secret Legacy of Male Depression, by Terrence Real, 1997

The Multi-Orgasmic Man: Sexual Secrets Every Man Should Know, by Mantak Chia and Douglas Abrams, 1996, 2010

The Multi-Orgasmic Woman: Sexual Secrets Every Woman Should Know, by Mantak Chia and Rachel Carlton Abrams, 1996, 2010

Pain Free: A Revolutionary Method for Stopping Chronic Pain, by Pete Egoscue, 1998

The Younger Next Year Back Book: The Whole Body Plan to Conquer Back Pain Forever, by Chris Crowley and Jeremy James, DC, CSCS, 2018

We Want To Live: The Primal Diet, by Aajonus Vonderplanitz, 1997, 2005

Community Facet
Creating A Life Together: Practical Tools to Grow Ecovillages and Intentional Communities, by Diana Leafe Christia, 2003

Federation of Intentional Communities (organization) - www.ic.org

Holacracy: The New Management System for a Rapidly Changing World, by Brian Robertson, 2015

More Than Two: A Practical Guide to Ethical Polyamory, by Franklin Veaux and Eve Rickert, 2014

Polysecure: Attachment, Trauma, and Consensual Nonmonogamy, by Jessica Fern, 2020

Sex At Dawn, by Christopher Ryan, Ph.D. & Cacilda Jethá, M.D., 2010

Sex At Dusk, by Lynn Saxon, 2012

We The People: Consenting To A Deeper Democracy – A Guide to Sociocratic Principles and Methods, by John Buck and Sharon Villines, 2007

Spirit-Self Edge
Iron John: A Book About Men, by Robert Bly, 1990
Of Water And The Spirit: Ritual, Magic, and Initiation in the Life of an African Shaman, by Malidoma Somé, 1994
Peace Pilgrim: Her Life and Work in Her Own Words, by The Friends of Peace Pilgrim, 1992
The Knee Of Listening, by Franklin Jones, 1972 [I recommend only this original version]
The Michael Handbook: A Channeled System for Self Understanding, by Jose Stevens & Simon Warwick-Smith, 1988
Waking Down: Beyond Hypermasculine Dharmas — A Breakthrough Way of Self-Realization in the Sanctuary of Mutuality, by Saniel Bonder, 1998

Self-Community Edge
Children: The Challenge, by Rudolph Dreikurs, M.D., 1964
Connection Parenting: Parenting through Connection instead of Coercion, through Love instead of Fear, by Pam Leo, 2008
How Can I Get Through To You?: Closing the Intimacy Gap Between Men and Women, by Terrence Real, 2002
Hunt, Gather, Parent: What Ancient Cultures Can Teach Us About the Lost Art of Raising Happy, Helpful Little Humans, by Michaeleen Doucleff PhD, 2021
Infant Communication: Raising Babies Without Diapers...and More, by Natec, 1990-2001
* *Nonviolent Communication: A Language Of Life*, by Marshall B. Rosenberg, 1990, 1998, 2003
Parenting From The Heart: Sharing the Gifts of Compassion, Connection, and Choice, by Inbal Kashtan, 2004
* *Star Wars Episode III* [Movie], 2005
* *The Continuum Concept: In Search of Happiness Lost,* by Jean Liedloff, 1975
The More Beautiful World Our Hearts Know Is Possible, by Charles Eisenstein, 2013
The Multi-Orgasmic Couple: Sexual Secrets Every Couple Should Know, by Mantak Chia, Maneewan Chia, Douglas Abrams, and Rachel Carlton Abrams, 1996, 2010

Community-Earth Edge
Permaculture: A Designer's Manual, by Bill Mollison and David Holmgren, 1988

Earth-Spirit Edge
The Hidden Messages In Water, by Masaru Emoto, 2005
The Natural Way Of Farming: The Theory and Practice of Green Philosophy, by Masanobu Fukuoka, 1975

Self-Earth Edge
Cho's Global Natural Farming, by Cho Han-Kyu, 2011 [About Korean Natural Farming]
Earth-User's Guide to Permaculture, by Rosemary Morrow, 1993
How To Grow More Vegetables Than You Ever Thought Possible On Less Land Than You Can Imagine, by John Jeavons, 1974 - 2012
* *Instinctive Eating: The Lost Knowledge of Optimum Nutrition*, by Zephyr (aka Ano), 1996
Instinctive Nutrition, by Severen L. Schaeffer, 1987
The Humanure Handbook: A Guide to Composting Human Manure, by J.C. Jenkins, 1995, 2005

Spirit-Community Edge
The Spiral Dance: A Rebirth of the Ancient Religion of the Great Goddess, by Starhawk, 1979, 1999
The Spirit of Intimacy, Ancient Teachings In The Ways Of Relationships, by Sobanfu Somé, 1997

A Closing Thought

The human world we see everyday, the social-economic structures, how resources are shared, how families interact, how governments behave -- all the "invisible" structures that generate what's visible in our cultures -- are re-created every morning when people rise from sleep. Just think about it: Who's president, who owns this property, why someone can have access to goods in a store, who can park where, what teachers teach in school, what's "cool" -- all of it is re-created every morning by each and every person participating in that culture. And even though they are just thought forms, beliefs, and emotional responses, they are also recreated with the same dependability and rigidity that the buildings, roads, sewers, and electric grid of each city and suburb re-emerge every morning.

This can be thought of as our inner Matrix, or the golden handcuffs, or a collective social fiction, or mind games, or Maya. Whatever metaphor you prefer, the truth is that these are not rigid structures -- rather, they are highly mutable thought forms and relationship patterns that can be changed. We can be liberated from all of this and stand free, truly free, in *True Human Freedom*. We can stand alone in this, or better yet, we can stand with others. We don't have to keep recreating the same world that doesn't meet our needs, or meets our needs at the cost of others' needs not getting met. We are powerful creators, and we can create something else... If we have a different vision, teaching, and practice that is "designed" to create something else.

I said something similar in the closing thoughts of *An Intro to GaiaYoga* and earlier in this book. The first step for each of us is to realize that "I am actually planting the seeds (the patterns of life and consciousness) everyday that are manifesting as the life I have," and that "To create a different experience I need to STOP what I've been doing," then each of us needs to get some new seeds that contain patterns that when manifested work for everyone over time, and then start planting those. It's like the old adage in The Bible: we reap what we sow.

While I cannot guarantee that the vision I've expressed in this book will "work," I can say with total confidence that I have no hope that anything else I'm aware of will produce the results I (and many others) want. This is the only approach I have inspiration to invest into. I deeply trust in this vision that I've been pregnant with for the last 25+ years. Moreover, I am perpetually inspired to put everything I can into manifesting this vision. It's what I wake up every morning devoted to create. I cherish and trust in this inspiration.

Maybe in a generation or two there will be further re-visioning of GaiaYoga by people who've been able to go farther into this process than I will be able to as a first generation pioneer, coming out of Domain 8. But for now, I'm thrilled to have these new seeds to plant and saplings to tend to and very curious to see what will arise. I hope you will join me in co-creating GaiaYoga Culture and True Human Freedom and I send you blessings regardless of what you choose.

With love and devotion,

Ano Tarletz Hanamana

About The Author

Ano Hanamana has devoted his life to GaiaYoga®, which includes articulating the GaiaYoga Vision, pioneering and manifesting GaiaYoga Culture, and co-founding GaiaYoga Gardens (www.gaiayoga.org). He is also a father of two children born in 2011 and 2012, a coconut free-climber, a Nonviolent Communication teacher, an eco-entrepreneur, and an author of three other books: *Instinctive Eating: The Lost Knowledge of Optimum Nutrition* (1996); *An Introduction to GaiaYoga: A Holistic Vision for Living Sustainably as Spirit, Self, Community, and Earth (2001);* and *The Dharma In Song: The Complete Lyrics of Nagdeo* (1987 - 2017). Ano is also the principal songwriter and rhythm guitarist for the progressive, shamanic, folk-rock band, Nagdeo.

Ano moved to Puna, Hawaii in 1992 searching, at first, for a place he could eat raw food all year round. He found that, and as the years went on, his vision broadened to include all aspects of life and the desire to recreate human culture from the ground up. Now, with a lot of grace and help from fellow GaiaYogis, he is co-founding a well-researched, dynamic, sustainable-and-holistic community and cultural template, in the lush, Hawaiian, permacultured rain forest, right now☺

Also Published by Pan Piper Press

Books:

Instinctive Eating: The Lost Knowledge of Optimum Nutrition, by Zephyr (Ano's previous name), 1996
Infant Communication: Raising Babies without Diapers, and More..., by Natec, 2000
An Introduction to GaiaYoga®: A Holistic Vision for Living Sustainably as Spirit, Self, Community, and Earth, by Ano Tarletz Hanamana, 2001
The Dharma In Song: The Complete Lyrics of Nagdeo (1987-2017), by Ano Tarletz Hanamana, *2017*
True Human Freedom: The Inspiration and Argument for GaiaYoga® Culture, by Ano Tarletz Hanamana, 2016, 2017, 2019, 2021

Albums:

CocoPele, by CocoPele, 2001 (5 song mini-album)
Living The Dream(s), by Nagdeo, 2013 (10 song album)
The Pan Piper, by Nagdeo, 2018 (12 song album)
Pray Yang for Yintegrity, by Nagdeo, 2021 (12 song album)

All are available through www.gaiayoga.org.

Made in the USA
Middletown, DE
30 December 2023